Of Course You Can Have Ice Cream for Breakfast!

A Journalist's Uncommon Memoir

Ron Cohen

Order this book online at www.trafford.com
or email orders@trafford.com

Most Trafford titles are also available at major online book retailers.

Print information available on the last page.

ISBN: 978-1-4907-8241-6 (sc)
ISBN: 978-1-4907-8240-9 (hc)
ISBN: 978-1-4907-8242-3 (e)

Library of Congress Control Number: 2017907868

Trafford rev. 06/12/2017

www.trafford.com
North America & international
toll-free: 1 888 232 4444 (USA & Canada)
fax: 812 355 4082

DEDICATION

*For Kamille, Rivka, Sara Malka and Shlomo
(Stretch), the best grandkids a Grandpa ever had.*

ALSO BY THE AUTHOR

Down to the Wire: UPI's Fight for Survival
(1990, with Gregory Gordon)

CONTENTS

ACKNOWLEDGMENTS

Writing can be very lonely, but nobody can do it alone.

Among those I must thank are all my friends and family whose interest, enthusiasm and encouragement kept me plodding on for seven long years. You know who you are.

Mike and Mikal Schneider, who so generously loaned their cottage in Pemaquid Harbor, Maine, where much of this was written.

And Marlene Loznicka, in whose old schoolhouse home in beautiful New Harbor, Maine, the first 30 chapters were written in 30 furious, snowy days in January, 2010. (Some even survive, if in radically different form!)

Thank you, Richard Lerner, for your trenchant and thoughtful suggestions. They absolutely made this a better book.

Thank you, Millard Cherry, my old high school pal. You served double duty as sounding board and constant irritant, needling without surcease: "When is it going to be done, already? I want to read it **before** I die. And before you do." Well, Mil, here it is. Guess we both made it.

Thanks Allan Papkin, old friend and colleague who flawlessly steered this clueless computer klutz through the final editing throes.

Finally, without Jill's patience and encouragement and reading over my shoulder whenever I asked I probably still would be hunched over the keyboard making yet 19 more "final improvements." Thanks, Honey. I love you.

🍦 🍦 🍦

PREFACE

This memoir was conceived to divide seamlessly into professional and personal. Yet early on, characters and events mischievously erased those lines, criss-crossing and overlapping seemingly at will.

A scribbler may designate, but life tends to defy assignment.

In the end, the memoir managed to assemble itself into chronology — of a sort. But no demerits will be assessed should you choose to color outside the lines and select chapters randomly.

My life has been filled with unforgettable characters who disregard artificial borders and hop-scotch over an enchanting landscape. This volume chose to follow their caprice.

I found the journey delicious fun. May you, as well.

Ron Cohen
2017

FOREWORD

Kamille, Rivka, Sara Malka, and Shlomo Shimon (Stretch):

Get a map of New England, my precious grandkids, and look where the top of New Hampshire disappears into the bottom of Maine. Run your pointing finger up the coastline, past Ogunquit and Kennebunkport, past Portland, and Freeport and Brunswick and Bath, and past Wiscasset, which calls itself the "Prettiest Village in Maine" and gets no argument from Grandpa. Up a tiny bit more, to Damariscotta. Then turn your finger to the right until it dips into the Atlantic Ocean.

That is Pemaquid Point. Grandma Jill and I have been known to sit on the rocks for hours listening to the soothing symphony of thrust and parry as the surf pounds Maine's "stern and rockbound coast."

I am here for the month of January 2010, house-sitting for Marlene Loznicka, an artist friend who has fled to warmer climes. My aim is to paint for you, in story form, a portrait of who your Grandpa is and how he got that way.

Most grandparents don't need a memoir to introduce themselves. If we didn't live so far apart, our relationships could just evolve slowly and naturally, and you would get to draw your own pictures without me butting in. I did that with my own grandfathers, whom you will soon meet in these pages. But we see each other far too infrequently, and I worry that someday, when I am gone, you will be left with blurry recollections of a balding guy who loved you to bits, popped into your lives for a few days, then popped right back out like a bagel escapes a toaster. He was fun, and he loved to hug and make jokes and push you on swings and take you riding in his convertible and stare and marvel at your beauty and your smarts when he thought you weren't looking — and hug you even harder when he knew you were.

So I decided to "write myself down," hoping you will get to know me better, as well as our family and my friends. And to understand the things I've done that brought me to where I am -- 73 years old, a retired journalist searching for a meaningful project. I have written many words over many years, but have an inkling that collecting remembrances for my grandkids will turn out to be the most important.

New Harbor, Maine, January 31, 2010

🐦 🐦 🐦

It is now 2017, and every word of this collection paints my life at the confluence of past and present, newly hatched and antique. This has been a wonderful roller-coaster, easily the most literary fun I've had in a lifetime of arranging and re-arranging words. Because this is my life, each chapter became an obsession. So I could only shrug and smile guiltily all those times people asked, "When the heck are you going to finish, already?"

It's been seven years, and maybe this book would improve with seven more of polishing and buffing. But I want to be around to see your faces when I hand you your copies.

🍦 🍦 🍦

This is what I wrote in 2010:

Kamille Sue Peralta, you just turned 7 as I begin this. You live 3,000 miles away in Daly City, California, where your mom, Rachel Cohen, my elder daughter, teaches English as a second language at San Francisco City College. You have raven hair and alabaster skin like your mom. You are impossibly tall and beautiful, and your heart is impossibly huge and caring, your feelings swim close to the surface. Again, very much like your mom.

I was in the next room at the hospital in San Francisco the morning you were born, and I got to hold you the very first day of your life, when you grabbed my big thumbs in your tiny hands and squeezed like you never wanted to let me go. I hope you never will.

You are serious and smart and inquisitive, and your eyes burrow deeply. You say things so far beyond your years that it takes my breath away. But you are also funny and sweet and loving, like the time you visited the orthodontist who is married to the secretary at your school. You greeted her the next morning, saying, "I want to tell you one thing about your husband. He is a keeper!"

Every time I see you, I am more certain you are going to be one fabulously terrific sensational person. I visit you in California once a year, and you and Rachel visit me and your Grandma in Maryland maybe twice a year. You love to sit in the kitchen with me and watch the cardinals and sparrows and blue jays and even our industrious local woodpecker at the feeder a few feet away. But the times between visits are way too long. We talk on the phone, but your life is busy, busy, busy — and no phone conversation can ever beat a hug.

🍦 🍦 🍦

Rivka Zilbershtein, you turned 5 on Halloween, which is like your Purim. You live 8,500 miles away on a pinpoint of a religious commune, Or HaGanuz, in northernmost Israel, just a few miles from the Lebanon border. Your mother, your "Imah," is Tziona Achishena (we named Jennifer Michelle Cohen and I will forever call her Zen no matter how many times she changes her name). She is my younger daughter, and she has chosen a fascinating, if difficult, existence in a place so distant that I only see you every year or two. Your Imah, as you know, is an impossibly talented musician who sings, taught herself to play multiple instruments, and composes the most beautiful songs—without being able to read or write musical notes. She teaches, gives concerts, makes CDs and music videos. I love her music—and I love it even more when you sing with her. And when you sing to me.

Rivka, your brown hair turns lighter and curls in the warm Israeli summer sunshine. Your sometimes crooked little smile reminds me of my favorite actress, Stockard Channing. You are smart, you remember everything, you bury your nose in books just like your Imah did at your age, and your second-grade teacher calls you a genius. The only other "genius" in your yishuv is your friend and next-door neighbor, Saralee. One day you both sat on the floor of your house and engaged in an intense, Talmudic-like discussion in Hebrew for more than half an hour. When I asked your Imah to translate, she replied, "They were discussing what happens to the soul when someone dies." Your interest in this perplexingly difficult subject was understandable. Just a couple of days earlier, a mother and father and five of their children from the adjoining village were killed in tragic car accident. The only survivor was a little girl. She is the same age as you and Saralee.

Your Hebrew flows a mile a minute, and although I don't understand much beyond *shalom*—hello, goodbye, and peace—your voice and your laughter are tinkly sweet. You speak a little English and are a fast learner, but you understand about love as if there were no language barrier. Remember what I wrote above about the town of Bath, Maine? Well, one day, I was on the phone with your Imah, and she asked you if you wanted to talk to Ba-Ba. "No," you screamed. You were just ready to get into your own "bath," and an unclothed conversation with me would not be "modest." Not modest -- 8,500 miles away! I laugh every time I think of that because I changed your diapers and helped give you baths when you were "little."

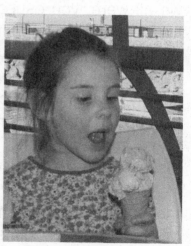

Rivka about to take a lick

Sara Malka Zilbershtein, you are 2 years old, and you are lucky--you live with Imah and Abba and your big sister, Rivka, in a wonderful new house in Or HaGanuz. *Lucky* because your sister was born in a tiny trailer several hundred yards away. It was ancient and drafty, and everyone had to sleep in the same little room without an instant's privacy. And there still is a crater in the yard where a rocket landed during the Israeli-Hezbollah conflict, the summer before you were born. Although it did not explode, shrapnel—small pieces of metal—pierced the walls of the caravan, some exiting the other side. How frightened your Ba-Ba and Bubbie were, so far away and helpless to do anything to make your parents and your sister safe. Malkie, you and I met in Israel in October, 2007, when you were just five months old. I remember how excited we all were, you especially, when during my visit, you huffed and puffed and finally turned over onto your back for the first time. Now, nobody can catch you as you careen around the house, exploring every nook and cranny, dragging a kitchen chair to the cupboard, and clambering aboard to reach the candy and chips. You delve into everything to satisfy your other hunger— discovering how things work.

You are a tiny dervish, blissfully unacquainted with the concept of contemplative walking. Your reddish-brown corkscrew curls look like you just stuck your finger in a light socket—entirely appropriate, since when you bounce into a room your smile makes it seem as though every light in town simultaneously has been switched on. The word *irrepressible* was invented for you. Your wild hair, your sly smile, and your big, conspiratorial eyes remind me of Harpo Marx. Tell Imah to let you watch a Marx Brothers movie, and see if you don't love Harpo the most. While you are at it, ask to see one of the old-time *Our Gang* movies. You would have fit right in. Like your sister Rivka and your cousin Kami, you are a beauty. (But what Grandpa would say otherwise!).

♟ ♟ ♟

It is now more than two years after that January in Maine when I began writing. Now comes Shlomo Shimon Zilbershtein, who, on April 26, 2012, became the first boychik in our immediate family since ... well, me. The jury is still out on you, little one-month-old Shlomo; that you are not a girl is going to take me a little getting used to. (This book used to be called "*Love Stories to My Granddaughters.*") But I am trying; my first gift to you was a variety of onesies, tiny hats, little socks, and burping cloths—all with sports motifs. You cut quite a handsome figure, even though you just got here, and you already offer tiny hints that you will turn out to be a "mensch." You are long and angular with shockingly big feet—I hope that portends basketball, not soccer. The former, your Ba-Ba can help you with; the latter makes him feel like he is watching grass grow. Or getting a root canal without Novocain.

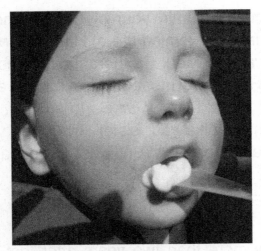

Shlomo's first goat milk yogurt

Pizza slice almost as big as little "Stretch!"

Well, kidlings, that's where you stand in life as I begin to write for you these little glimpses into what I have done, and seen, and experienced. You will paint your own portraits of me; surely, each will be quite different. I hope these chapters help make your imaginations soar.

As Tevye sang in *Fiddler on the Roof*:

"And that would be the sweetest thing of all."

🍦 🍦 🍦

Update, 2017:

Kami, you are on the cusp of high school, and everything I wrote a half-dozen years ago has proved prescient. You are now taller than your mom and your grandma, by loads. And by the time you read this, I will be gazing up at your chin. You are proof that wonderful things also come in tall packages. Best of all, you are growing even more terrific every day—beautiful inside and out. I am very proud of the amazing young woman you have become.

Rivka, what can I say? Your English is now superb. We carry on long, involved conversations and understand each other perfectly. I have already read several of these stories to you and Kami, and you both interrupt to ask questions and call me out when things don't seem to quite fit. One night we were on my deck and I was telling you about a chapter, and you two ganged up on me to interrupt with questions and commentary, some quite pointed and jokingly snarky. The teacher who said you were a genius has been proved a genius herself. You and I have a very special bond that warms both our hearts, and who could ask for anything more?

Malkie, you are a rare package of giggle and introspection. You are the only person in the world who makes me laugh every time I look at you. You are fiercely loyal, a fervent protector of your kid brother. Your brain is whirring constantly, hunting for why things happen and how things work and where you fit into this world. What other eight-year-old girl, given her choice of presents in a toy store, would immediately gravitate one of those hand-held metal detectors old folks use to scrounge for coins on the beach? When your mom asked what you want to be when you grow up, you answered, in English, "A mad scientist." Peering into my crystal ball, I see an outstanding engineer, or a famous inventor. Or prime minister of Israel. Or all three. Why not?

Shlomo, your English is better than your sisters when they were your age. You are smart and funny all at once and a handful indeed—just like any five-year-old boy. I nicknamed you "Stretch," because Shlomo seems a mouthful for someone so young. And you seem to get a kick out of it. When I asked your name a few weeks ago, you replied, "I'm Stwetch." And so you are; I can't wait to see how you grow up.

🍦 🍦 🍦

Kami and Ron at Nats' Park

Rivka and BaBa

Sara Malka and BaBa

Shlomo and BaBa

Chapter 1

WINE AND RAVIOLI WITH CARLO AND FILOMENA

Earliest recollection of my grandma, Filomena Monzione Figliuolo:

I am about 2, stubby chubby legs struggling up what must be the world's steepest, darkest staircase, at 16 1/2 Rowland Street in Newark, New Jersey.

One tricky step after another, grasping the bannister poles with my right hand, stepping up with my left foot, Millie right behind in case I stumble. (My mom always had my back, right to the day she died.)

Finally, the summit. Sir Edmund Hillary could not have been more excited atop Mount Everest.

Out of the hallway's darkness and into the light—Grandma's sun-splashed second-floor kitchen, the tiny fiefdom where she performs her miraculous alchemy.

She is at her familiar battle station, her battered stove. With metronomic precision, her right arm guides a wood spoon the size of a small oar through a bottomless vat of gravy. Olfactory overload -- garlic, basil, tomatoes, assorted pork products -- embracing magically, blissfully.

She has monitored my snail's-pace ascension up the stairway to heaven, but feigns surprise as I burst into the kitchen. Dropping the oar into the gravy pot, she spins and picks me up.

"Ron-nie, Ron-nie," she croons. "You wanna *sang-weech-a*?"

Of course, I want a sandwich. Even at that tender age I have learned the immutable Figliuolo law: When Filomena offers, "no" is never an option. She fills a sub roll with slices of meatball, then ladles in gravy. She sits me at a Formica kitchen table battle-scarred by thousands of family meals, and tucks a large napkin into my shirt collar.

We both know it is a pious gesture. Even a shower curtain could not have protected me from splatters of blood-red gravy. She salutes my first bite with a single Italian word, *"ben-u-ree-ga"* (spelling phonetically here), which in later years I discover is almost a sigh of satisfaction — "enjoy."

Which I certainly did.

There was no queenly throne in Filomena's kitchen, but she managed to reign supreme despite hardly ever sitting down. The fulcrums of her little world were the gas stove and the adjoining refrigeration unit, her *"ice-a box"*—which got its three-syllable name from an 18-square-inch block of ice delivered three times a week on a horse-drawn cart that plied Newark's all-Italian North End.

"Ice-a-man! Ice-a-man! Getta you ice-a heah!" the driver would sing, grabbing a block off the cart with

fierce-looking tongs and depositing it in the place of honor, the middle shelf, with a pan underneath to capture the devolution back to its original liquid state a couple of days later. Invariably, as the last sliver gave out, we could hear the cart clackety-clacking with replenishments.

That was pretty much the way you did business back in the late 1930s in the North End where for dozens of square blocks my grandparents lived cheek to jowl with their *"paisani"*—countrymen from Italy. Besides the *"ice-a man,"* there was the knife sharpener guy, who every couple of weeks pushed his cart down Rowland. When they heard the whirring wheel of his whetstone, Italian matriarchs carried every knife in their utensil drawers down the stairs and out into the street.

Then there was the milkman, also in a horse-drawn cart, delivering actual glass bottles (not cardboard) topped with three inches of thick cream -- to add to coffee or churn into butter. Still in bed, I took comfort in the clinking melody of full bottles replacing empties. The symphony provided reassurance that there would be a cold glass of Becker Dairy's moo-juice with breakfast. He also delivered fresh eggs; Grandma had a huge standing order because eggs were cheap and she had 10 bellies to fill.

My favorite tradesman was the legless war veteran who traveled atop a sturdy four-by-twelve wood plank, roller-skate wheels attached to each corner. From a small, wood-burning stove in front, he extracted freshly roasted chestnuts and luscious hot-baked yams wrapped in several sheets of newspaper to protect my little fingers. When I became a baseball fan I would connect that memory to the term *hot potato,* a batted ball too hot for an infielder to handle.

Yam guy propelled himself along the street, hands tucked into thick gloves to protect knuckles. He sang, in a deep bass you started hearing a block away, the heart-shattering World War I ballad, *"My Buddy."* To this day I cannot hear that song without recalling the mournful keening of that brave, legless man.

"My buddy, my buddy,
Nobody quite so true.
Miss your voice, the touch of your hand,
I long to know that you understand.
My buddy, my buddy,
Your buddy misses you."

🍦 🍦 🍦

Filomena's hair, dark and thick in the fading photos that dotted the small apartment, now was thin and gray. Wrinkles had begun creasing her soft features, but the sweet smiles lovingly bestowed on her grandchildren never faded. She was a quiet woman, befitting a hard life caring for five daughters, three sons, and a stern husband. She struggled to acclimate herself to a strange new world far from Napoli, carefully marshaling money, wasting nothing. Her English was not so much broken as fractured.

If one word could describe life on the second story at Rowland, it would be *abbondanza*—abundance. Filomena always managed to find something in a far recess of the ice-a-box to construct a *"sang-weech-a"* for Ronnie, her moon-faced first grandchild. Fixing my snack was a stroll in the park compared to the daily grind of feeding her family—and any other passing friends and relatives who knew just what door to rap on for leftover spaghetti.

Sunday dinners were the jewels in Filomena's crown. Beginning Thursday, clad in an old but immaculate-patterned dress protected from the bubbling gravy vat by an apron of great age, she would all but take root at a stove that countless thousands of meals had rendered the color of midnight.

In her neighborhood, everyone's last name ended in a vowel. Everyone had big families and spoke lilting Italian, spiced with pidgin English. And after mass every Sunday, women in black stockings hosted bacchanals featuring varieties of macaroni (never call it pasta) flavored by that sea of homemade gravy (never call it sauce), simmered for hours and flavor-enhanced with meatballs, bracciole, sausage, spareribs and assorted leftover pork that transformed the concoction from bright tomato red to a burgundy so dark it bordered on black, so thick she had to use both hands to stir.

Words cannot convey the joy and love that embraced Sunday dinner in Filomena's kitchen. The day before, while she "rows" the thickening gravy, the Figliuolo ravioli "assembly line" reports for duty—every able-bodied man, woman and child. That would be me.

From a hiding place somewhere (under their bed?) materialize two giant wooden boards, three feet by five, balanced precariously on the kitchen table and dusted with flour. Various aunts and uncles with interchangeable skills claim dough-making, dough-rolling, dough-cutting jobs. Various others mix the pot cheese (don't call it ricotta) with eggs, milk, flavored breadcrumbs, and parsley and stuff it into the individual ravioli pouches (cheese, never, EVER meat!), and crimp the edges with fork tines. Each board held 100 of those plump little beauties.

The full boards are entrusted to my sure-handed uncles, Cush and Rudy, huge, granite-hard semi-pro football players you always wanted on your side of the scrimmage line. They gently lay their precious booty on the bed so the dough can dry slightly before being covered with damp dish towels. These pockets of paradise will claim center stage Sunday, their supporting cast consisting of platters piled high with gravy and meats. Where, I wonder in retrospect, did my grandparents sleep on Saturday nights?

Nobody ever knew how many relatives/friends might drop in after Mass for sustenance, laughter, and arguments replete with wild Italian gesticulations more richly communicative than words. (To render an Italian speechless, cut off his hands.) Nobody could guess how many people would consume how many "ravvies," but, astonishingly, the food never seems to run out. Or how much of Grandpa Carlo's homemade red wine would help wash everything down.

Despite looking tiny alongside my mom's brothers, my Jewish Uncle Mac could really pound down Italian food.

One Sunday he showed up unexpectedly, but no brother-in-law of Millie's ever would be turned away from the groaning board.

Mac's prodigious appetite that day earned him a niche in Figliuolo family lore, and, even more important, a permanent Sunday invitation. He methodically tucked away about four dozen ravioli, not ignoring the various meats, and, like a starving stranger who had just wandered in from Napoli, sopped up gravy with giant slabs of crusty bread.

Delighted shouts of "Where are you putting it?" and "The Jewish guy must have a hollow leg!" greeted Mac's feats—hearty appetites were always applauded, even if one's old country is Russia, not Italy.

Happily, the Italian "stuff-'em-'til-they-burst" gene seemed not to have skipped generations. Filomena's kids grew to adulthood and continued the tradition of "Nobody leaves hungry, nobody leaves empty-handed." That would have been the motto on the Figliuolo family coat of arms—if we could have afforded one.

The tradition lived on in both me and my sister, Diane, and our 12 Italian cousins. Ditto for the 21 great-grands that Filomena, sadly, didn't live long enough to feed.

Food assembly lines were always a Fig specialty. Although the family was rich in love and tradition, nobody ever became "rich" rich. Just "getting by" required planning and ingenuity.

When my youngest uncle, Rudy, became engaged to Aunt Rose, the large numbers of extended family and friends necessitated a big wedding. But nobody could afford a "big" wedding in the traditional sense.

Uncle Rudy's fabulous wedding at Club Harmony,
the Italian social club in the north end of Newark. L-R,
Best Man Uncle Cush; "Red" Aunt Rose's best friend and
maid-of-honor, last name forgotten; and the bride and groom.

So the reception was held at the neighborhood Italian
social hall, Club Harmony. Fare consisted of Italian cold-cut
sandwiches washed down with quarts of Brookdale soda
and kegs of beer. I recall stacks of crates, each holding a
dozen quart soda bottles, being carried by Rudy's strapping
young *amici* up the stairs of Club Harmony early in the
week and tucked away in a closet. On Saturday afternoon,
the ice-a-man delivered blocks of ice that joined the soda
bottles in enormous galvanized tin tubs.

The sandwiches? Another assembly line on the ravioli table.

We stuffed hundreds of oval Italian rolls with endless combinations of meats and cheeses—hot *gabbagool* (capicola, without the dialect—a type of Italian ham); nonspicy *gabbagool* (for the very few Italians cursed with delicate digestive tracks); Genoa salami, sopressata, mortadella, prosciutto, provolone, mozzarella. (My mouth waters as I write this!) We garnished the sandwiches with mustard, cherry peppers, and olive condit—bits of olive, celery, carrots, cauliflower, and fennel soaked in olive oil and spiked with oregano.

We wrapped the filled-to-bursting rolls tightly in wax paper, contents marked in heavy black ink. There was enough activity around that kitchen table to keep a half-dozen enthusiastic volunteers busy.

Big boxes were filled with sandwiches, and Rudy's friends carried them to the Club Harmony. Henry Ford may have invented the assembly line, but the Fabulous Figs elevated it to an art form.

The memory of that Saturday night wedding party almost seven decades ago still burns bright. Best damned wedding ever. Guests are so jammed on the dance floor that snaring a sandwich from the food table is impossible. That's when I realize why the *"sang-a-weechas"* were wrapped tightly and labeled.

"You're the starting quarterback. I'm your backup!" my Uncle Cush, clad in a tuxedo as his brother's best man, shouts from the far end of the small stage we share with the tiny band. At our feet are the boxes filled with football-shaped sandwiches, ready for tossing.

"Ron-nie, hot gabbagool and provo!" cousin Rocky bellows from the right side of the dance floor. The "starting quarterback" reaches down, grabs the properly labeled spheroid, and sends it arcing to the general vicinity of Rocky's voice. Cush does the same as orders are shouted from the left side of the hall.

Sometimes one of those little footballs falls short or drifts wide left. But my completion percentage is pretty darned good for a 10-year-old, and even the errant tosses quickly find their way to the hands of the intended receiver. How people managed to get their beer and their Brookside creams and sarsaparillas, I have no idea.

I had another pretty important job that night—helping stash "La Busta," another delightful Italian wedding tradition.

La Busta refers to the envelopes containing cold, hard cash guests give the newlyweds for a needed financial "boost." Cush and I stuff the "La Busta" envelopes into our pockets.

It is altogether fitting that, at evening's end, I hand Rudy the loot. Because for years, my sweet, strong, silent uncle, every single time he saw me —***every single time***—slipped a five-dollar bill into my shirt pocket.

Afterward, back home from Club Harmony, Grandpa Carlo cracks out liquid refreshment so the Figliuolos and their relatives can more formally toast Rudy and Rose. And it isn't Brookdale cream soda: it is Grandpa's Dago Red—vino *rosso* lovingly concocted every fall in his basement, always just enough to last a year of ravioli-dappled Sundays.

When I was about seven, Grandpa decided it was time to entrust me with his winemaking secrets. One autumn morning I clutched his hand, and we walked a couple of miles to where Broadway turns into Broad Street, then we hung a left to Penn Station. There Grandpa collected eight crates of red grapes shipped via train from California's Napa Valley, 3,200 miles west of Newark—grapes grown and harvested by *paisani* who settled on the Left Coast.

We walked because Grandpa, after investing in grapes, had only enough for bus fare home, plus several dimes to pay a stranger to help get the crates at the station to the bus stop two blocks away.

It took several round trips—I was too small to be much help with the three-by-five wood crates. When we were all done and the hired guy had been paid, Grandpa and I sat with our treasure on the corner of Broad and Market, Newark's main intersection, to await the Broad Street bus.

When the driver stopped he could only watch with admirable patience as I staked out a couple of rows of empty seats, and Grandpa hefted the crates, one by one, onto the bus. Then he dropped his last dime in the fare box.

When the bus stopped at Broad and Rowland, I ran down the block and fetched Uncles Cush and Rudy to help carry our treasure to our finish line, the basement.

There, Grandpa and I sat on a grape crate so he could fortify himself with the final bottle of last year's vintage. My reward was the very last sip from our "goblet," one of the old jelly glasses that constituted the entirety of the Figliuolo "stemware" collection.

Grandpa and I then removed our shoes and socks, scrubbed our feet, and stepped, hand-in-hand, into the huge metal tub reserved for his oenological endeavors.

Stomp vigorously.

Repeat for eight crates.

Feet turn deep purple.

"*Piccoli diti melanzone,*" he says to me.

Translation later, via mom:

"*Little eggplant toes.*"

Chapter 2

GRANDPA JOE

My other grandfather, my dad's father Joe, was difficult to love. Sometimes even harder to like.

His stiff, formal, old country mien that made it impossible for him to warm to his grandkids meant we could never warm to him.

Joseph Cohen brought his wife, Rebecca, and his young sons, Sam and Maurie (my dad), to Newark, New Jersey, late in the first decade of the 20th century, because Ukraine had become frighteningly dangerous for Russia's Jews. Cue the plot of *Fiddler on the Roof* to understand the perils facing our family and countless others whose survival depended on the whim of Russia's tsar.

In America, a third son was born. Dear, sweet Uncle Mac.

Clockwise, from lower left: Joseph Cohen and his three sons,
Maurie (my dad), Sam (the eldest), and Mac (the baby).

Rebecca died young among millions who perished in one of mankind's most dreadful scourges, the global influenza epidemic in 1918. I was born almost 20 years later, so my memories of her consisted solely of a few faded, dog-eared photos. Daughter Zen (Tziona) named her first child, my granddaughter Rivka, after Rebecca.

My joy compounded when Zen named my other Israeli granddaughter Sara Malka after my great-grandmother, Malka Cohen. And my middle name comes from my great-grandfather Eli Cohen, Malka's husband. So there was no shortage of family ties to my dad's side.

But back to Grandpa Joe. Rebecca's death left him alone and lonely, raising three young sons in a strange land where he never became comfortable. Trying to provide a stable home he remarried twice, unsuccessfully. His assimilation difficulties mirrored thousands of other immigrants who, dreaming of a safer and more welcoming world, flocked to America around the turn of the 20th century.

His lifelong struggle with an unfamiliar language kept Grandpa Joe socially uncomfortable, painfully silent. Our conversations were halting, stilted. I never could be sure he understood much of what I said, although he would nod and crack a little smile as if he had. And I certainly was lost when his pidgin English lapsed into Yiddish.

Grandpa Joe's uniform, worn unfailingly every day, consisted of a natty suit with trousers creased sharp as razor blades. The long sleeves of his heavily starched white dress shirts were secured at the wrist with flashy cufflinks. Even on the hottest summer days, he knotted his necktie tightly against his Adam's apple, with a jeweled stickpin on a collar so stiff that it seemed about to strangle him.

Yes, Grandpa Joe was a dandy. I'd say he never had a hair out of place—but like his follically challenged sons and grandsons, Joe had little to muss. And although his carriage was stiff and erect, he always seemed tinier than his 5-foot-5.

Joseph Cohen, my "Grandpa Joe."

Rebecca Malamud Cohen. Joe's first wife died before
I was born. Granddaughter Rivka was named after her.

After stopping for a prayer each morning at B'Nai Jeshurun, his temple on Newark's South Side, he made his way downtown to Imperial Outfitters, the retail store his sons had launched in the 1930s. He brought lunch from home every day—two hard-boiled eggs and a sleeve of Saltine crackers, a meal that always seemed incongruous for a man dressed so fussily.

Joe spent hours on a chair tucked in a corner by Imperial's front door, reading his *Daily Forward*, the Yiddish-language daily that was the lifeline of Jewish emigres. He could barely conceal his pride that his sons had seized a chunk of the American dream. Periodically, he would perform his only work-related task: Neatly folding his newspaper, he carefully placed it on the seat of his chair, picked up a broom and long-handled dustpan, and swept the display floor 'til it shined like his patent leather shoes.

My Italian grandpa, Carlo, also struggled with the language and could be a reserved disciplinarian. But you always could sense love flowing both ways. (See Chapter 1, about making wine with Grandpa.)

My mixed feelings about Joe were further jumbled by a terrible and, to this judgmental teenager, unforgivable flaw.

Dad was Jewish, while my mom grew up in a large and boisterous Italian-American Catholic family. Nowadays, marrying outside your faith is commonplace. Plus, Dad was never particularly religious, and Millie had discarded all religious beliefs early on. But their relationship grated on Joe.

Her family—mom and dad, aunts and uncles, brothers and sisters—fell in love with Maurie the instant he crossed the threshold on Rowland Street. He was smart and funny and handsome, and most important, absolutely adored Millie. And she adored him right back. Their love survived–thrived–through many years when poor health prevented his working, confining him to his library when he wanted to be playing tennis with his pal, Irv Schultz, or tossing a football with his son.

Maurie's brothers, Sam and Mac, also loved Millie. Bachelors at the time, they could always count on a wonderful Italian dinner at a moment's notice. And sure, bring a date.

The holdout in this interfamily love fest was Grandpa Joe, who refused to accept that his son had wed outside his faith. And it was my mom who bore the brunt of Joe's disappointment.

All the years my younger sister Diane and I were growing up, twice a week like clockwork Grandpa Joe came for dinner. He didn't drive, so he caught a bus from Newark to West Orange, then walked several blocks to our house.

Mom always went all out, often preparing his favorite —brisket with roasted potatoes and vegetables. We ate in the dining room, best dishes and silverware, table impeccably set. My mother, the consummate hostess.

Yet to Joe, she remained all but invisible, her efforts to please never piercing his Eastern European reserve.

My parents made allowances—they adored each other far too much for Joe to drive a wedge. And Millie knew how much Dad loved and respected his Pop, who largely had raised him as a single parent.

My parents, the Italian beauty and her handsome Russian Jew.

Millie and Maurie at Grossinger's, in the Catskills.

So she endured stoically as the price of their storybook marriage. That couldn't have been easy. Mildred Figliuolo Cohen was strong-minded and strong-willed, qualities that only reinforced my dad's devotion. So far as Maurie was concerned, Millie had hung the moon.

Mom was nobody's fool. She had a fiery temper, true to her Latin roots. A tough cookie, she also was gracious and generous—so long as you stayed on her good side. Mount Vesuvius to my dad's Lake Placid.

But Millie forever gave Joe a get-out-of-jail free card. Hiding her indignation at his silent treatment, she patiently placed his dinner plate before him, week after week, year after year.

Sundays at Chez Cohen meant a traditional Jewish brunch—lox, bagels, whitefish, smoked sturgeon, kippered herring. The works. Lively conversation, bottomless glasses, good cheer stretching through to dinnertime, when Millie magically transformed the smoked fish table into a groaning board of Kosher meats—knockwurst, pastrami, corned beef, salami— on rye or pumpernickel. But only spicy brown deli mustard, never French's, that ersatz yellow glop. Baked beans, kraut, potato salad, cole slaw, sour pickles, sour tomatoes. Family and friends knew where the hospitality flag flew on Sundays, and the Cohen salon was always packed.

Including Joe.

Millie and Diane would pick him up at his apartment in Irvington on Sunday mornings and take him back home Sunday evenings, a drive of nearly a half-hour each way.

I always marveled at Mom's self-control, a commodity she generally rationed jealously. But now, seven decades late perhaps, my hard heart has begun to soften. Maybe Mom realized something I had been too immature to comprehend.

Because my grandpa's world consisted entirely of family and a very few Jewish friends, he was hurt and bewildered that Maurie had married a "shiksa." Her Italian family was a demonstrative, lust-for-life bunch–polar opposite to Joe's narrowly structured existence.

I came to realize that perhaps it wasn't so much that he ostracized Millie but that he could not comprehend nor deal with the unfamiliar culture and religion she represented.

So, Grandpa Joe, far too late to do you any good, I am cutting you a little slack (okay, a LOT of slack). It may well be revisionist history, but I'll give you the benefit of my doubt—that what you put my Mom through was less malice and more the angst of a soul struggling for a foothold in an alien land--even though you lived in America far longer than in Ukraine.

I've become quite fond of this softer scenario because it also cuts *me* some slack for finding it so hard to love Grandpa Joe.

Wait. There is a surprise postscript. When Dad died in 1959 after open-heart surgery, Millie found she suddenly had become Grandpa Joe's best friend.

Really.

Not only did he begin acknowledging her, but he also started confiding. And with no effort on her part, this daughter of Italian-Americans became Joe's "rabbi."

"Millie, I am in luff," he confessed one day. "What should I do?" (He was 85.)

"If you are sure you're in love, go for it," advised "Dear Abby".

And so he did, proposing to his "luff," Rose Ellenstein, the 77-year-old daughter of Newark's only Jewish mayor.

Way to go, Grandpa Joe! Marry up, like all the Cohens!

I've never seen an odder couple. Rose was New World; Joe, Old Country. She articulate, he tongue-tied. She social extrovert; he shy and reticent. She urbane, sophisticated. He? Not even close. All they seemed to have in common was a love of elegant clothing.

Meet Mr. and Mrs. "Jim Dandy."

Our family was wildly happy for him, although we suspected it could not last.

And it didn't. For Rose, the bloom faded in a couple of years. "Take him back. I'm out of here," she basically told us. And sure enough, she was. And we did.

Not long after, Grandpa Joe died at 89 and we buried him in the family plot in Lyndhurst, New Jersey. Next to his beloved Rebecca.

He departed impeccably dressed, of course. Best pressed suit, shirt impossibly starched, faultlessly knotted tie, bejeweled cufflinks and stickpin, shoes buffed so brilliantly that, had he been able to raise his head and open an eye, he most surely would have seen his smile reflected back.

Joe's oldest son, my Uncle Sam, also married late. On Jill and my wedding day in Chicago in 1961, Sam demanded of me, with trademark brusqueness, "Getting married next Sunday. Be there."

Sam had chosen another spirited, fierce-willed Italian beauty, Caroline Pennachio. Joe welcomed her warmly into the family.

Hadn't Millie the Amazing already performed the heavy lifting?

🍦 🍦 🍦

Chapter 3

THE FABULOUS FIGS

Sure, sure, I know. Everybody thinks their family unique.

Well, mine *is*.

And because they were so abundant, so uninhibited, so ... so vigorously and relentlessly "there," my Italian side always seemed more colorful, more fun than the (usually) more sedate Jewish side.

I already have introduced you to matriarch and patriarch, Filomena and Carlo, in Chapter 1. Now, the complete tale of the Fabulous Figs.

In 1909, Carlo Figliuolo left the village of Fischiano, Italy, near Salerno, and sailed to America on the good ship *Duca Dacosta,* with Michael Monzione, his wife's brother.

A year later, Grandma Filomena and their little son, Carl, joined them in Newark, New Jersey, to begin a new life in the New World.

In Italy, Carlo would travel the countryside peddling his hand-made knives, copper pots and pans. One day, in the hamlet of Volturro Urpino, near the province of Avellino, he espied the fair Filomena, and Carlo's wandering days ended—more or less.

But perhaps Grandpa Carlo had not been all that anxious to return to his own town. Just why will never be certain, but family lore goes something like this:

Carlo's father, my great-grandfather whose name also was Carlo, had been a guard in the court of Queen Margherita of Savoy-Genoa—and, perhaps, had "guarded" her a trifle overzealously. An affair was insinuated, and Carlo the elder banished from the Royal Court. I like to savor the possibility that, however salacious and tangential, a few drops of royal Italian blood still trickles through the family's veins.

And, apparently, like father like son. My Grandpa himself was a ladies' man of some repute until he lost his heart to Filomena. And mayhaps even post-Filomena?

Many, many years later, my cousin Connie asked our Aunt Kay the name of Carlo's hometown. She replied that Grandpa, a man of few words, was even less talkative about his personal history. Where there's smoke …?

But wait. Seems the whiff of **scandale** might not be confined to Grandpa's side.

Besides Michael, her husband's sailing companion to America, Filomena Monzione had another brother who, family lore (again) has it, hustled himself out of Italy a step or two ahead of the **carabinieri** (precise transgressions lost forever), and did not look back until he reached South America. Where he stayed.

And, too, there was Filomena's sister, Tzia (Aunt) Marie, who (here again "family lore" raises its ubiquitous head) never was completely right mentally after a horrific incident as an infant.

Seems that one day, after the baby had suckled, her mother placed her down and did not notice when a small snake slithered up the little girl's body, into her mouth, down her throat, and drank of the mother's milk she had just consumed.

Now here is perhaps where I ought part company with "family lore." But the "mother's milk" story is so deliciously outrageous I simply cannot bear to discard it. So following an honored journalistic tradition … I report, you decide.

I will add only that, in the early 1960s when Millie and Diane visited my maternal grandparents' home towns, they discovered Tzia Marie living alone in squalor in a dirt floor hut in Volturro Urpino.

After that, my mom and her sisters and brothers periodically sent money to the DeMaos, prosperous owners of the villa across the road, to help care for their aunt.

🍦 🍦 🍦

The decision by Carlo and Filomena to emigrate, entirely voluntary or not, surely required more than a fair dose of courage.

Forsaking home and hearth to sail a dangerous ocean in search of a new life in an alien land is … well, gutsy.

But my grandparents, modest and practical, probably harbored few illusions of New World fame and fortune. Lacking formal education, surely they realized language barriers meant they would realize scant personal achievement. But Carlo managed a living with his metalworking skills, and they nurtured high hopes for their kids.

Their eight children—three boys and five girls—all reached adulthood. Ultimately, perhaps, they fell a little short of parental dreams.

My aunts, The Fig Girls. L-R: Rose Figliuolo,
Rudy's wife; Grace Figlio, Carl's wife; Violet Figlio,
Cush's wife; and sisters Anne Pagano, Amelia Cappadona,
Kate Rancitelli and Millie Cohen, my mom.

The Rowland Street Mafia: L-R, Top: Bill Rancitellii, Cush Figlio and Frank Pagano; Middle: Carl Figlio, Carlo Figliuolo (my grandpa) and Nick Cappadonna; Front: Rudy Figliuolo and the author.

The Fig men: Cush, Carlo and Rudy, Carl standing behind.

For they left no huge footprints. No inventors, no teachers, no business magnates, no college grads. Just good, smart, solid, honest American citizens. Truck driver. Waitress. Nurse. Factory worker. Stay-at-home mom. No fame, no fortunes, but rich in family and friends. College would be left to their children and grandchildren.

None of the siblings strayed far from the nest, a very modest duplex in Newark's Italian North End. When they married, they moved to other North Jersey towns—South Plainfield and Finderne and Springfield and Belleville and Glen Ridge and the Oranges, East and West—easy drives from Rowland Street.

The Fig siblings had friends and coworkers, but family was—by far—their own best pals. Weekends and holidays fairly burst with activities, all revolving around tables groaning with the peasant foods of their ancestors. They gathered for parties, dinners, picnics, swimming at the lake. I remember occasional weekday outings in summer to Coney Island, which to this little guy seemed a galaxy away—it required changing trains four times. You really had to want to be there, and I always did. It seemed so exotic. And imagine—young enough to slip into the ladies' locker room with my aunts to change into my trunks.

Drink hearty, lads. The author flanked (L-R)
by my uncles Carl, Rudy, Cush and Frank.

Grandma Filomena, with the two eldest cousins,
Ronnie and Connie, in their Easter finery on Rowland Street.

While the sibs practiced mutual adoration, being Italian their occasional disagreements took place at maximum decibels, especially with strong beverage in the vicinity.

Arguments generally involved whose memory was more accurate on a topic so arcane it made my teeth ache. Which route would get you home faster. The name of the butcher on Stone Street when they were kids. Voices often were raised loudest over such minutiae as who better remembers the exact year Marinella got married, or when did Rocky's great-aunt die.

But the arguments were short-lived and quickly forgotten, winners never crowned. With everyone too stubborn to concede defeat, we kids watched the same arguments, with minor variations, recur and recur.

Aunt Kate occasionally flashed her dreaded *mal occhio* (evil eye) at a wayward *fratello* or *sorella*. But woe betide an outsider to even hint a Fig might fall shy of perfection.

Like many immigrants, there was a second-generation Americanization of the surname. Carl and Cush shortened it to Figlio, far easier to spell and pronounce. Rudy, like his dad, kept Figliuolo, pronounced the Italian way, the "g" silent: *Fill-yew-low.*

It makes a great computer password, easy to remember if not spell, certainly unhackable.

Here, chronologically, the Fig sibs:

🍦 🍦 🍦

The eldest, Carl, very smart, loud, opinionated, dead certain he was right—oh, wait. I just described all of them! He was a master woodworker—every family member treasured his creations, lovingly crafted, lovingly given. After Jill and I married, he made us a gorgeous, 100-bottle, all-wood wine rack, each cubby connected by tiny dowels. Nary a screw or nail. It still sits in our basement, the most beautiful piece of "furniture" I ever owned. Going through boxes of memorabilia when I retired, I happened across a scrap of notepaper containing an intricate, hand-drawn blueprint. "In case you ever need to fix anything, here's how it was put together," Carl had written. "Of course, you can always call me, and I'll come down." I wish that were possible— I didn't rediscover the note until 25 years after he died. On it was his old phone number, in South Plainfield.

Cush, the family glue. Born nine months after Filomena joined Carlo in Newark. (A towering figure in my life, you'll hear much more about him in subsequent chapters.)

The author and his hero, Uncle Cush.

Millie, my mom, eldest sister, strong-willed and tough, tender and relentlessly sentimental. You wanted to be on her good side because the alternative was fierce. Millie and Cush, closest in age, looked shockingly alike and simply adored one another. Much more about her later.

Kate, at once big-hearted and judgmental, the sister closest to Millie in age and temperament. The family joke: "Who would you rather have mad at you, Millie or Kay?" If Kate loved you, she loved you unconditionally, forever. If not … duck.

Amelia (Amy), marginally quieter but capable of rivaling her elder sisters' volatility, particularly after her first few belts at Christmas and New Year. Made the best sausages and peppers.

Rudy, strong, sweet, silent, who always—and I mean every single time—slipped a $5 bill into my shirt pocket when he hugged me goodbye. Never a word, just slipped it right in there. In those days $5 was a not insignificant sum, either for me or for my truck driver uncle. I always felt funny accepting it, but what the hell. When your Chrysler convertible "Woodie" gets eight miles per gallon every buck comes in handy. It was our own little secret. Until many years later, when the next eldest cousin, Connie, revealed he also had been slipping her fivers. Ah, the perfidy.

Annie, next youngest, became the "baby" sister when Helen died. Annie was fun, fun, fun. Party gal. Warm heart, the smilingest sister. Never, ever, stingy with the hugs.

And beautiful, sweet Helen, everybody's favorite, in her early 30s when she succumbed to tuberculosis. Uncle Paulie, her husband, never stopped coming to family functions. He and his second wife, Betty, always arrived to shouts and hugs—for decades after Helen's death. Those were the Figs. Once you basked in the familial glow, you never could get out. And never want to.

Aunt Helen, who died of tuberculosis in her early 30s, with her husband, Uncle Paulie.

My big-hearted aunts were an opinionated flock of magpies. When I was a kid, Amelia and her husband Nick occupied the first floor of the Rowland Street house; Filomena and Carlo still lived upstairs.

The sisters, all married by then, would gather at Amy's for gossip and coffee. And arguments, always arguments! A Fig girl never lacked for an opinion, nor shared it at less than a roar.

And my goodness, the smokes! Morning fog in San Francisco had nothing on the air in Amy's kitchen. Shoo away the haze just to see who was sitting next to you. It was particularly scandalous because in the 1940s good girls didn't smoke. Certainly not in authoritarian Italian households where immigrant parents enforced Old World values.

Whenever the sisters heard footsteps on the stairs they frantically sprang into action—emptying ashtrays, opening windows. Even to this little kid it was hilarious—grown women flinging open windows and doors and firing smoldering butts off the back porch, flailing in vain to dissipate any incriminating fumes. Even more hilarious were the many times it all proved for naught; the footsteps skipped the downstairs apartment and headed straight out front door.

Once, half-convincing myself it was purely research and not a mean little kid ratting out his aunts, I asked Grandpa, "Why is it okay for men to smoke, but not girls?"

His English might have been shaky, but Carlo was no dummy. "We *know-a* the girls smoke," he replied with a smile. "They no *fool-a* us."

When I mentioned this to Kate years later, she confessed the sisters always knew their parents knew. But even as adults there was respect—and a dollop of fear.

Aunt Kate, in particular, was wonderfully unforgettable. A character for the ages. One summer I worked at my dad's appliance store in downtown Newark, and she was waitressing around the corner at the old Novelty Bar and Grill on Market Street.

A couple of times a week I would go for lunch. When Kate spotted me at the door, she leaped into action, shouldering aside the woman dishing out the cafeteria line chow and hissing, "He's my nephew. I'll take care of him." Then without bothering to ask what I wanted, she piled meats, potatoes, veggies, and bread so generously that lunch spilled over onto a second dinner plate. Plus several desserts. And a carton of milk—or four.

Again whispering, "He's my nephew. I'll take care of him," she slipped into the cashier's chair and hijacked the register.

"Two dollars and 23 cents," she would say, eyes flashing me a "shut up, kid" warning.

I hand her a fiver—probably one of those from Uncle Rudy. Then came her most audacious act. She would slip it back to me—plus several bucks change.

In one swoop she handed me a gut-busting meal practically free—and gas money, to boot.

She seemed unconcerned the boss might discover the familial larceny. After all, wasn't she just performing my aunts' life's work? And Filomena's? Stuffing Ronnie like a Christmas goose?

The most personally painful example of their manifest destiny occurred the summer after I graduated high school. My folks had moved from West Orange to Florida, hoping a climate change might benefit Dad's health. I stayed back north with my pal, Stan Lowenberg, who lived up the street.

With no Mom around to feed me, I largely was on my own. Normal fare consisted of overstuffed deli sandwiches at Stash's, a bar and grill on Valley Road in Orange whose regulars literally cried in their beers when the place shut down.

Anyhow, Millie's sisters had convinced themselves that without home cookin', my starvation was both inevitable and imminent.

Reveling in the most freedom I had ever enjoyed, I eluded their repeated entreaties to feed me until at last I ran out of excuses. Back to the wall, I hatched a flawless strategy: Telescope all three invites into a one evening and be done with it.

Executing this screwball game plan, I arrived at Annie's house one early evening in July. My youngest aunt awaited with ravioli, gravy and assorted pork products.

Feeling like a goose's liver being plumped for fois gras, at 7:30 I rang the doorbell at Amy's, to be assaulted by the aroma of sausage and peppers cooking in her omnipresent electric fry pan.

Stifling moans of intestinal anguish, I staggered into Kate's kitchen around 9, apologizing for my tardiness and pleading that I wasn't too hungry--a small plate would do. The words *"small"* and *"plate"*, of course, were absent from Kate's lexicon.

Pondering the unlikelihood of scoring an air sickness bag, I dispiritedly watched Kate deposit under my exhausted jaw a Brobdingnagian platter of lasagna, sausages, meatballs, and spareribs. Fumbling with my fork, I spotted her shooting me that glare capable of sending shivers up every spine in the Garden State.

"So how were Annie's ravioli? Amy's sausage and peppers? Good as my lasagna?"

Had I really fancied that I could hoodwink the witches of Rowland Street? Their phones had been buzzing for days as my aunts gleefully plotted their assaults on my digestive tract. And for years later, at every family function, they never tired of trotting out their merry tale and watching me squirm.

As I left that night, Kate lovingly pinched my cheek and handed me . . . a doggie bag. My pal Stan would love his midnight snack of lasagna and cold meatballs.

🍦 🍦 🍦

The Fig family's yearly highlight was the Christmas Eve *"abbondanza,"* a freewheeling bacchanal of food, drink, merriment, song.

Way, way more than a party, it was akin to opening night at the circus. The only acceptable absence was a notarized note signed in blood by a head nurse in the local Intensive Care Unit.

For many years the venue was Amelia's flat on the first floor on Rowland, central and convenient. For attendees of midnight Mass, St. Michael's Catholic Church was but a few steps away. The pious departed when it was still Christmas Eve and returned an hour later to find the heathens a little drunker, a lot louder. I never went—no religious needs could compare to the Italian tradition of The Seven Fishes—one variety for each of the disciples.

Everybody contributed. Fish of every description, gilled and non-gilled. The Holy Trinity of *"S"* fish—shrimp, scallops, scungilli (conch). Calamari. Three iterations of cod—baccala salad, baccala stew, fried baccala. Smelts. Anchovies. Linguine with clams and mussels.

Nobody left hungry when my family gathered, especially on Christmas Eve.

Booze flowed. Annie and Amelia sipped cloyingly sweet Brandy Alexanders, seemingly harmless until the fourth one decked you like a short left from Cassius Clay.

After her second, Annie would begin dancing a jig and crooning, "This is such a n-i-i-i-ce party," repeating repeatedly. Even after she passed on to that great *abbondonza* in the sky we would reprise her joyous cry. In fact, at a family reunion years and years after her death, cousin Connie and her son Ted printed T-shirts bearing likenesses of Carlo and Filomena and the words, "This is such a nice party!"

Amelia, our hostess, was quiet and reserved until her sixth Brandy Alexander. Then she morphed into the Amy we impatiently had been awaiting, sexily belting out, "Frankie and Johnny were lovers"—seven regular verses, plus a couple off-color ones of her own composition— all delivered from her version of center stage. Atop the kitchen table.

But the musical highlight was Uncle Cush and his ukulele, a cheap contraption of indeterminate age that all but disappeared in his enormous hands. Cush had taught himself just enough chords to ensure the revelers' enthusiasm and endurance would overwhelm his musical shortcomings.

He insisted I sit beside him as we croaked our way through every old song extant. My voice was lousy but I was loud and knew all the words, religious and secular. He particularly favored my off-key assaults on "Red River Valley" and "Down by the Riverside."

About an hour before midnight, as the true believers surrendered forks and knives to troop out to St. Michael's, things turned serious. Cush's fingers, gnarled from semi-pro football, would segue from "Sweet Adeline" to "Hark, the Herald Angels Sing"—a cue for Amy's husband, Nick, to begin clearing his throat.

Nick was movie-star handsome, with a pencil mustache and a silvery-black mane. The quietest man I ever knew sat all night in silent bemusement at the clowns and their hijinks. His contribution: Quirkily hanging a fully trimmed Christmas tree upside down from the living room ceiling.

Every so often, Amy would shout, "Nick, shut up!" His response always was a small smile plying the corners of his mouth. Nick knew his moment was coming soon enough.

At midnight, as the bells of St. Mike's began pealing, Cush sounded a chord signaling the arrival of our magic moment:

Silent Nick singing "Silent Night."

The room fell dead still. Although we had heard it every Christmas for years, his deep, lush voice never failed to produce shivers and tears. He acknowledged our plaudits with a nod and another small smile, then retreated into his shell until same time next year.

After my grandparents died and Amy and Nick had moved to the suburbs, the party migrated west to Cush's and Vi's home in central New Jersey, quite a drive for most in a season of uncertain weather. But don't dare make other plans. This is your family. We are The Figs. And this is Christmas Eve.

Different venue, familiar festivities. Long tables in the low-ceilinged basement, and constant stair-climbing to replenish platters of fish. But same songs, same corny jokes, same hoary stories provoking the same loud discussions about whether Route 22 or 28 was the faster way home. Same gorging on seafood, stuffed artichokes, linguine. Same hugs, same kisses, same Brandy

Alexanders, same "Nick, shut up!", same "This is such a n-i-i-i-ce party!"

Same old "Red River Valley," still loud and still off-key.

Annie and her husband Frank, who had Lou Gehrig's disease, had moved to Phoenix for his health. Beautiful Barbara, Cush's youngest, had settled in Denver with her perfect husband, Jim. But whenever humanly possible, family members returned for ***"The Party."***

As my aunts and uncles grew older, the drive to Cush's grew longer and more uncertain.

Luckily I had a solution. In 1968, we bought our first house, and that's when "Christmas Eve with the Fabulous Figs" moved yet again to 220 Grove Street in Montclair. As a toddler in the late 1930s, I had snoozed through the festivities. Thirty years later, I am host.

The sweetness of generational continuity delighted my aunts and uncles who partied reassured the family tradition was in good hands.

My party tried to replicate its predecessors—quite successfully, it turned out, even without ready access to Midnight Mass. At the first one, after ukulele madness and Nick's "Silent Night," after we couldn't possibly force-feed ourselves another morsel of fish, we noticed Amy missing.

An ad hoc search party discovered her, sweetly asleep, curled on a couch in another room. Thank you, Mrs. Brandy Alexander. That nap stamped the seal of unqualified authenticity upon the party's new venue.

Four years later, in 1972, we moved to Washington and the festivities shifted back to Cush's and Vi's. With our young girls, Rachel and Zen, in tow, we made the trip every year until the party expired of old age—its founders' "old age." The next generation was left to begin fashioning its own, very different holiday memories.

As for me, our new tradition retains some of the old, although it is far less boisterous. We host dinner for a few friends, replete with seven, eight, ten, fourteen varieties of fish, depending on our mood. Our cramped dining room ensures that an invitation to our holiday dinner is highly coveted.

Di drives down from Jersey, having soaked dried, salted baccala until it is fat and plump and juicy. She bears cans of sliced scungilli and other holiday aquatic pleasures largely obtainable only in the Italian enclaves of North Jersey. The rest of the fish comes from Costco's Christmastime "Seafood Festival," and we occasionally ignored the budget to kick things up a bit with fire-red king crab legs.

We sing "Happy Birthday, dear Di,", and she always jokingly grouses that Christmas Eve iis the worst possible birth date. Should the Jewish and Christian holidays overlap, the reflection from the menorah candles dance gaily, reflected in the Christmas tree lights.

I pour grappa for the brave, we toast our good fortune and good health, and conclude the festivities before midnight. Nick is long gone, but cousin Connie has unearthed a treasure: A scratchy recording of "Silent Night" which I transferred to my I-Pod.

"Frankie and Johnny," belted out from atop a kitchen table, is no more. The happy cries of "This is such a n-i-i-ice party" are gone. And our blender never has seen a Brandy Alexander. No more carols, no more hokey jokes, no more off-key '40s songs. Saddest of all, no more Cush's battered fingers plying the uke as I croak, "From this valley they say you are leaving, we will miss your bright eyes and sweet smile ..."

We enjoy ourselves, but I profoundly miss the "bright eyes and sweet smiles" of the Fabulous Figs. Good times and wonderful memories exist because of the good and wonderful relatives who nurtured them.

Improbably, by virtue of longevity, I find myself de facto Fig "Godfather."

Right before Christmas a couple of years after Cush died, I received a FedEx box. Connie and Barbara (middle sister, Helen, was taken by cancer) had sent his old ukulele, protected by so much Bubble Wrap you'd have thought it a Stradivarius. A note declared that after one year I must pass it down our fast-dwindling line of cousins.

Fat chance. They're going to have to pry Cush's uke from my cold, dead fingers.

And Connie and Barb knew that all along.

🍦 🍦 🍦

Chapter 4

DAD, VIOLINS,
AND GEORGE SISLER

I was in second grade when Dad got this crazy notion I should play the fiddle.

Maurie really loved the violin. The sweet, dreamy notes of *Spring,* from Vivaldi's *The Four Seasons.* The frenzied dance of bow over strings in Rimsky-Korsakov's *Flight of the Bumblebee.*

So nothing else would do, he decided, but that his baseball-crazed kid set aside his new first-baseman's glove long enough to entertain him in our living room with a little Bach or Beethoven. A hand-cranked Victrola would have been cheaper and infinitely more musical.

First, a little about the glove.

Dad was really neat, the sweetest, most gentle man ever. He was so different from other dads—for one thing, he talked to my friends like adults capable of carrying on a cogent conversation. Consequently they congregated at our house after school, vying for his attentions. It didn't hurt that my Italian mom's fridge was filled with snacks bearing exotic names like *scamorza* and *soppressata*.

My friends still howl recalling the afternoon we gathered in our breakfast nook, chattering about our school day, when I yawned and stretched arms high. Bang. A salami smacked my forehead.

This foot-long Genoa beauty, stashed behind the window curtain, was yet another lost skirmish in Mom's lifelong war to conceal processed meat from her son.

Dad's wildly misplaced faith that I could learn a musical instrument was typical. Although he never graduated high school, he was remarkably well educated. Poor health ruled out anything more strenuous than a rare set of tennis, so he spent countless hours in his extensive library. Fiction, biography, poetry, history. Old favorite authors, aspiring newcomers. Newspapers, magazines, specialty periodicals with obscure themes. He read voraciously, conversing brilliantly on multiple and disparate topics. And he loved classical music.

But he was not the reclusive bookworm. Our door was always open to friends who loved both Mauries: The quietly erudite intellectual and the happy-go-lucky party maven whose fridge and liquor cabinet always were bulging.

When I was about 11, Dad established a drinking and eating society made up of a few of his closest friends, and his brothers Sam and Mac. He dubbed it *"The Munners Trenchermen and Stube Society"* -- *Munners* after our street in East Orange, Munn Avenue; and *Trenchermen* because all were prodigious eaters. *Stube* is German for beer garden. He outfitted the inductees with cone-shaped, feathered, variously-colored felt Robin Hood hats.

Beer flowed generously at their weekly meetings, as did heated discussion—loud, long, opinionated. And boy, those hats were way cool.

Dad knew I would covet one; at the inaugural club meeting of the six adults, he reached behind his chair and pulled out a hat so big it swallowed my ears.

"You, Ronald, are now an official member of *The Munners Trenchermen and Stube Society,* entitled to all the honors and emoluments thereof."

With that, he gave me a sip of his beer—out of Millie's sight, of course.

And to ensure that I wouldn't feel lonely among the adults, he proffered honorary memberships—and hats— to Stan Lowenberg and Mike Schneider, lifelong friends whom I chose some years later to be co-best men when Jill and I married.

But the very things that made my dad so interesting to his friends and mine often proved taxing to his son. Other kids played catch with their fathers, but he rarely felt well enough. Other kids spent hours in front of a fascinating new invention, television, which back then offered more test patterns than real programs. We were among the last families in the neighborhood to acquire a TV--even though they were sold at my family's appliance store.

Even when our tiny-screen TV arrived, he rationed our consumption so stringently that watching *Howdy Doody* became the rare treat. Instead, Maurie made me memorize Mark Antony's speech from Shakespeare"s *Julius Caesar,* which begins:

"Friends, Romans, and countrymen, lend me your ears; I come to bury Caesar, not to praise him. The evil that men do lives after them, the good is oft interred with their bones. So let it be with Caesar."

Almost 70 years later I remember most of that long speech. But I resented back then that, while carefree friends were playing ball, my grudging nose was oft buried in The Bard.

The author and my Dad.

So it was something of a surprise one spring afternoon when I was about eight that Dad met me at school and we walked a few blocks up Central Avenue to a sporting goods store. He had been watching my pickup baseball games from our fifth floor apartment window and noticed I always was banished to right field, where nobody hit the ball. Because I was the only kid without a glove.

We stroll, my hand in his, through the narrow aisles of a kid's fantasy world—bats, gloves, balls, caps, spiked shoes. I barely notice the equipment of other sports—golf, tennis, football, basketball. Even then, baseball is my life.

I try on every mitt. How to choose from this cornucopia? Bookworm Dad suggests: "All the other kids have five-fingered fielders' gloves. You'd be the only one with a first-baseman's mitt."

His logic is unassailable. The light tan—almost blond — beauty he holds has a place where the thumb goes, and a much larger compartment for the other fingers. They are joined together by an interlocking criss-cross webbing of leather straps that surely will trap all errant throws. Move over, George Sisler. Cooperstown, here I come.

The autograph of Sisler, the greatest fielding first baseman of his time, is burned in cursive on the heel of the mitt, an inspiration for anybody lucky enough to wear this behemoth, which is five times the size of my little hand.

"You know about breaking it in, the Neatsfoot oil?" asks Dad.

Of course I know Neatsfoot oil, a magic yellow elixir made from the shin bones of cattle. You rub it nightly into a new glove until, many weeks later, the stiff, unyielding leather turns soft and supple as a baby's bottom. But how does Dad know that?

"And you'll need a new ball, to form the pocket."

This guy who makes me memorize Brutus and Cassius knows about Neatsfoot oil? And how to fashion the perfect catching zone?

Then he launches into a paean to his baseball hero, his fielding statistics and his lifetime batting average.

George Sisler once hit .420. he says reverently, "One of the rarest feats in baseball."

A few years later I would venerate Gil Hodges, Duke Snider, Pee Wee Reese, Jackie Robinson, the Brooklyn Dodger stars who were *MY* "Boys of Summer," just as Sisler, elected to baseball's Hall of Fame a few years earlier, had been Dad's.

I am surprised and delighted to learn that Billy Shakespeare isn't my Dad's only vice.

The salesman packs up the glove, a tin of Neatsfoot, and a shiny new National League baseball. (I never would choose a ball from any league Those Damn Yankees played in).

At home with my golden beauty, I massage in the Neatsfoot until my fingers ache, then tightly bind twine around the ball and the pocket.

I place it under my pillow, fetching the first of a long string of uncomfortable nights. But nobody ever promised a Yellow Brick Road to Cooperstown.

I had planned to keep my mitt secret until it was perfectly broken in, but I am fairly bursting to show off my treasure. So next afternoon my friends gather around for the unveiling ceremony. From behind my back I produce, in all its blonde loveliness and its sweet, snare-trap pocket glory, my brand spanking new Rawlings George Sisler Genuine No-Errors First Baseman's Mitt. The boys rush over, begging to be first to try.

"Not until it is ready," I brush them off with as much of a sneer as such a happy child could muster as I trot out to—no, not right field—*First Base*!

From there I sneak a glance at our apartment where Dad is leaning out the window to watch the magic moment. Surely I have the best pop, ever.

♗ ♗ ♗

But all those warm feelings dissolve when discussions turn to violin lessons. After all, aren't I already overburdened with second-grade homework, afternoon emulations of Mr. Sisler, and rote recitations of Mark Antony? I might as well be talking to a Rodin statue, for Dad knows someone who knows someone else whose sister had once (unsuccessfully) auditioned for the Newark Symphony Orchestra. She will be coming to the apartment for twice-weekly lessons as soon as I have a fiddle of my own.

Let me assure you picking out a violin is far less fun, involving much less father-son quality time, than selecting my Sisler had been.

While that mitt fits my left hand like, well, a glove, the second-hand violin my father chooses feels like a sack of potatoes. No matter how I position it under my chin, even the Sisler/hardball lump under my pillow is more comfortable.

As the encounter with violin virtuosity approaches, my mood darkens. None of my friends is forced to play some dumb musical instrument, I grouse--always out of Pop's earshot.

My imagination runs wild. This wretched teacher will turn out to be a harridan who insists I spend six months playing scales before she turns me loose on *Fur Elise*. She will be fat and old, with hairy, sweaty armpits and, unquestionably, multiple chin moles. By the time our doorbell rings, I am in a frenzy.

In walks Leah.

George Sisler and all he represents fly from my brain. The creature standing before me is slim, young, darkly beautiful. No mole hairs. No moles, even. Arresting smile. Perfectly straight teeth, gleamingly white as Chiclets. (Google it, kids.)

She has me at "Hi, Ron, I'm Leah." I am hopelessly, cruelly in love — although since I am eight I have no actual clue what that means.

Although I silently vow right there on the spot to make her proud, it becomes painfully apparent I am even lousier than I had expected—actually, numerous rungs down the musical ladder from "lousy." Even Leah's loveliness cannot lift me to musical heights that even approach dreadful.

I dutifully practice an hour a day under Millie's baleful stare, but as the weeks fiddle by, inconceivably I regress. My scales resemble a hundred bellyaches.

Our flat at 18 South Munn Avenue sits directly across a narrow courtyard from 22, its mirror-image sister building. This far predates home air-conditioning, so on sweltering summer days every window is open, hoping for a hint of breeze.

Thus, dozens of neighbors are subjected to my puerile squealings. One particularly aggrieved fellow leans far out of his living room window one night to shout at Mom, "Hey, lady! Have a heart!"

And Dad stubbornly refuses to face the music.

So Millie reluctantly, and against her far better judgment, signs me up for the Nassau School talent show, where I will attempt to play "My Country 'Tis of Thee".

"Talent" is a word best not uttered in the same breath with *"Ronald"* and *"violin."* Had there been elimination rounds, I would have been spared the public mortification that lingers seven decades later. But, apparently, if your Dad says you have talent, that's good enough for old Nassau.

Which is why, on an otherwise delightful spring afternoon, I stand in the wings of the very auditorium where a few weeks earlier the great opera star Paul Robeson had sung *"Old Man River."* That I would be committing musical homicide on Paul's stage might have struck me as travesty had I been old enough to be acquainted with that word.

"And now our next talent, Ronald Cohen of Mrs. Doyle's second grade class, will play *America'* on the violin," comes the off-stage voice of a hapless teacher wondering what depredations had won her the job of emcee for "The Afternoon From Hell."

Numb with fear, and with the whole world seeming to be out of focus, I stumble to center stage and begin scratching away. It feels like I have been standing there forever, but like a dentist's drilling my public humiliation finally, mercifully, concludes. Before they can actually give me the hook, I peer into the audience trying to spot Mom.

Although she is quite tall, the humiliated woman has slumped so deeply in her seat to be nigh invisible.

That night, I catch snatches of stage-whispering from behind the parental bedroom door.

"That's it, he's finished. It's over. I've never been so mortified in my life."

"C'mon, honey. It couldn't have been that bad."

"How would you know? You very conveniently weren't there."

"He's no Jascha Heifetz, but he isn't **THAT** horrible."

"Yes, he's **THAT HORRIBLE**! Not a single note right! If they hadn't announced it, nobody would have had the vaguest clue what he was playing. He played *America--* and *America* lost!"

No audible response from Maurie. He again has thrown in the towel in the face of my Italian mom's wrath.

Thus did the violin disappear.

Alas, so did Leah.

🍦 🍦 🍦

Chapter 5

SOMEONE'S IN THE KITCHEN WITH MILLIE

Mom didn't spend her whole adult life in the kitchen. It just seemed that way.

She was no Julia Child, nor Marcella Hazan. She didn't cook fancy, nor pore over fussy, glossily illustrated recipes.

Millie cooked by memory—her's and Filomena's—and by experiment, by instinct, by gut.

She shined brightest with the simple Italian peasant food of her heritage. A magician. Her three-meat meatballs—beef, pork, and veal—disintegrated at the touch of a fork, tiny garlicky, garlicky, garlicky bombs. Marinated in her peerless San Marzano tomato-based gravy (never say sauce!), they could whisk you off to Napoli at first bite.

Lasagna, gnocchi, ravioli, manicotti—all blissfully married to that otherworldly gravy, in which simmered delicacies beyond just the meatballs. Italian sausage. Bracciole. Spareribs. A brace of pork chops. Each added distinctive flavors to embrace gravy so darkly red that it almost was black. Enter that kitchen and be prepared for an odor that at once was enveloping and congratulatory.

To this day, in a small plastic box in our kitchen, reside three-by-five-inch recipe cards containing her secrets to penne arrabiata, pasta puttanesca, and, yes, gravy and meatballs. In ink, in her lyrical cursive.

But though justly famed around North Jersey for her Italian specialties, Millie didn't neglect my dad's Jewish heritage. Nobody ever made a better brisket, simmered agonizingly slowly, peerless root vegetables the supporting cast.

And she effortlessly handled our Sunday ritual— bagels and cream cheese and a variety of smoked fish for brunch; pastrami, corned beef, Kosher knockwursts for dinner. We never knew how many semi-regulars might show, but somehow Millie never ran out.

Drop-in visitors, a regular occurrence in the Cohen home on Cobane Terrace in West Orange, never left disappointed. Mom always could whip out of the freezer containers of those meatballs and gravy; presently, they were arrayed on a heaping platter of macaroni.

She genuinely loved to cook, but even more loved watching friends eat, drink and make merry around the Cohen table. *"Mangia, mangia, mangia"* could have been—should have been—the motto on a Figliuolo coat of arms.

Yet for all her culinary successes, I most fondly remember Millie's occasional gaffes.

First you have to understand that she was a neat freak, a trait she handed down to Diane but not to me.

Millie's home was immaculate—tables and lamps and knick-knacks dusted, beds made, floors swept, rugs vacuumed, kitchen eat-off-the-floor spotless. Disorder disoriented her.

The very first thing she did after walking through the front door of our newly acquired house on Grove Street in Montclair was to polish three hanging doorbell chimes in our foyer. That clearly was their introduction to Brasso.

So that should put into some context the following tales.

In a Thanksgiving fiasco that instantly became family lore, Millie lined her oven with aluminum foil so turkey splatter would not despoil its pristine interior. Hour after hour she checked on the progress of old Tom, who remained very dead—and also very raw. In her zeal for cleanliness, she had not realized that foil may keep an oven clean, but it also shields the turkey from the heating element.

We didn't starve, of course. A few hours earlier we had polished off the first course—lasagna and all the trimmings.

Then there was the time Jill and I picked up Millie at Kennedy Airport in New York and drove to our apartment in East Hartford, Connecticut.

Just back from Italy, Millie was itching to try her hand at zeppole—little balls of dough deep-fried golden brown, then powdered liberally with confectioner's sugar and wolfed down piping hot.

Barely dropping her valise, she commandeered our garden apartment's narrow kitchen. Before long, little zeppole balls were erupting like Vesuvius, splattering the ceiling with boiling vegetable oil and chunks of half-raw dough. She had neglected making the little pinholes in the dough to relieve pressure that builds up during the frying process.

When the excitement concluded, we returned from our hiding places to assess the damage. The ceiling was doomed—even Millie, who possessed the magic to remove the most persistent stains, was helpless in the face of the carnage.

So we did the only sensible thing. We moved to a new apartment across town.

But perhaps nothing embodied Millie's spirit of cooking and cleaning like the time Jill and I treated ourselves to a three-week vacation, having asked the Montclair Police Department to keep an occasional eye on our premises.

An officer, driving down Grove in his cruiser one afternoon noticed our front door ajar. He entered warily, right hand nervously suspended over holster.

Imagine the shock when he reached the kitchen doorway to discover Millie, on hands and knees, scrubbing our oven.

"Don't shoot!" she cried. "I'm his mother!"

"Of course, you are," he replied gently. "Lock the front door when you leave."

🍦 🍦 🍦

Mama Cohen's Meatball Recipe (The Whole Megillah)

In a large cast iron pan (doesn't work as well with nonstick), brown two pounds of Italian sausage, hot, sweet or both, in a little olive oil. Set aside. Next. brown some country spare ribs and several pork chops in the same pan. Then fry some beef bracciole, which tastes great and darkens the gravy (recipe below). Set all the meats aside and begin on the meatballs.

For the meatballs:

3 pounds ground beef, pork and veal combination
2 Tbs olive oil
6 slices white bread, crust removed, soaked in water or milk and squeezed dry
Milk for proper consistency
Italian flavored bread crumbs for consistency.
6 (minimum) cloves of finely minced garlic
12 or so leaves of Italian flat-leaf parsley, finely chopped
6 eggs
Salt and pepper to taste

Gently mix everything in a large bowl until well combined. You are striving for a very moist consistency that barely holds together. Too moist, add bread crumbs. Too dry, add milk.

Make sure the moistened bread is distributed well throughout the mix, you don't want big chunks in some meatballs, none in others.

If you like cheese in your meatballs, you can add a cup or so of grated parmesan into the mix. Do not over-handle, nor pack the meat too tightly.

Form into balls approximately the size golf balls, or a tiny bit larger. This is important. Don't make them TOO BIG!

In the pan you used for the other meat (leave any stuck meat bits), heat enough olive oil to cover one-third of the meatballs. (Fry a small test meatball, let it cool a little, then taste it). Adjust seasonings as needed.

Once you are satisfied, begin frying meatballs. Don't crowd the pan; cook them in batches if necessary.

When the bottom gets nicely browned (but not crusty), carefully rotate the ball by one-third. When the second third is brown, rotate again. So, in essence, instead of having perfectly round meatballs, they will be sort of triangle-shaped.

When the meat has browned, drain excess olive oil from the pan but be careful to leave ALL the bits of meat that have stuck.

Then, over a very low flame and add a teaspoon or so of sugar, and swirl it into the dregs of the pan until it starts to foam. Carefully add a can of tomato paste and swirl again to completely incorporate. Put a little warm water in the tomato paste can to get all the paste, and add mixture to the frying pan. Repeat with two more cans of tomato paste.

In a couple of minutes everything will darken into a beautiful, almost ebony color from the burning of the sugar and the retrieval of the meat flecks. When well incorporated, turn off the flame.

Place the contents of four large cans of imported Italian tomatoes (San Marzano are best, but make sure whatever you use are imported from Italy) in a 7-quart stockpot. If the canned tomatoes do not contain basil, drop in a half-dozen large, fresh basil leaves. Add the tomato-paste/sugar/meat dregs to the pot. Incorporate well and bring to a boil. Reduce heat to a simmer and carefully place in the pork products and beef bracciole. Simmer gently, covered, for about two hours. Periodically, gently stir to make sure no meat sticks to the bottom. The lid can be adjusted to release a little during cooking.

The last half hour, carefully add the meatballs.

🍦 🍦 🍦

Millie's recipe for beef bracciole:

Pound a half-dozen pieces of thin-sliced butterflied beef (you can find it in a supermarket or an Italian specialty store) to a very thin consistency. Sprinkle with chopped garlic, minced parsley and grated parmesan, then roll into cigar-shape rolls about 4-5 inches long and gently tie in several places with thread. Brown in olive oil, then add to gravy with other meats, except meatballs.

NOTE 1: You can adjust ingredients depending on how many you are serving. But remember, every time you reheat gravy it improves—so you really can never make too much.

NOTE 2: The meatballs NEVER come out exactly the same. Any Italian cook will attest to that. The most important thing is to make sure they aren't TOO DENSE. Better they should be too moist than too dry -- dense ones sit sullenly in the bottom of your belly, light ones seem to disappear as they pass the taste buds.

Serve with your favorite pasta (great with ravioli and lasagna, too).

Mangia bene -- and don't forget the vino rosso!
Ciao, bambini.
Mellina Cohen (nee Figliuolo)

🍦 🍦 🍦

Chapter 6

LONGIE AND THE HERSHEYS

We always are well-stocked with candy treats when the ghosts and goblins and ballerinas of Hallowe'en ring our doorbell.

For I have fond memories of a Hallowe'en more than 70 years ago, when somebody was extremely generous to me.

My benefactor was a man named Abner "Longie" Zwillman, stepfather of my slightly older playmate on South Munn Avenue in East Orange.

I was seven, far too young to be aware of the gangsters and hoodlums that populated Longie Zwillman's nefarious crime kingdom.

Google him and read his 747-page FBI dossier. It identifies Zwillman as "boss of New Jersey's underworld, beginning in 1935 and ending in 1959, when he 'committed suicide.' He was one of the six bosses of Murder, Incorporated."

Those FBI files are chockablock with allegations of "illegal liquor, racketeering, waterfront extortion, income tax evasion, jury tampering, obstruction of justice, contempt of court, and corruption of public officials." Quite the bill of particulars.

But absent is the fact that on Halloween night in 1944, Longie stepped out of character long enough to add "kindly benefactor" to his relentlessly ghastly resume.

Costumed as a ghost and bearing an empty pillowcase to transport my goodies, I left our apartment with this admonition from Mom: "You can go in this building, and to 14 and 22 next door. But don't cross the street to 32."

So I canvassed the three identical apartment buildings as she had instructed, then returned to empty my sack and to beg to go to my Uncle Sam's off-limits apartment at 32 South Munn—just to show him my costume, of course. She relented, and I headed off to a magnificent building that dwarfed its dowdy neighbors, including ours.

Uncle Sam was impressed by his ghostly nephew, but he had no candy—nothing in his bachelor fridge except Scotch, a bottle of club soda whose carbonation had long since returned to the atmosphere, and the detritus of a jar of pickled herring. In cream, not wine sauce.

But while he had no goodies, he did have an inspiration.

"Go knock on Longie's apartment. I bet he'll have stuff."

Up to the Penthouse I went—because I couldn't reach the top button Uncle Sam punched it for me, then slipped out before the elevator door could close on him.

Longie is dressed in a red smoking jacket.

"Whaddya want, kid?" he growls, perhaps unnerved that I have pierced the lobby's security force—an oldish guy in a far less elegant red jacket.

"Trick or treat," I cleverly reply.

Longie gazes at me suspiciously, as if my sheet might conceal a belt of explosives, or a gat. Then he shrugs and disappears, returning a couple of minutes later with a box of 48 Hershey bars.

Plain, no almonds.

"Open up, kid," he commands, and dumps the entire box into my pillowcase.

Be still my heart! This bonanza will last until New Year's!

Happily, I ride the elevator down to the lobby—(I can reach *that* button!)—cross the street, and run home to show Mom my treasure. Twenty yards from the safety of our front door, disaster. Three bullies (maybe they were a couple years older, I couldn't tell exactly because of their masks) mug me for my pillowcase. I am angry and scared and teary-eyed— all understandable reactions to such a heinous deed. But one emotion trumps the others.

Greed.

I return to 32, con the one-man security force into pushing the penthouse button, and soon I am again confronting Longie.

"What the hell, kid? Whatsa' matter?"

"The big kids stole my Hersheys," I whimper.

Longie spits a word I recognize because it once earned me a mouthful of Octagon soap. Then he wheels and disappears down the hall. In a few moments he is back carrying one of his own silk pillowcases stuffed with 48 replacement Hersheys. No almonds.

And a bonus. From the hallway shadows materialize two of the meanest-looking torpedoes on planet Earth.

"Walk the kid home, and make sure nuthin' happens to him," Longie orders his stevedore-sized bodyguards.

Which they did.

🍦 🍦 🍦

Fifteen years later, Longie Zwillman, his coin-operated machines rackets under fire from the feds and with G-Men after him for taxes, was found in the basement of his home on Beverly Road in West Orange, a few houses from where my Uncle Sam now lived. Longie was hanging by a clothesline noose. Suicide, the authorities said.

Yeah, right. How many gangsters live long enough to commit suicide?

As often happens after sinners depart, stories began surfacing about Longie's generosity—with which, of course, I was intimately acquainted. Seems that during the Depression, he had bankrolled the Mt. Carmel Catholic soup kitchen in Newark. Needy Jews always got holiday food baskets at Hanukkah. And he dressed up as Santa with a well-stocked bag of presents for Christian kids on Christmas.

And he was particularly good to the ladies. A special squeeze was Jean Harlow, a legendary platinum blonde movie star so dazzling that she won the nickname "The 'It' Girl."

Longie secured a two-movie deal for her with a $500,000 cash "loan" to film mogul Harry Cohn; he also gave Harlow, godmother to racketeer Bugsy Siegel's daughter, a jeweled bracelet and a red Cadillac.

"The 'It' Girl" really loved that big red Caddy.

Probably almost as much as I loved those Hersheys. No almonds.

🍦 🍦 🍦

Chapter 7

CRAZY FOR BASEBALL

Slow and languid under the summer sun, baseball is an insidious mistress.

I fell in love with her at age seven at the Grove Street Oval in East Orange, New Jersey—and never fell out.

My wonderful granddaughter Kamille also was seven when I took her to her first game at a far grander venue where the San Francisco Giants play.

On the bus to Pac-Bell Park in the summer of 2010, she looks up at me, big eyes open wide, and says, "Grandpa, will you catch me a ball tonight?"

Now I have attended thousands of baseball games at all levels of competition for more than seven decades, and guess how many balls have I caught?

Just one. When I was in college keeping statistics for the guy broadcasting the University of Illinois game, a high pop foul behind the plate would have hit him smack in the head had I not stabbed it barehanded. "Ladies and gentlemen, Ron Cohen just saved my life," Harvey Wittenberg informed his vast listening audience— perhaps a few dozen indifferent souls.

Yet every time I enter a ballpark, I delude myself that this is the game I get lucky. A phenomenal, one-handed twisting grab, and, as 45,000 roar, I selflessly present the ball to the nearest little girl with curly red hair. Never a glove. For sissies. Bare hands, damn the consequences.

I was in the upper deck in left field at the Polo Grounds in New York in 1949 with my Uncle Sam when a batter cracked a homer—right at us. Sam, perhaps 5-feet-7 on tip-toes, lunges to score a souvenir for his nephew. The pain of failure (no ball!) is assuaged by the fact his two broken fingers are courtesy of that rarest of creatures, a Jewish slugger. Sid "The Yid" Gordon.

I try to explain to Kami the astronomical odds against my catching a ball, but I spy a look familiar to guys with seven-year-old granddaughters, the one that says, against all reason, "My Grandpa can do anything." A look that, like the first crocus of spring, will be short-lived as she gradually matures into the world of the real: Grandpa would walk through a wall of fire for you, my darling, but he is quite fallible and often doesn't know what to do—or how to do it.

So I tell her of course I'll try to catch you a ball, then divert her attention with a San Francisco Giants cap and certificate certifying she is attending her first major league game. I shell out for a monster hot dog that could feed our whole section behind home plate, a super-sized soda and a huge swirl of cotton candy dyed a blue so garish that Mother Nature would wretch.

Oh, that was a glorious night, Kami. Before we left for the game, I tried to give you a crash course, with crude drawings. I wanted you to understand at least enough to keep you interested; games these days can last four hours and try the patience and loyalty of the most rabid fan.

I could have saved my breath. You forget your lesson before we even reach our seats—well out of range of even the foulest of foul balls. It doesn't matter. You sweet-talk an usher into taking our picture, and your unalloyed cuteness led the lady sitting next to me to declare, "You must be some wonderful Grandpa."

And you never are bored. You charm me out of my skull when, every time the crowd cheers or groans, you ask, "Are we happy, Grandpa?" I assure you that, yes, Kami, we are happy, and you squeeze my hand and say, "Grandpa, I'm having so much fun ... Thank you."

Five years later, simultaneous with the final out of the World Series, I answer the phone and hear, "Giants win the series! Giants win the series!" A huge grin creases my face, for the excited voice belongs to my Kamille Sue.

We have gone to many more games since then, Kami, and will continue to have "so much fun." That night in San Francisco, you were four years younger than I was on a September evening in 1948 when my Dad, your great-grandpa Maurie, took me to the Polo Grounds for my first game, New York Giants hosting the Brooklyn Dodgers.

I had been a Dodger fan since I was six, my fate sealed the day I came home from kindergarten, switched on the radio, and caught the last inning of the game against our hated rivals, the Giants. Dixie Walker, the Dodger star, hit into a double play to end the game.

In what would become a lifelong (and reliably heartbreaking) habit of rooting for the underdog, I immediately became a Dodger fan. And Dixie became my favorite player, at least until the unspeakable racial slurs he directed at his own teammate when Jackie Robinson became the first black major leaguer. No wonder Walker's nickname was Dixie.

Our apartment in East Orange was a few blocks from the Grove Street Oval, where I saw my first games. I did not realize until years later I had been present at history in the making.

Back then, blacks were not allowed in the major leagues, or even the minors. So Negro League teams formed in heavily black cities like Baltimore, Pittsburgh, Kansas City, Washington. These teams included players skilled enough for the majors, but that career avenue seemed permanently closed. So they spent their most productive playing years barnstorming America against each other before a few dozen spectators in dusty one-horse towns that made East Orange seem like Gotham.

The Oval was frequent host to teams like the Homestead Grays, the Baltimore Elite Giants, the Kansas City Monarchs. I saw Negro League legends like Satchell Paige, Josh Gibson, Roy Campanella, and Cool Papa Bell—some of whom made the big leagues past their primes after Robinson broke the color barrier in 1947. Other greats—and Cool Papa was one of the greatest—never did.

The Oval sometimes had a special attraction, one of the Negro League teams playing a squad called The House of David whose players—beards so long you couldn't read the team's name on their uniform fronts—were billed as Orthodox Jews.

It is doubtful any actually were Jewish, never mind Orthodox. Even at my tender age, I suspected they had been chosen less for religious beliefs than beard-growing prowess.

I "made" the majors a year after Jackie Robinson had, when my dad took me to that first big league game at the Polo Grounds. Dodgers vs. Giants. Every seat was occupied for this bitter rivalry. Of course it rained. Hard and long.

With drops splatting on the infield tarp like Gene Krupa on drums, the start is delayed. In truth, the game should be postponed, but the home-standing Giants are loathe to lose the revenue from 50,000 paying customers when the game is made up as part of a double-header.

The first pitch finally is delivered around 9 p.m., after a 90-minute delay. Dad and I are soaked and shivering, but we are 20 miles from home and unwilling to forfeit the symbolism of a first father-son ball game. So we hang tough—and wet.

Rain comes and goes; twice more the tarps roll out, are rolled back up, and roll out again. It is almost 1 a.m. when Dodger catcher Bruce Edwards squints through drizzly mist to catch the foul pop that brings merciful conclusion. Wringing wet and exhausted but caring only that "The Dodgers Won!", we arrive home after 2.

Carrying our soaking shoes and my new blue-and-white Dodger pennant, we tip-toe into the apartment, hoping not to awaken Mom.

Fat chance. The lightest sleeper on the planet confronts us immediately in the darkened vestibule, arms folded across her chenille bathrobe and shooting her death-ray glare, the dread Italian *mal' occhio*.

Our very own one-woman police force, judge, and jury. Mildred Delores Figliuolo Cohen is on the warpath.

Even under normal circumstances, Millie cuts a formidable figure. Angry, she is a force of nature.

No couple could be more dissimilar. She a fiery Italian, nobody to mess with. He soft-spoken, far more comfortable with cajoling than confronting. I never met two people more in love.

But love is a foreign concept to Millie right now. She struggles to keep her voice below a shout, in deference to our neighbors—and perhaps the entire population of North Jersey.

"Young man, to bed!" she orders. My heart says hang around to help Dad, but I am young, not stupid. He alone will have to face this epic eruption of Mount Millie.

I listen from behind my bedroom door, but out of respect for the hour, she employs a low hiss even more menacing than the roar I had expected.

"What do you mean keeping him out to all hours? He has school tomorrow., He's only 11, for heaven's sake?" (Paraphrasing to sanitize the flood of Napolitan epithets.)

Soaked and shivering, Dad is silent. He has learned it does little good to interrupt.

"He will flunk out. He won't make it through high school. How is he ever going to get into Yale?"

With this last I must stifle a guffaw. When Mom gets on a roll, logic is a non-starter. That I could even dream of Yale is preposterous, no matter how brilliant my kindly fourth-grade teacher, Hester Switzer, thinks I am.

Poor Dad, I think as I drift to sleep, but at least his co-conspirator seems to have eluded maternal wrath.

Mom is right, as always. I sleep-walk through class next day, but after school things seem fine. Can it be that punishment for the sins of the father will not be visited upon the son?

Attacking my after-school snack, I open the now long-defunct Newark Evening News to relive last night's glorious Dodger triumph.

In huge black type on the first sports page:

BARNEY NO-HITS GIANTS, DODGERS WIN 2-0.

Fourteen hours after Bruce Edwards snares the final pop-up, I learn from THE DAMNED NEWSPAPER that my first Major League game was A NO-HITTER!

Enraged, I rush to where Dad is sitting.

"Why didn't you tell me?" I demand, waving the headline inches from his nose. "Why do I have to find out from the paper?"

It turns out Maurie hadn't realized it, either.

⚾ ⚾ ⚾

Rex Barney was a flame-throwing right-hander of such prodigious talent that insiders predicted he might mature into one of the truly great pitchers. His fastball had been clocked at 100 miles per hour, meaning that almost before he releases it the batter must decide whether to swing.

Or duck. For, sadly, Rex was possessed of a crippling weakness. He had no clue where his pitch would end up—four feet outside, four feet inside, bouncing three feet in front of the plate or sailing six feet over the catcher's head.

Or rarely, right down the middle.

Hitters normally dig their spikes in the batter's box, weight distributed for maximum balance and power.

Against Barney, "digging in" was out of the question. Batters hoped merely to survive.

"We barely can see it. How are we supposed to get the hell out of the way?" more than one hitter would grump on the trudge back to the dugout.

Utter wildness is why his no-hitter shocked the fans, the Giant batters, his own teammates. Rex Barney perhaps most of all. Yet for a brief moment in the cold, vast dampness of the Polo Grounds, Barney had realized that enormous potential.

But fame disappeared as quickly as his fastball could travel the sixty feet, six inches to the plate. Never solving the mystery of how to keep his aspirin tablets in the strike zone, Barney drifted out of the majors two years later, completing a mediocre career with 30 wins and 31 losses--and hundreds of jelly-kneed batters praying for another base on balls.

A sports writer quipped that Barney might have become the greatest pitcher in baseball history "if only home plate were high and outside."

His no-hitter, the only one in the majors in 1948, was a feat that would not be replicated for two more seasons. But history was lost on Mom, for it had been a school night, and I was only 11.

Yes, I got a high school diploma, and no, I didn't get into Yale. I could almost hear the admissions officers in New Haven slapping their thighs in the spring of 1955 as they flipped my application into the wastebasket marked "The Kid Must Be Joking!"

But I would always have a priceless memory—a no-hitter with Dad a decade before he died, at age 49.

On my first pilgrimage to the Baseball Hall of Fame in Cooperstown 55 years later, I picked up only one souvenir: a copy of the box score of Barney's masterpiece, my first big league game.

Wait. There's a postscript.

Rex Barney's big league playing career may have been largely unremarkable, but he enjoyed a far happier second act for two decades as the Baltimore Orioles public address announcer. His corny routines appealed to the citizens of "Charm City," many of them working-class cornballs themselves.

When someone in the stands made a good catch of a foul ball, Rex would shout over the PA, "Give that fan a contract!", and an usher would materialize carrying a pen and a phony, if official-looking, souvenir.

And after the final out at each home game, Barney would intone a signature "Thank youuuuuuuuu!" to the fans for coming, milking "you" for all it was worth.

But he remained sad and bitter that he never had lived up to the hype.

"Believe me," he once wrote, "there isn't a day goes by that I don't think of what I could have and should have done. It still hurts."

Yet Barney clearly loved basking in the Orioles' reflected glory, until he suffered a debilitating stroke that sidelined him for almost a year.

Frail and pale, he returned to the Orioles press box on Sept. 9, 1997, to a standing ovation.

I was among the 50,000 fans that day, positive that Rex Barney and I were the only ones there who had been at the Polo Grounds one fateful night precisely 49 years earlier.

And I needed to tell him that.

Leaving my seat near the right field foul line, I snuck onto the media elevator and up to the press box level. Although my U.S. Congress press pass had absolutely no standing at the ballpark, I flashed it and hurried past a couple of stadium ushers too quickly for them to read the small print.

When I found Barney's press box seat, I squatted so that my face was at his level.

"Sorry to disturb you, Mr. Barney, but I just had to let you know. I was there that night at the Polo Grounds for your no-hitter. It was my first big league game. Thank you so much for that memory. I'll never forget it."

Rex Barney stared for an instant in disbelief, then shut his eyes and quickly jerked his face to the side.

But not quickly enough to hide his tears.

🍦 🍦 🍦

Chapter 8

MYRNA AND THE CHICK

It was in fourth grade at Nassau School in East Orange that I discovered that whatever my future held it surely would not include animal husbandry or veterinary medicine.

Because Easter school break that year brought a horrible self-revelation. I was scared of a baby chick.

As a science experiment, Mrs. (this was long before somebody invented Ms.) Switzer's class endeavored, starting on a cold, wintry January day, to hatch our very own Easter chick.

This small, kindly grandmother, my favorite teacher of all time, brought into class the closest thing she could find to approximate an actual hen house—a rectangular wooden box with slanted roof, wire mesh, and a smallish light bulb that glowed fiercely yellow.

The bulb was the fulcrum of the experiment: If we kept it constantly shining on a regular normal old egg 24 hours a day for a number of weeks, would an actual baby chick emerge?

If so, the class would adopt it—feed it, water it, and altogether welcome it into our world. Mrs. Switzer decreed that on weekends, on a rotating basis, she would choose one particularly well-behaved pupil to serve as adoptive parent.

Well, the light bulb did its stuff. On Monday before Easter, an infinitesimal beak cracked through the eggshell, followed by the rest of the creature—a tiny soaking wet, thoroughly bedraggled black lump.

To our surprise and delight, the critter somehow survived its first few days. So lavishly did we tend its biological needs that by Thursday afternoon it had noticeably bulked up, with nascent feathering.

Hester Switzer rapped her pencil on her desk just before dismissal bell and made an announcement that would rock my world: Over the 10-day Easter recess, none other than Ronald Cohen would be the initial guardian of the new chick's future—should it survive to have one. I was Mrs. Switzer's favorite, just as she was mine, and neither of us took pains to hide it.

"Oh great! Oh no!" was my dueling reaction. Honor and responsibility locked horns like stags impressing a doe. My initial day with the new chick would be Good Friday, and even this budding atheist knew that might not be the most propitious coincidence for our new friend.

I was to be first! But what if I murdered it? Racing through my brain were all sorts of potential calamities that might await Chez Cohen.

Just before we added new straw to the box that I would be carrying four blocks on my walk home, Mrs. Switzer announced that each bird-sitter would have the honor of bestowing the chick a temporary name. And re-naming rights would fall to the next well-behaved classmate; Chicky X would be rechristened each weekend. Since most chickens had no names at all, we were pretty sure not having a permanent one would cause no harm.

"Ronald, what are you going to name him?" Mrs. Switzer asked.

I gazed at our new coal-black mascot and peripherally spotted the current object of my fickle elementary school hormones—Myrna Fletcher, tallish, thin, sad-eyed. Like our pet, she possessed shoulder-length coal-black locks.

"Myrna," I blurted, noting that she was blushing prettily as I headed for the door.

Perhaps I should have named it "Trouble." Next morning when I opened her tiny cage door, Myrna the chick hurtled past me to relative freedom behind the stove.

When I informed Mom, her response was zero sympathy. I wasn't surprised. When I had carried Myrna and the box home, this was Millie's approximate welcome:

"*Managgia mia!* How long is that little rat going to be here?"

She hadn't mellowed overnight. "Get her out from behind the stove before she gets cooked! I'm making Easter lasagna."

"What, me? I'm supposed to get her?"

"It's your pet. Your responsibility. Figure it out!"

I took my case to appellate court—my father, usually the more patiently understanding parental unit.

"Dad, can you get Myrna out from behind the stove?"

"No, son, it's your pet and your responsibility."

Drat! Those two must have stayed up all night rehearsing.

Gingerly I reached behind the stove, but when Myrna brushed against my hand en route to her terrified getaway, I screamed in most uncourageous fashion.

How foolish. How could I be afraid of something I could crush with the light pressure of one hand?

Logic stood no chance against pure fear. Myrna, equally petrified, chased me from the kitchen into the living room. Cowardly Lion in *The Wizard of Oz* was braver than I.

Mom and Dad could have called me "chicken" and ordered me to just pick the damn thing up. They could have pointed out that—like the Wizard—I was great and terrible and Myrna was small and meek. But to their credit they sensed my inchoate state demanded tenderness, not tough love.

So Mom gathered me in a hug while Dad re-caged Myrna. For the next 10 days they cared for the chick as if it were their own. The Monday after spring break, Dad carried the cage into the classroom. I trailed quite a safe distance behind.

"It was a great experience," Maurie baldly lied to Hester Switzer. "We hate to give him up."

That Friday, just before dismissal, Mrs. Switzer prepared the announcement we had all been awaiting. Dramatically, she toyed with us, prolonging our tension. At last she drew herself up to her full 4 feet, 10 inches.

"In reward for exemplary comportment all week, the winner of 'Chick-Sitter for the Weekend' is … Myrna Fletcher. What are you going to name him, Myrna?"

Myrna the Bigger Chick hesitated briefly, then slyly smiled and replied "Why, Big Ronald, of course."

I could have sworn she winked at me.

🍦 🍦 🍦

Chapter 9

DORIS AND THE BROKEN LEG

Doris Kraus was a classmate at Nassau School in East Orange, a sweet little girl whose parents came from Germany. It was kind of exotic having a German-American friend during World War II when adults were saying bad things about those awful "Krauts."

But you couldn't regard her wildly bouncing blond curls and her shy smile and think anything except, "How unbearably cute!"

One day in fifth grade Doris was absent and Miss Hood delivered shocking news: Doris had been struck by a car on Central Avenue, her right leg was shattered and she might even miss the rest of the school year.

"We need a volunteer to bring her homework, someone who lives not too far from the hospital," declared Miss Hood.

My hand shot up. I liked Doris. A lot. And I kinda thought she "liked" me back.

East Orange General Hospital was on my block, I told my teacher, and Miss Hood agreed. I was perfect for the job.

Carrying our books that day after school, I visited Doris in the very hospital where, a couple of decades later, my daughters Rachel and Jennifer would be born.

Her room was a torture chamber. Tiny Doris, all but swallowed up by her enormous hospital bed, was prisoner to cranks and pulleys and wires. Her leg disappeared in a plaster cast that reached her hip.

It wasn't easy maneuvering around this mechanical monstrosity to deposit the homework. We both were embarrassed: She to be seen like this; me by how vulnerable she looked. I blurted a bit of nonsense and fled.

But I returned next day and the next, every school day for three weeks. Less awkward each time, I stayed longer and longer. She was an industrious student with nothing else to do during long hours of hospital isolation. Each afternoon I brought her new assignments and picked up the completed work for Miss Hood to grade.

When they discharged Doris doctors cautioned her not to put too much weight on the reconstructed leg. She could not leave her apartment for another four or five weeks, almost to the end of the school year.

So Miss Hood needed a replacement volunteer for after-school homework delivery chores, someone who lived near her apartment.

My raised hand drew her raised eyebrow. Didn't Doris live on South Harrison Street, at least a mile out of my way? "Milton Strauss lives right next door. Perhaps it would be easier for him to carry her homework."

Rats! Milton Strauss!

Kraus and Strauss!

My warped and hormone-addled young mind conjured a euphonious Kraus and Strauss wedding a few years hence, myself slumped broken-hearted on the sidelines like a lump of liverwurst.

I stood no chance against Milton. He was tall and ruggedly handsome, with chiseled nose, strong and square jaw, a pillow of blond hair just like Doris. A perfect match.

Me? Even in elementary school the first traces of the hereditary Cohen widow's peak were painfully apparent. A cold-hearted classmate once described my profile:

"His forehead is like a ski jump, and his nose just keeps on going."

Milton was quiet and studious, Ron loud and distracting. A few weeks earlier he had beaten me by a nose—even with my Cyrano de Bergerac advantage—in the hundred-yard dash, the featured event at Nassau School's Spring Jamboree.

Before finishing my tale of Doris, let me tell you a little bit about the aftermath of that race. As runner-up, I too had won a large orange block letter *N.* I rushed home so Mom could sew it on my front-button cardigan. Soon I would be wearing my very first "letter sweater!"

Walking into the apartment, I waved the *N* as if it were an acceptance letter from Yale. Millie seemed underwhelmed.

"I'll sew it on, but I don't see the big deal."

No big deal? Didn't she remember back several centuries to her own teens when athletes wearing varsity letter sweaters strutted the halls of Barringer High, trailing legions of starry-eyed co-eds?

"I bet you're not even all that fast," Mom taunted. "Bet I could beat you."

I stifled a guffaw. Was she nuts? This pitiable antique dared challenge Mr. Nassau School Hundred-Yard-Dash-Runner-Up? Absolutely not. I had no intention of embarrassing my mom.

She shot me the "look" that her Italian brothers and sisters, with respect and some jealousy, called Millie's *mal' occhio.*

The Evil Eye.

"Okay, we'll race someday," I muttered.

"We'll race right now!"

When she got like that, don't argue. A lesson painfully learned and relearned, even at my still tender age.

We walked five floors down from our apartment to the backyard, where Millie stepped off about 50 yards like a football referee marking a penalty and threw down a dishtowel to mark the finish line.

Swinging her arms and twisting her trunk vigorously to warm up, she walked back to where I was standing. I glanced down at her flat shoes, pitiable next to my gleaming new white sneaks.

"I'll count to five—give you a little head start," I offered.

Again the *mal' occhio*—second time in five minutes. Perhaps a new North Jersey mixed-marriage record.

Okay, I thought, *I will start slowly to make the outcome a little closer.* But she suddenly shouted, "Go!" and shot off like Mercury. I knew instantly I was doomed. Many races are decided at the starting line, and this was going to be one of them.

She won by five yards, and it could have been far worse had she not begun trash-talking me near the finish, theatrically slowing and twisting her head to make sure I would not miss her decidedly unmotherly gloat.

Millie had, ruthlessly, crushed her very own son. She would have crushed Milton Strauss. Hell, she might have crushed Jesse Owens.

I'll hand this to her. When I later showed my dad the sweater onto which she had stitched the spiffy orange *N*, Millie silently stood in the kitchen stirring the gravy and never hinting at my mortification.

"Nice going," Dad said. "You know your mom was quite a runner in her day, too."

"Oh, yeah?" I said, suspecting the saga of my backyard humiliation never would pass mom's lips or mine.

Until now.

🍦 🍦 🍦

But back to Doris. I had volunteered to re-up for five more weeks of selfless humanitarianism, fearful my blonde cutie would fall into the clutches of my matinee idol rival and end up Mrs. Doris Kraus-Strauss.

I guess Miss Hood must somehow have remembered about young love, because she agreed to extend my after-school gig.

But puppy love rarely survives the inexorable march of time. After sixth grade my family moved to West Orange to a new school system and brand-new best friends. There even were some new schoolboy crushes, passing of notes to new cute girls in class and teasing them mercilessly. Exact schoolboy behavior since puberty was invented.

Doris was equally busy adjusting to junior high in East Orange and a fresh supply of swains-in-training.

The new distance between us was small potatoes— maybe three miles from my house on Orange Mountain to her apartment on South Harrison Street, via the Public Service 23 bus. Yet we might as well have been inhabiting different planets.

I didn't really think about Doris again until autumn of my junior year in high school, the only season I wasn't involved in varsity sports. I really liked watching football, but play it? That was for oversized brutes from The Valley whose names ended in vowels and whose heads were empty save for the boulders. Jewish kids on the mountain stuck to intellectual pursuits like basketball and tennis, where bone pulverization was far less likely.

Also, I had just broken off yet another fickle crush. No girl, no sports. Nature abhors a vacuum, and into my personal vacuum crept memories of Doris Kraus.

It took her a few seconds to remember me when I phoned, but she agreed to a movie date that Saturday night.

The first visit to her building since my homework delivery chores, and it smelled as if I had never left. The first magic sniff of her mom's gut-busting German cooking wafted down the elevator chute. By the time I reached her door I felt myself transported back a half-dozen years to the memory of my plumpish little blond-haired cutie. I waited a couple of seconds and breathed a couple of deep whiffs of sauerbraten to bolster my courage, then knocked.

The door opened to reveal a taller, far more mature version of my grade-school infatuation. I tried to speak but ... gibberish. Even worse, gibberish delivered in a cracking soprano.

Now I had overcome the problem of "voice change" several years earlier, so this relapse had far more to do with my brain cortex than my vocal cords. Girls "way more mature than you remember" can reduce young men to blithering idiots.

The New Doris and I walked around the corner to the Palace Theater. I've long forgotten name of the movie, but the memory of holding hands for the first time still brings a nostalgic smile.

Afterwards we went to *Eppes Essen* (translation: Something to Eat), the best deli in the Oranges. Over pastrami and kosher dills, Doris and Ron tried to rekindle the old days.

She told me I had turned out "so cute" (the sweet little liar). And she smiled at how bowled over I was by this new, vastly improved Doris. But soon, our silences grew longer as we exhausted memories of Nassau School and the Springtime of the Broken Leg.

For Doris had her new world and I had mine. The world of "us" was merely a memory.

At her door she shyly raised onto tiptoes and softly kissed my cheek, perfume mingling with the lingering scent of schnitzel.

"Goodbye," Doris Kraus whispered, then turned and disappeared from my life forever.

🍦 🍦 🍦

Chapter 10

ME AND THE DUKE

Since seventh grade, John Dowd has been my pal. His nickname back then was Duke—why, I have no idea. Now we both are 80, and because we are almost grown up and because he asks me to, I call him John, not Duke.

Except when I forget, which is quite often.

Because even if we live to be 100, rocking on the porch of our nursing home and plotting fresh ways to get into trouble, Duke will always be "Duke" to me.

I still have many good childhood friends, but Duke stands out because whenever we get together—when we were teenagers and now that we are old and gray (at least Duke is, because *he* still has hair)—trouble clings to us like wet socks. When my mother would spot Duke headed toward our house, she'd say, "Well, here comes trouble." I am certain Mrs. Dowd said even worse about me.

Not terrible trouble. Nothing involving police or penitentiaries or being grounded for two weeks or having to give up ice cream. I did those things with other friends. With Duke, it was small potatoes stuff.

Like when we were 14 and living in West Orange. One day, Duke came back from the neighboring village, South Orange, our bitter rival in everything: Sports, disposable income—*everything*.

South Orange kids were rich and spoiled. West Orange kids were good and kind, the salt of the earth. They were snobs, we were regular guys. South Orange kids knew that when they turned 17, their parents would buy them new cars. West Orange kids knew that when we turned 17, we might be allowed to get drivers' permits. Our own cars? Dream on. Maybe a rare chance at the family buggy—but only when more important family members deigned.

If one of our gang got lucky enough to cadge a car on a weekend night, everybody piled in—sometimes 10 kids jammed in for a sundae with hot fudge at Gruning's. Or squeezing into the car (sometimes into the trunk so we wouldn't have to pay) and heading to the drive-in movie. (Ask your Grandma what that is, kids).

And those snots from South Orange often would bring their very own cars onto our home turf, West Orange, and drive away with ... are you ready for this? **OUR GIRLFRIENDS!** Many of these interloping Lotharios had convertibles; watching our girls defecting to an enemy driving top-down rag-tops only intensified our anguish.

One lout was particularly aggravating. Not only did he have a snazzy new convertible, but when he stopped the car in front of the house of the girl (**OUR GIRL!**), did he honk? He did **NOT**! He stepped on a button on the floor and activated a chime. *Ding-dong! Ding-dong,* like a damn ice cream truck guy! **OUR GIRL** would run from her house, jump in, and squeeze closer than was safe . . . for driving or for otherwise.

Oh how I wished I personally could "ding-dong" that creep!

Most annoying was his squeaky voice. He sounded like a girl himself, for crying out loud! Why would our smart and beautiful girls fall for a guy who sounded like Mickey Mouse? Sounded, in fact, like his damn car chime! They could have had *us*— our voices cracked only occasionally. It was the car and that chime and the fact his parents were rich. To West Orange girls, South Orange was Venice, Paris, Constantinople. (Look that last one up, too)

Years later, that guy and I wound up working for the same newspaper company. Turned out he was a really nice guy--now that he wasn't stealing one of **OUR GIRLS** and we could laugh over teenage angst. And though the car and the chime were long gone, he still had that squeaky voice!

Anyhow, Duke returned from South Orange with cuts and bruises the day I was talking about above, when we were 14. A bunch of South Orange "hoodlums" had jumped him.

Revenge must be ours! Those bums couldn't get away with something like that! Not with our Duke. Nothing would do but for us to march to South Orange and exact retribution.

So it came to pass that a dozen of us assembled fighting tools—"Sticks and stones will break their bones"—and began our trek, en masse, about three miles toward the center of South Orange Village.

Leading the pack was the smallest kid, Elliott Altman. He might have been short, but he was broad-shouldered and had muscles he later would put to good use as a dentist. Not only was Elliott tough, he also was armed with the ultimate weapon—a metal chain. Duke was right behind him, while I kind of lolled near the back, carrying a small stick. Well, okay. A twig. In truth I considered myself a lover, not a warrior, and didn't think this Armageddon march was such a hot idea.

With each step our confidence grew. Soon we were shouting catchy war chants, like "S.O. guys are Mama's boys, W.O. guys will kick your butts." Didn't rhyme, but sure sounded tough.

Onward and onward, heads swiveling to make sure our flanks were safe from sneak attack. Down Gregory Avenue to the town line, then left on Luddington Road past Mike Schneider's, onto Valley Road as it snaked into South Orange. Into Cameron Field, a beautiful suburban playground with probably more grass than existed in all of West Orange. Baseball diamonds, tennis courts, swimming pool—a wonder those rich jerks didn't own polo ponies.

Finally we hit South Orange Avenue, the main drag through the small village shopping area that rises up a steep hill to the mansions on the crest of Orange Mountain. Still no sign of the "hoodlums." Lucky for them, for they surely would have paid heavily for their transgressions against our Duke.

We shrugged, tossed our "weapons," and hit Gruning's for root beer floats.

🍦 🍦 🍦

Another time, on a hot and sultry summer night, Duke and I sat outside his house scheming how to get our underage fingers around some beer. The legal drinking age in New Jersey was 21, and we were only 15. Worse, we looked 13! What purveyor of beer would be stupid enough not to card us?

"But, what the heck," Duke says. Let's try the Central Tavern on Valley Road. What can they do? Kick us out?

Says I, always a trace less adventurous, they could call the cops. And the cops could call our parents. I know I don't want Millie finding out.

We kick around possible repercussions and the more we discuss it and the thirstier I get, the more fool-proof Duke's plan sounds.

So we make our way several blocks down Lawrence to Valley to the Orange town line. When we get to the Central Tavern, we stand outside a bit, ratcheting up our courage. The place looks far bigger and more forbidding close-up than the many times we'd driven past with my parents.

Duke screws on his best "I'm 21" face, pushes the front door, and strides in. I wait outside, ready to abandon him at the first hint of a cop car.

In a few moments, out walks my co-conspirator with his booty, a cardboard cylinder holding a precious quart of Miller High-Life. The Central Tavern conveniently sold quarts of draft beer to go, just in case you were in a hurry or had lost your church key.

There could be no chickening out now. Duke would rat me out to our friends, and I'd get ragged for weeks. I give the door a tentative shove and slip into forbidden territory, dark and gloomy, redolent of stale beer. When was the last time this joint had seen a mop? Garish neon signs extolling various brews pierce the darkness with a ghastly, otherworldly light. On one, a raven-haired lovely announces, "My beer is Rheingold, the dry beer." And there is one for Shaefer lager, much smaller than the one on the right field scoreboard at Ebbets Field in Brooklyn where my Dodgers play.

The cigarette haze is so thick that I bump into a barstool — and apologize. Then a deep voice comes from the vicinity of the bar, and I squint and spy a guy who looks like the giant in *"Jack and the Beanstalk."*

Although my heart is racing, I catch the words "Whaddya want, kid?" My fears vanish! This guy doesn"t care how old I am! All he wants is my 75 cents! He'd give me a quart of Miller even if I were 10! Or wearing diapers!

Outside, Duke and I suck those babies down like grape Nehis. Then, like seasoned veterans, we casually march back in for refills.

Halfway through our second quarts we realize we might be too drunk to ride our bikes home.

🍦 🍦 🍦

You get the idea. There were plenty of other times when Duke and I got into minor league trouble, alone or with our friends.

But these hijinks didn't end with our teens. Fast forward many, many years, when we were almost 70. Duke—excuse me, John—and I were spending a long weekend with a bunch of high school friends.

Our hosts for this every-June reunion, Dave and Lucy Trebour, have a gorgeous weekend home on the Piankatank River in Virginia, near the Chesapeake Bay.

It can accommodate our nine high school friends and spouses, and features a swimming pool, hot tub, games of every imaginable variety, a movie theater-sized popcorn dispenser, boats and other water toys, lots of good food and drink, and nonstop laughing and reminiscing.

The Duke-Ron trouble that particular year starts with each of us hopping on one of Dave's jet-skis for a long, fast ride up the river. The subsequent travails include, but are not confined to, the following:

- A side trip into a shallow, narrow tributary of the Piankatank, where the exhaust pipes of our machines become choked with mud and reeds, and shudder to a halt.
- We try pushing the jet-skis back out to open water but slip in the mud a la Humphrey Bogart straining with "The African Queen." (Rachel and Tziona: Rent it for the kids)
- Finally get Duke's vehicle to start by yanking mud out of the tail pipe. But mine seems irreparable, and we abandon it in the reeds.
- Both ride on Duke's crippled craft back to the broader part of the river, chugging along at a snail's pace.
- Shiver in our bathing suits as the sun disappears behind black clouds, and we hear the menacing sound of thunder.
- Thunder rumbles louder — we must hurry to shore; open water the worst possible place to be in a lightning storm.
- Chug to someone's dock and scramble to the safety of land, as torrential rain begins.

- Seeking a place to call for assistance, we knock on door after door. But this is a clutch of unoccupied weekend vacation homes.
- Finally find someone who, regarding us soaked and shivering supplicants, lies that he doesn't own a phone.
- Get back on the jet-ski to seek another dock, and perhaps a greater display of human kindness.
- Ron falls off and hits his head on the dock as Duke guns the jet-ski's engine.
- Duke pulls Ron back onto the ski. Both attempt to just ignore gushing blood.
- Re-dock downriver, beg a woman who answers the door to ignore our wet and hideous selves. Phone Dave for help, with the home's owner protesting that it might be a long-distance call. We tell her to send the bill to our millionaire friend.
- Dave and Bob Shippee rescue us with the Trebours' party boat.
- Duke and David take the barely useable jet-ski back into the tributary and retrieve the one I had abandoned.
- Finally we arrive back home, tired and hungry, bodies all achin' and wracked with pain.
- And there is my beloved Jill, clapping derisively, as a "welcome home" from our four-hour misadventure. Duke's wife, Aggie, a far more humane creature, has been worried sick, but Jill cannot contain laughter at the pathetic wreck of a husband standing before her. The difference, I guess, is that—compared to us—Aggie and Duke are virtually newlyweds.

We bedraggled adventurers may have returned with fallen crests, but we took pride in one thing: Our reputation for courting disaster is unsullied.

Even if we live to be 100, rocking on the porch of our nursing home, we will be devising fresh ways to get into fresh trouble.

And I'll still be calling him Duke.

🍦 🍦 🍦

Chapter 11

"WE SHUDDA' LET YA DROWN!"

Thoroughbred racing, "The Sport of Kings," never has been able to shake its whiff of larcenous possibility, like banks, insurance companies, used-car salesmen, hedge-fund operators.

Ah yes. And politicians.

Losing bettors love to concoct conspiracies. Crooked trainers. Owners tanking horses for better odds next time. Doping. Bribing jockeys. Theories of collusion always abound when lots of money is involved, be it at Saratoga or on Wall Street.

Before smart phones became ubiquitous, it was impossible to find a pay phone at the track; bettors with larceny in their hearts would game the system, phoning bets into unsuspecting bookies on nags that already had won. This foolproof little scheme earned its own name: Past-posting.

There's always someone willing to risk short-cutting the rules, especially with new exotic wagers offering payoffs that make win-place-show bets seem like so much horse manure.

A few years back, three Drexel University engineering students hatched history's biggest swindle in a sport that is no stranger to elaborate scams.

They targeted racing's premier gambling day, the Breeders' Cup. Bettors smart or lucky enough to pick all or most of the winners of six consecutive races stood to gain riches beyond imagination.

The Drexel wise guys, determined to eliminate luck from the equation, used computers and an inside conspirator to scam the system for a cool $3.1 million.

Greed proved their undoing. Had they cashed one or two winning tickets instead of eight, they might have pulled it off. But the breathtaking scale of their thievery alerted track authorities, who immediately froze their winnings and launched an investigation. The result?

Jail.

🍦 🍦 🍦

Avarice on a much more plebeian scale was central to my first encounter with, as Prof. Harold Hill says in *The Music Man*, "horse-race gambling."

Dramatis personae: me, age 10; my father, Maurie; my Uncle Sam; and a tiny guy named L.C. Cook. Three decades later, Sam carried to his grave boundless enmity for Mr. Cook.

Now Sam was a generous, sentimental man whose crusty exterior masked those traits. "Brusque" does not even begin to describe him.

Sam minced no words — he alone determined when a conversation had concluded. A telephone was for communication, not pleasantry—whether he had initiated the call or not, he abruptly would end it with a hang-up when *he* chose. Sometimes it took 15 or 20 seconds to realize, in mid-sentence, that he was gone.

Sam was an avid, if pedestrian, tennis player. Each weekend, he and I bounced around in his little Triumph convertible until we found an open court. Short and stocky and spotting me 35 years, Sam's mobility was a mere memory. I was merciless, but each defeat fed his thirst for revenge.

In winter, we often swept snow from the courts. On really cold days, we built a small bonfire near the net posts, un-numbing our fingers between points.

This is the kind of stand-up guy Uncle Sam was:

— In the upper deck in left field at the Polo Grounds in 1949, he broke two fingers trying to catch me a souvenir—a homer off the bat of Sid Gordon of the Giants. Though he dropped the ball, Sam was proud his injury had been administered by that true rarity, a slugging Jewish major leaguer.

— When I was a senior in high school, Sam gave me his 1948 Chrysler Town and Country, a woodie convertible. No sexier car ever left a Detroit assembly line. Teenage girls thought so, too.

— When I embarked on my newspaper career after college, he wrote me a check for a new car. (The Town and Country had to be junked because termites had transformed its wood panels into sawdust piles on our garage floor).

— At my wedding reception in Chicago in 1961 Sam told me, "Getting married next Sunday. Be there."

Now this was a big deal. My Jewish uncle, 57 years old and a confirmed bachelor, at last was taking the plunge. And like my father before him, he had chosen a beautiful young Italian woman.

In short, Sam was a mensch, although he would have denied it bitterly.

But back to the aforementioned L.C. Cook.

On a walk one morning in 1947, while vacationing in Hollywood, Florida, we heard a weak cry—"Help, help I can't swim!" And we spied a small boy thrashing in a canal.

Uncle Sam and my dad waded in and rescued him. This is not as courageous as it sounds. The water is barely thigh-high, the boy light and frail.

When everyone is back safe on the walking path, Sam noticed that the "boy" needed a shave.

When Sam inquired about his beard, the lad lifted himself to full height (4-feet-9) and proudly announced, "I am L.C. Cook, a jockey at Hialeah."

That was all Sam needed.

"Got any tips?"

"Puchinello, eighth race. I'm riding. Can't lose."

Listening, Damon Runyon?

Uncle Sam, race track aficionado, holding a picture
of the infamous glue factory nag, Puchinello.

Sam sprang to action. He phoned my Uncle Mac,
back in Jersey guarding the family store, and told him to
"wire a thousand bucks, quick."

Now in 1947, $1,000 was a small fortune. It could buy
a new car with gas money to spare. But his eldest brother
would not be denied, and Mac agreed to scrape up what
he could.

Soon, with me in tow and 800 smackers via Western
Union burning holes in their pockets, Sam and Maurie
pushed through the turnstiles at the Hialeah Race Track,
floating on dreams of imminent riches.

The wait seemed interminable, and to pass time they
warmed up for the big race with a deuce or two on the
early card.

Finally, we claimed positions at the rail near the finish
line as the bugler summoned horses for the eighth.

And there he was. Number 7, Pucinello, a handsome, muscular three-year-old chestnut colt. Aboard, jauntily oblivious to his recent flirtation with The Grim Reaper, was L.C. Cook himself, wearing the owner's silks—red shirt with big white polka dots.

Sam checked the tote board and quickly did the math. He had spent a year at Harvard, after all! $800 at 12-1 odds—almost ten grand! A year's income! On the nose—the Cohens were in no mood to hedge with lousy place or show wagers.

"We're going for broke!" Sam exclaimed.

And broke we soon were.

Puchinello "ran" like his next stop was the dog food factory. Dead last by 40 lengths.

When Cook returned to the finish line on "The Pooch" after the race, he gave the traditional wave of his whip to assure the owner that his horse had emerged unscathed.

But Sam mistook that "everything's okay" signal for undeserved bravado. Cook might as well have been waving a red cape in a bull's face.

My uncle's roar, audible a furlong away, must have sounded like a thunderclap to the ears of L.C. Cook:

"We shudda' let ya' drown, you sonofabitch! We shudda' let ya' drown!"

🍦 🍦 🍦

Chapter 12

SHATTERED GLASS

Why do good kids go bad?

Who knows? It has been happening since dirt was invented.

But I do know what made good kids like Bosco O'Connell, Mike Farrell, and myself "go bad" in the summer of 1950.

Boredom. Stinkin' boredom.

I apologize in advance to my grandkids. They can't imagine how painful it is to recount events embarrassing enough that they continue to haunt me 65 years later.

I have no idea which of the three "good boys/devils" on that hot night in early August suggested it might be fun to toss a rock through a window of Theodore Roosevelt Junior High. Or which knucklehead threw first. Or how long it took for insanity to become epidemic. It matters naught. Culpability must be apportioned equally.

The first tinkle of broken glass unleashed a flood of evil—beyond comprehension now, but an unstoppable force that night.

One rock begat another, and a third. In short order we had exhausted the supply of visible missiles, and began pawing the hard dirt at Woodhull playground for more ammo. The barrage seemed to go on forever. Wearied, it took the combined strength of all three of us to hoist one last Gargantuan boulder onto a ground floor window ledge and roll it in. That monster not only shattered all nine panes of glass; but it also reduced the wood partitions to toothpicks.

Spent, we drifted to our respective houses on Cobane Terrace. No blood drawing, no vow of silence. We knew that if our heinous deed were exposed, a death oath would be unnecessary. Our parents would take care of that.

The enormity of our stupidity didn't click into my addled brain until I tried to fall asleep. Of course we would be caught. A given. The real question: Which official entity would mete out punishment? The FBI? The state police? The Supreme Court? A firing squad?

Please don't let it be Detective Palardy, the West Orange Police Department's very own *Javert*. But any and all would be preferable to the fearsome retribution duo of Maurie and Millie Cohen.

I avoided the crime scene next morning, too discombobulated to understand that my absence from the regular daylong baseball game might rouse suspicion. Not to mention hanging around the house all day, offering to do odd jobs for Mom. The unprecedented nature of that behavior would certainly have been admissible evidence at any trial.

Mike and Bosco also lay low, separately. But a couple more days pass with no thunderbolts from above. Dare we hope to beat the rap?

Fat chance. On the third P.W. (Post Windows) evening, a sharp rap at our front door brought my parents face-to-face with my second worst nightmare—Detective Palardy, whose scowl for years had set miscreant West Orange teenagers wondering whether a stretch in juvey actually might be preferable.

Two years later, when I entered high school, I discovered a reason for his fierce demeanor—my new classmate, Barbara Palardy. If ever a father needed to protect a daughter's honor, it was the detective. Miss Palardy surely was the most tempting female east of Marilyn Monroe.

I heard Palardy at the front door introducing himself. Knowing I was doomed, I slithered out of sight into the kitchen and listened to his opening argument.

"We recovered 100 pounds of rocks from inside the building, including a 25-pound boulder."

Wow. I had known that sucker was heavy.

Snatches of the officer's Bill of Particulars floated into the kitchen, words like *window casement shattered* and *maybe the worst vandalism I've ever seen.* I did not hear him say any words like "Alcatraz" or "electric chair," -- but I certainly felt crushed by this one: $875 damages. He might as well have said "Ten million bucks."

In 1950, 875 dollars was a stupendous sum. We had recently purchased our house, a three-bedroom, 2.5 bath stunner with fireplace, den with built-in bookcases, full basement, nice kitchen, Florida room, garage, attic, corner lot in prime residential area: $14,500. Our four-door 1950 Buick Roadmaster cost $1,500, new.

I would be an old man before I finished reimbursing Dad. And I found scant solace that the debt would be split three ways.

Maurie broke my parents' stunned silence.

"How many others were involved?"

"Two."

"So our share is about $300?"

"Yes, sir."

"And that will be it?"

"Yes, sir. Your son's name will be on a juvenile record sheet that will be expunged in one year. If he stays out of trouble."

Stays out of trouble? I'm not even going to be allowed **OUT OF THE HOUSE** in the next two centuries!

As my folks ushered Palardy out, I steeled myself against the anticipated outburst from my disciplinarian mother. But this time, judge, jury and executioner turned out to be my gentle, usually forgiving Dad.

You'd have loved your great-grandfather, kids. Since he was unwell most of his life, he was home far more than other fathers. After school, my friends congregated at our house. It was close to school and stocked with exotic Italian snacks. Plus, my dad was there.

Maurie talked to my friends the way he conversed with everyone, for they were soon-to-be adults and thus entitled to grown-up opinions. This did not mean subjects like basketball with the boys, or hairdos and crushes with the girls, were excluded. But they also ranged much farther afield. My lifelong pal, Evalyn Zoda Shippee, remembers how the girls would cluster in the first floor den to listen to Maurie read poetry.

But poetry was the last thing on his mind this night. I slunk into the living room when I heard him call "Ronald," the form of address reserved for the most severe occasions. That his voice was calm and measured only terrified me more.

Trial was swift, sentencing immediate. Court adjourned in about eight seconds. No opening arguments, no evidence presented, no closing statements. Nobody on my side to suggest a mistrial.

Punishment meted out, effective immediately. I was banished to the attic for the four weeks until school started, downstairs to the second floor only to use the bathroom. Millie would bring meals three times a day, and retrieve the dirty dishes I would place at the bottom of the attic stairs. No visitors. No phone. No radio. No reading material. No nothing.

The "no" he didn't have to mention was "no air-conditioning." We don't own one. The stultifying attic will be my San Quentin, solitary confinement. I won't even guess the temperature. The relentless heat of the blistering Jersey sun, trapped by the roof shingles, mingles with the hot air rising from the rest of the house and hangs suspended, motionless and fetid, over my cot. The Ninth Circle of Hell cannot possibly have been worse.

Perspiration pours off me day and night, but Dad's prohibited list includes showers. Mom brings up meals, holding her breath against the intensifying smell of sweat. Her eyes projected sad sympathy, but she was helpless to soften my sentence.

I count the days until the start of eighth grade and escape from my attic Attica. Will I be able to spot the new window panes at Roosevelt Junior High?

Two weeks into tedious exile and desperate for diversion of any kind, I begin investigating nooks and crannies.

`In a closet with no light switch, I poke around for a deck of cards or an old magazine — anything to alleviate the tedium. Then, on tip-toes and reaching on the back of a high shelf, my fingers touch something rectangular. It turns out to be an old shoebox, top thick with dust.

Inside are dozens of envelopes wrapped in bunches and tied with red ribbons.

I extract a single sheet of paper from an unsealed envelope. There, in Dad's recognizable if almost unreadable scrawl, lies my salvation.

A love letter to Millie Figliuolo. Gushy and mushy. Filled with my-darlings and I-love-yous and I-miss-yous, and I count the moments until we meet again. And a lot of more erudite stuff, too. My father, a huge romantic, is a devotee of great literature. And in these letters he summons the feelings espoused by the Shakespeares and the Elizabeth Barrett Brownings of yore as he pledges eternal love to his exotic Italian beauty.

Mesmerized, I cannot stop reading. For once, I even ignore my blast-furnace Elba; this is my dad, and this is my mom, and it is beginning to dawn on this self-centered little punk that they had been actual humans before my sister and I disrupted their private Eden.

I don't hear Mom's footsteps on the stairs delivering dinner, but cannot mistake her volley of Italian expletives when she discovers my discovery. She drops the tray on the cot, snatches the letter from my hand, stuffs everything back into the shoebox, and flees downstairs, slamming the attic door behind her.

"He found the letters!" I hear her wail despairingly two stories below. "He found the letters!"

"What letters?" asks my bewildered dad.

"The damn letters, the goddamn love letters! I want him down from the attic! Now!"

Dad, as always, is defenseless when Mount Millie erupts. His love letters turn out to be my "Get Out of Jail Free" card.

No, I couldn"t distinguish the new window panes from the old at Theodore Roosevelt Junior High.

And yes, I did pay my debt—surrendering half my weekly $5 allowance. It took a little over two years to amortize that horrible August evening.

And no, I never did ask out the stunningly constructed Barbara Palardy. That would have required encountering Inspector *Javert.*

In *his* living room.

🍦 🍦 🍦

Chapter 13

HARRY AND CARY

I was a pretty fair athlete when I was younger, faster, thinner. Taller.

At West Orange High in the early 1950s, I won varsity letters in three sports. Tennis captain. Second in scoring in basketball. Left fielder on the baseball team that blew the state championship with two outs in the ninth. That one still really hurt.

But even world-class athletes with skills I never could dream of emulating have days they'd sooner forget. And that is how I try to console myself over two nightmare basketball tales.

The first came early in my junior year when we took a school bus a few miles to the adjacent town to play Montclair. Because our coach, Al Lawrence, had an almost pathological aversion to playing anybody but his most experienced seniors, I had an unobstructed view of the proceedings from the farthest end of the bench, a vantage point I had absolutely no prospect of relinquishing.

In football, a sport I was far too chicken to play, Montclair's state champion powerhouses perpetually annihilated poor little West Orange. But we always were tough in basketball, and figured we had a chance. That is, until we watched the Mounties pour out of their dressing room onto the court. When did the Boston Celtics start wearing blue and white?

It was a rout from the opening tap. Montclair's tall, tough, veteran team soon transformed a basketball game into a demolition derby, nailing basket after basket from impossible angles. Most of them came from Harry Zingg, a sure-fire college star.

Five minutes into the game, with the scoreboard showing us down by 16 and Zingg replicating Larry Bird, I hear Coach Lawrence bark from what seemed a mile away: "Cohen!"

The only Cohen on our team had been riveted to the bench all year, with zero chance of making his varsity debut against the likes of Montclair. So Lawrence's summons did not immediately register.

"COHEN!" Even louder.

Now I heard. I just couldn't process.

"NUMBER 7!"

A fellow scrub poked me out of my trance. I looked down at the big white "7" on my shiny maroon visitors' jersey to be sure that still was my number and ran in what my befogged brain hoped was the general direction of coach's voice.

"Get in there, Cohen, and cover Zingg like he was your girlfriend. Don't let him even touch the ball."

Oh my god! I had been preparing for and dreaming about this only . . . FOREVER!

All those hours shooting baskets past midnight until my best friend's dad, who had generously erected floodlights so I could practice after dark, leaned out his bedroom window and suggested I go home to bed.

All those afternoons dribbling alone in my low-ceilinged basement, pretending the pillars were so many Wilt Chamberlains.

All those years haunting playgrounds whose netless rims made it impossible to know whether I had fired up a "swish" or an air ball.

The icy winter days I had ridden my bike to sneak into the driveway of State Senator Mark Anton's sprawling estate. I cleared off the snow with my sneakers and practiced free throws and engaged in solo last-second, game-winning heroics.

But now, at last, my moment has arrived! Coach is sending me in!

I gulp, swallowing my wad of Juicy Fruit.

Nervous? Me? No. Far, far beyond nervous. Totally, completely, absolutely, irreversibly petrified. Legs? Twenty-minute linguine.

On my best day, on tip-toes, I was 5-11, a half-foot shorter than Harry Zingg. Nearly a foot shorter than Montclair's star center, Dave Fulcomer. Half as fast (charitably) as their blue blur of a point guard, Everett Christmas.

The whistle blows and I stumble onto the court, searching frantically for Harry — any Harry — only to hear the Montclair cheering section erupt again. Finding himself completely unguarded, Zingg had casually tossed in a 20-footer from the top of the key.

Okay, the long and the short of it (Harry meets Ronnie): I am on the court less than two minutes—and Zingg torches me for five buckets.

Apoplectic, Al Lawrence calls time, his face the color of our snazzy road unis, the veins on his head bulging alarmingly. My only hope: he strokes out before he can throttle me.

"Cohen, you **NUMBSKULL!** I told you to stick to Zingg like **GLUE!** What in God's name are you **DOING** out there?"

Rather than treat this as the rhetorical question it certainly was, I compound my mortification.

"I couldn't find him."

My coach grows sclerotic. Definitely on the brink of a seizure—and not some rinky-dink little minor league, insignificant, wussified seizure either.

The Mother of All Strokes.

"**NOT FIND HIM! NOT FIND HIM!** He's 6-5 and weighs 235! This is a little court. There only are five opponents out there—**AND THEIR UNIFORMS ARE BLUE!** How the hell could you *MISS* him!"

Could this be another trick question?

I slither back to the end of the bench. Perennial second -stringers have concocted an entire thesaurus to describe the seats from which they watch sporting events they rarely are invited to join.

"Grab some pine."

"Splinter City."

"Ride the wooden trolley."

"Plank spank."

My "friends," rather too joyfully I think, employ these to describe my exile, plus far more colorful ones not fit for youthful ears.

No, Al Lawrence did not die on the spot. Nor did he follow through on his homicide threat. He made sure, though, that for a whole month, I would not so much as smell the court during a game.

Mortification No. 2, a couple of months later:

🍦 🍦 🍦

The highlight finale of our season, the Essex County Tournament at Seton Hall University's gym in South Orange. Dramatis personae include: Ronnie Cohen (me) and Cary Wills, star guard for the Orange High Tornadoes.

Wills was, quite simply, a magician. He could palm a basketball like a grape, twirl it on either index finger, dribble blind behind his back, feather no-look half-court passes to teammates for easy baskets. His sleight of hand was marvelous to watch—from the visitors' bench. He also looked like he was about 24 years old, and a hardscrabble 24 at that.

We trail badly late in the third period, and several of our best players are in danger of fouling out. Al Lawrence rises to scowlingly contemplate his limited options. I pray silently, "Please, Hashem, not me."

His hard eyes scan the bench, resting when they reach my scrunched body. He points. No histrionics, no barking my name. Just a finger. I groan inside, then slouch toward doom.

Lawrence's instructions are succinct.:

"Cohen, this guy is shorter than Harry Zingg, but for Chrissakes, find him anyhow. He's killing us. Tackle him. Maybe we'll get lucky, and he'll brick the foul shots. But just stop him, damn it!"

Stop Cary Wills? Might the refs fail to notice if I carry a baseball bat out in an attempt to stop Cary?

Al Lawrence is correct about one thing. Because of his thick coal black stubble (nobody on either team employs shaving cream and razor more than weekly) I immediately locate Wills.

Big mistake. But although I will never ever forget what followed, there was one saving grace. It was mercifully brief.

Cary Wills receives the inbound pass under his own basket and dribbles slowly over the half-court line. I pick him up at the top of the key, striking the classic defensive pose—one arm extended toward his waist, the other behind me to detect one of his teammates setting a pick that would give him clear sailing to the basket.

Crouching like a starving mountain lion, I bounce lightly on the balls of my feet, ready to spring in any direction. Legs about a yard apart, I am prepared for any movement, left or right. I laser-in on Wills's legs and feet. You can feint with your eyes and your arms and your torso, but your body must follow your feet.

Had I glanced north to Cary Wills's face, I would have detected the look of abject pity he surely flashed ... ***THE INSTANT BEFORE HE DRIBBLED THE BALL BETWEEN MY LEGS!***

Wills then whirls around me, retrieves the ball on the other side, and sinks his layup before I can say "Harry Zingg."

I reclaim my ride on the "wooden trolley" almost before Coach Al can scream "Time Out!", before he can yank me, before he can stump me with any more stupid rhetorical questions.

For there could be no questions. Al Lawrence had seen precisely what 3,200 fans had seen, what my teammates had seen, what my mom and my dad and my five uncles in the bleachers had seen.

In broad daylight on the largest stage we ever played on, in our most important game of the season, Cary Wills had publicly undressed me.

Exchanging post-game handshakes, Wills, almost old enough to be my grandfather, offers grandfatherly consolation.

"Listen, kid, don't feel bad. Even if I warned you I was going to dribble between your legs, I'd **STILL** have dribbled between your legs."

If he guessed that would afford solace, he guessed dead wrong.

I still hate him.

Chapter 14

DAD, IMPERIAL, AND CHRISTINE JORGENSEN

In my growing-up years, Maurie and his brothers Sam and Mac owned Imperial Outfitters, an appliance/everything-under-the-sun store on Broad Street, Newark's main drag.

My dad's contribution largely was wisdom, empathy and moral support. Rheumatic fever at birth had severely damaged his heart and mostly consigned him to watching life from the sidelines.

On rare occasions he felt strong enough for tennis, which he loved and played extremely well. But there were long stretches when he wasn't well enough to even come watch my high school games.

Yet he was a great dad, so smart that people would have been astonished to learn he never finished high school. He read voraciously, practically taking up residence at the East Orange Public Library, just a few steps from our apartment. And he was psychologically incapable of walking past a second-hand bookstore.

Before I reached my teens, on days when he was feeling pretty good, a typical Saturday goes like this:

We take the bus or trolley from East Orange and spend a couple of hours in the magnificent Newark Museum.

Then we check in with Sam and Mac at Imperial, who adore their brother and listen patiently to his suggestions about enticing customers. Although they were far shrewder businessmen, people loved Maurie from his first word, and Sam and Mac were smart enough to realize that.

Imperial was huge—three stories and very deep. The brothers sold all sorts of appliances—refrigerators, washers, dryers, and a mesmerizing new invention called television. The showroom occupied most of the first floor; in back was the business office where Mac and Sam had desks. A third desk, lonely and underused, was Dad's.

Unquestioned queen of that domain was a beautiful young woman named Caroline Pennachio, the engine that powered Imperial's train.

Raven-haired and Italian, Caroline possessed both a heart of gold and an eviscerating mein. At Imperial, she lived on the telephone, softly but menacingly dealing with tardy inventory suppliers—or softly but menacingly dunning customers delinquent on their dollar-a-week installment plans.

Caroline's telephone skills were wondrous. To both the deadbeat from Jersey City and the regional distributor for Bendix washers, she could be tougher than two-buck chuck. Rarely did she need to raise her voice; even more infrequently did she feel it necessary for a reminder phone call.

Imperial's implicit business model was "buy now, pay forever." When balances slipped below triple digits, we would peddle something else. The markup was huge because the installment business was fraught with peril. A dozen salesmen working on salary plus commission took to the road on regular routes six days a week, knocking on doors and collecting on balances while sweet-talking customers more deeply into debt. For Imperial's cash-poor clientele, the installment plan was the only way to obtain new-fangled gizmos like TVs and window air conditioners.

Our hefty prices reflected a stark, if sad, reality of the installment business:

Deadbeats.

A large filing cabinet at Imperial was marked P&L— "profit and loss." It should have been just *L*. Customers whose names resided therein never had the slightest intention of contributing to my family's *P*—they were ghosts who left no forwarding addresses when they vanished into the industrial pall perpetually hanging over North Jersey.

The second floor of Imperial was a rabbit's warren of dry goods and small appliances, clothing and slipcovers and sheets and pillowcases and toasters and silverware. Name it, we sold it. Or we'd get it for you. Sure, it was far cheaper elsewhere, but that would require cash—a commodity with which our customers were largely unfamiliar.

It truly was a symbiotic relationship: Everyone knows we overcharge, but you get a really long time to pay while we pile on more treasures of the great American dream you probably don't need.

The musty and sunless third floor, whose grimy windows had never encountered an actual cleaning product, was the realm of "Accounts Receivable." That would be Ceil, a blonde fireplug perched on a towering three-legged stool, the genius operator of a "posting" machine probably larger than her apartment.

Say a customer gives salesman Sid Corson her $2 weekly payment on Monday and also purchases a $39.95 set of "silverware"; Ceil posts both transactions on a ledger card. She is a sight to behold, legs suspended two feet above the ancient and warping floorboards, her fingers a blur over a giant keyboard. Acrid fumes from chain-smoked Camels halo her peroxide curls, further befouling the room's infinitesimal oxygen supply. I always wonder how long after quitting time it takes Ceil's eyes to adjust to daylight, and whether her flat reeks as horribly as her workplace.

"The Boys" know that Imperial could not function without the skills and institutional memories of impossibly loyal Caroline and Ceil. Carol proved so indispensable, in fact, that the week after attending my wedding in Chicago to Jill, Uncle Sam married her. He was 57, she 34. It was the only marriage for both.

After my dad is satisfied his brothers have things reasonably under control, we head next door to Chet's, a tiny takeout deli with a few stools in the lobby of the next-door office building. It is a good place to stop for coffee and a bagel. Or grab a sandwich on a nice day and head for a bench in nearby Military Park.

On a stool next to Dad, I always follow his lead— hot pastrami on rye with spicy brown mustard. Still my favorite sandwich.

When I got to junior high a few years later, I anticipated languorous summer days hanging with pals at Woodhull playground, down the block from our house. But Dad decreed I must learn the family business; his "Report to Ceil's third-floor dungeon" order was not up for discussion.

The first morning, Ceil instructed me how to file, alphabetically, the ledger cards on which she had posted the previous day's transactions. A garden slug could have mastered this unspeakably tedious task.

Yet mistakes were made—lots. Was I just plumb dumb? Or did I so resent my indentured servitude as to intentionally sabotage Imperial's customer lifeline? I lean toward answer B.

Could you blame me? My friends were home playing baseball in sublime summer weather that I could only imagine—because even the brightest midday summer sun could not pierce the encrusted filth on my garret window. And though Imperial sold air conditioners, not even a small fan stirred Ceil's Camel-polluted oxygen supply.

But however against my will, I now was a full-fledged member of America's Work Force, and thus entitled to a lunch break. So Dad informed Chet I would be visiting every day at noon, and he would settle up at week's end.

Exactly at noon that first Monday, starving and bored crazy, I am swirling a 360 on one of Chet's stools.

Chet, who often came to our house to play cards, was not just "pastrami dispenser extraordinaire." Old Chester was canny as well, and quickly eyed me as an opportunity to recoup poker losses.

"Hey, Ron. Do you want to king-size that pastrami on rye (an extra buck)?"

The very least I deserve after that torture-chamber morning. "Sure."

Potato salad? Certainly. Cole slaw? Pile it on. Large Coke or small? Large. Apple pie? Yeah, and a scoop of vanilla. Bring it. Bring it all. I deserve no less.

Chet's eyeballs morph into dollar signs, and his heart pounds to the rhythms of "Ka-Ching, Ka-Ching!"

The first bill goes directly to Sugar Daddy, nearly five bucks a day—a monumental sum in 1948. By comparison, our three-bedroom corner lot house on a quiet West Orange street cost $14,500.

"Forget Chet," Dad decrees. "Your mother will pack your lunch."

Anyhow, back to "Saturdays with Dad." Sated on pastrami, we wander Market Street, a heaven of second-hand bookstores whose delighted proprietors greet us— well, him—by first name.

Their emporiums of dusty dreams share a down-at-the-heels downtown block with a couple of burlesque houses, the Empire and Minsky's.

Later as teens my friends and I, risking being grounded for eternity, occasionally visited these exotic wonderlands of sin, lying about our ages and plunking down fifty cents to enter to a magical, mystical world inhabited by bawdy, seltzer-down-the-pants comics and their "second-banana" straight-men.

But the real objects of our hormone-addled pubescent brains were the strippers, some already famous, like Blaze Starr and Lili St. Cyr (no saint, she!); others hopeful, like Cupcakes Cassidy and Princess Domay.

However, those deliciously forbidden nights lie far in the future. Now, with my hand in Dad's, I don't even glance at the lurid posters. My companion's great joy is books, not ecdysiasts. At least not to my knowledge.

We slowly stroll dark, narrow aisles where overburdened bookshelves fairly groan in distress. Tiptoe lest you collapse the leaning towers of overflow volumes piled precariously on the floor.

Dad gently plucks an antique volume whose spine is tattered from decades of un-shelving and re-shelving. He brings it close, closes his eyes, inhales deeply.

"Nothing smells like an old book," he whispers, lowering it to my face for affirmation.

I cannot argue; nothing smells quite like an old book. The musty odor conjures its original owner, lounging long ago in a yellow leather chair in robe and slippers, teeth clenching a battered old pipe. Just like my dad.

We head home with an armload of treasures, at least one of which I "simply must read." Inevitably, Dad's choice proves too dense, and I seek explanations. Years later, I realize this was his way of connecting with his sports-crazed son, hoping I would recall and treasure our discussions long after my meager athletic skills had withered.

Mom greets us with a resigned look that says "We already have way more books than shelf room." But she can never hide her pleasure at our pleasure. And I still cannot encounter an old book without giving a sniff — and missing Pop.

Anyhow, this chapter was not meant to be totally about shopworn books or hot pastrami or Ceil's dusty-musty third-floor domain at "Imperial Outfielders," as my friends dubbed it. Or even the workplace magic of Caroline. The title includes "Christine Jorgensen," and while she has yet to make an appearance, hang in there. She will arrive soon enough.

❦ ❦ ❦

After my freshman year of college, the brothers Cohen decide to make one more stab at testing my aptitude for the family business. Nothing mundane like filing. I was marked for bigger things--substituting on a rotating basis for salesmen taking summer vacation.

That proved even more depressing than Ceil's counting-house. I was okay collecting a buck or two, not that hard if you actually could get someone to open the door. But my shortcomings as an actual salesman could bankrupt a lemonade stand in the Sahara.

I simply had no stomach for peddling furnishings and appliances to people who would be forking over a dollar or two a week for maybe forever.

They greet me expectantly, like kids on Christmas Eve. What have you got for me on special?

"Nothing special," I lie, although I realize my reluctance to exacerbate their credit woes will adversely affect my family's bottom line.

I had never heard the term *"bleeding heart liberal,"* but already I am one. Dad and my uncles don't love me less despite such injurious moral rectitude, but soon conclude they probably will need alternative long-range plans for Imperial.

My beat that summer includes the shabbiest tenements of Paterson, Jersey City, Newark, and a dozen other oppressive and depressing North Jersey communities. Had our customers been able to afford the air-conditioned suburban homes and immaculate lawns of Montclair and Westfield, they wouldn't need us.

My worst selling nightmares involve "custom-made" slipcovers. Customers choose a fabric from a catalogue, then I carefully measure their battered living-room furniture.

But when I deliver them the following week, **THEY NEVER FIT!**

No matter how I push and tug, pull and coax, curse and cajole. Not even close.

I promise to fix things the next week, cunningly booting the problem to the regular salesman returning from vacation. When he discovers the damaged relationships in my wake, he curses his bosses' idiot nephew.

One blistering August Saturday afternoon, I climb four brutal flights in Hoboken to discover the lady of the house still at the breakfast table, swilling lukewarm coffee and stabbing still another cigarette butt into a stomach-churning saucer of rancid cream.

Dishes scattered in the sink are spackled, perhaps permanently, with hardened egg yolk. This morning's breakfast? Last week's?

Three snot-nosed toddlers scream in delight as a cur with protruding ribs sizes me up for dinner.

"Can you come back later?" the mom begs. "We'll have our unemployment."

🍦 🍦 🍦

My psyche screaming for repair, I take a break in a gin mill in Weehawken that is blissfully cool—and perhaps dark enough to conceal how underage I am. As if the barkeep cares.

The first frosty schooner of Rheingold stings my tongue. As my eyes transition from the sunlight, if I strain I can discern the only other customer, at the far end of the bar, is a blonde in a red dress.

I am on my second beer when (Here it finally comes, folks) she brushes past and heads for the ladies room. "Know who she is?" the bartender asks conspiratorially.

"She? How can you tell it's even a woman it's so dark in here?"

"Well, I guess you could call her a woman. That's Christine Jorgensen."

Now he has my attention. And curiousity. Everyone has heard of Christine.

A few years earlier a guy named George William Jorgensen Jr. decides that, although he has lived several decades as a man, deep inside lurks a woman desperate to breathe free.

So he undergoes the first sex-change operation. George William leaves for Denmark; Christine returns to North Jersey.

Although changing sexes now is commonplace (Google Bruce Jenner), back then Christine caused a sensation. "Ex-GI Becomes Blonde Beauty" shout the front pages of the New York City tabloids.

And here's little me, sharing a cozy little dive bar in Weehawken with none other than Christine her/himself!

As she returns to her bar stool, Mr. Big Spender calls out cleverly, "Buy you a drink?"

Okay, I know I should be making callbacks on the customers who had hidden silently behind locked doors, but for almost an hour I hang on Christine's every word. Smart and glib, she soon would be peddling her story for cash money to college kids and medical meetings. But right now, the journalist I didn't know I'd become gets her for the price of a gin and tonic. Our conversation goes something like this:

"How long did you want that operation?"

"Ever since I first heard about it. But really? All my life."

If I had known back then what the "lede" of a story meant, that would have been it.

"The best part about being a girl?"

"I am now a whole new person, and I like her. George was kind of wimpy. Christine has balls, so to speak."

Or that's the lede, maybe?

"Biggest adjustment?"

"Some of the guys I used to hang around with are hitting on me."

No. **That** *really* is the lede. I'm sure of it.

But the last bit of information is far too much for an impressionable teenager to process, and I feel almost nostalgic for the Hoboken mom with the egg-encrusted breakfast dishes and the savage little Schnauzer. I bid Chris goodbye and head for the sauna on other side of the saloon door.

"Hey, thanks for the drink," she calls. "Watch for my cabaret show. I really belt out 'I Enjoy Being a Girl.'"

Old Christine is pulling my leg.

I think.

☃ ☃ ☃

Chapter 15

ICE CREAM, YOU SCREAM

I had a lot of interesting jobs growing up—some fun, some boring but instructive. One just plain boring—my family's business. (Check the previous chapter).

But nothing compared to my brief fling as a purveyor of summertime dreams.

On a beautifully sunny day in 1954, needing money for my gas-guzzling Chrysler woodie convertible, I scan the want ads in the Newark Evening News. My research ends quickly: "Ice Cream Truck Driver: Reliable."

Those five words float me to a world populated by guys in white pants, white short-sleeved shirts, white captain hats. The beloved *Good Humor* Man.

Soon I would be joining them, I exulted, dreaming of becoming an immaculately clad angel of mercy dispensing toasted almond and coconut bars and garishly colored, rocket-shaped frozen ice bombs on a stick.

The address turns out not to be the Good Humor factory, but a modest ranch house on a quiet street in Hillside, a working-class suburb of Newark — the very block where my Uncle Mac and Aunt Norma live.

It doesn't take long to acknowledge that my summer transport is not likely to be the square white truck with the bigger-than-life image of a chocolate-covered vanilla bar, one large bite missing from the top left corner—a vehicle whose approach is heralded by the crystal clear tinkling of silver bells.

Instead, I learn I will be captaining "The Little Red Wagon," cramped and low-slung and begging for a restorative paint job. In the world of mobile ice cream, TLRW is quite a few rungs down the evolutionary ladder from *Good Humor*—or even *Mr. Sof-tee*.

Interviewing me in their living room, John and Dolly Johnston, a retired couple supplementing pensions with the summer earnings of TLRW, ask a couple of simple questions and satisfy themselves I am neither an axe murderer nor a complete math idiot. (I a*m* the latter but apparently disguise it cleverly). On the road test I manage to aim TLRW around the block without hitting anything moving or stationery. Happy to have so quickly found their man, the Johnstons hand me a scruffy blue Dodger baseball cap and the keys to their fleet.

One truck.

Per instruction, I will arrive at 1:45 p.m. (no days off) and load up TLRW's refrigerated rear end with popsicles, cones, and Dixie cups from the basement freezer, restocking as necessary. A dollar an hour for a 10-hour day. (This was long before the invention of minimum wage and maximum hours.) My lagniappe: One free "personal treat" a day—sweet, if fleeting, balm from Jersey's blazing sun.

TLRW's entire musical repertoire consists of a scratchy calliope version of "The Daring Young Man on the Flying Trapeze." Try as I might, I never can disable that sucker. In self-defense of my eardrums, I invent bawdy lyrics that I remember even today. But "musical" monotony stands no chance against the joy at finding myself gainfully employed outdoors—surrounded by ice cream.

Trouble begins almost with the first calliope screech. The crafty little buggers—er, customers—soon discover I am a softer touch than a melting Creamsicle.

Here comes a sad-eyed ragamuffin spinning a mournful tale about losing the quarter his mom had given him for a fudge bar. And here comes a ginger-haired rascal promising to pay tomorrow if I would advance her a vanilla cone topped with chocolate and sprinkled with peanut dust.

They are so cute and it is *so* hot. Only a concrete heart could deny a kid desperate for a double-stick raspberry. The sort where you suck out the Red Dye No. 2, leaving shimmeringly pale white twin towers of semi-pure ice?

The first week, I turn in $138—not bad, until you realize the Johnstons have to pay my $70 salary out of that. I had given away all my freebies and more—even then, curly-haired little girls were my weakness.

The fixed-income proprietors of this family enterprise seem far from overjoyed. After salary, gas, and inventory, they barely break even and gently but firmly emphasize they expect better—far better. And fast.

But trouble degenerates to disaster. As dusk falls the first day of my second week, a kid about nine appears and orders a double-stick banana fudge. Armed with a semi-professional-looking telescope, he introduces himself.

"I'm going to be an astronomer. My name is Frank, but my dad calls me 'Sirius', after the Dog Star near Orion. Sirius is the brightest star in the sky."

"You're not serious," I parry.

"Am too."

"Well, my name is Mr. Cone," I say, taking a tiny liberty with the pronunciation.

"An ice cream man named Cone? You're not serious!"

"No, you're Sirius!"

And with this delightful repartee, my fate is sealed. He lets me peer, close-up, at the crescent moon. I comp his double-stick banana fudge.

Next night, he offers a peek at Jupiter's moons. I slip him a Dreamsicle.

My world begins to unravel completely the third night, when "Sirius" shows up with about seven of his closest friends. The night is crystal clear and I simply must have a glimpse of Saturn's rings. So I cave in to the pint-sized extortionists, hoping against all common sense that the Johnstons won't notice my arrears.

Fat chance. When the pluses and minuses are toted Saturday night, I owe them my entire salary—plus $11.

"We're really sorry," says sweet, blue-haired Dolly Johnston. "As much as we like you, we can't afford to have you in this job."

"I understand. I can't afford to have me in this job. either."

In my "civvies" at the corner of Voorhees and Liberty the next night, I inform "Sirius" the jig is up on his juvenile extortion racket. "But I will miss you almost as much as the close-ups of Andromeda's spiral nebula."

In the distance comes the familiar, cringe-inducing notes of the calliope as TLRW approaches, bearing its new skipper.

Declining to wait around to share my X-rated lyrics, I gift Sirius my last quarter for a farewell double-stick banana fudge and slip off, leaving my Ice Cream Man career behind.

The first time I ever was fired would not be the last.

🍦 🍦 🍦

Chapter 16

WHEELCHAIRS, SPUD-NUTS, AND PO' BOYS

I am jolted awake by a horrible metallic grinding, like speeding locomotives smashing head-on. I rush to investigate, but apparently someone has moved my door during the night and I bang into the wall. It begins to dawn on my sleep-fogged brain that this is not the comfy, familiar West Orange bedroom I can negotiate in my sleep. It is my first night in a college dorm.

Or an unreasonable facsimile thereof.

It is 6:15 a.m. on an early September Saturday in 1955. Welcome, Ron Cohen, to the University of Illinois. You will read elsewhere in these pages of a wondrously weird array of undergraduate sleeping arrangements, but none will top where I find myself right now.

The Parade Grounds Units. The PGUs.

Barefoot, I hurry into the hall to divine the source of the racket, wondering if I should head back to the relative safety of Mafia-friendly New Jersey.

At dusk the previous evening, an Ozark Airlines double-prop from Chicago deposited me on a ribbon of runway rendered all but invisible—even from the air—by what surely must be history's most prodigious cornfield.

The U of I hadn't exactly been my first choice. Never even an afterthought on the "Okay-since-I-won't-get-into-Yale-I-better-make-another-list" list. Only when the state universities in Virginia, North Carolina, and Michigan give me the brushoff do I begin to comprehend how deep a hole I had dug at West Orange High, memorialized by three years of report cards on which my academic efforts had been airily, if succinctly and accurately, dismissed as "Capable of Doing Better."

In near panic that I might be dragooned into the family retail business, I grabbed an atlas. Every state had a university. Just how hard could this be?

My finger lighted on Champaign-Urbana. What did I know about Illinois? Well, I admired the orange and blue uniforms on TV as we demolished UCLA 49–0 in the 1951 Rose Bowl, during which a modern-day Red Grange named Johnny Karras ran over, under, around, and through helpless defenders from the lesser coast.

Plus, I was intrigued that the university apparently couldn't decide exactly where it was. Maybe if I hated Urbana I'd love Champaign?

Upon such a thin reed does desperation lean. And that's how I find myself that morning, rushing toward that terrifying sound.

I discover no actual locomotives are involved; rather, wheelchairs are being yanked off storage shelves in a clanging, banging symphony, war chariots that my new

PGU compatriots soon would be crashing violently in a surreal game of football.

I ponder the (literal) irony. Football drew me to the University of Illinois, and football would be my noisy welcome.

Wheelchair football.

For, you see, of the dozen guys in my barracks unit, only three could actually walk, and one of those would drop out before the first bright leaves of autumn. Everyone else traveled by cane, crutch, leg braces, wheelchair—or assorted combinations thereof.

Why had I, with four sturdy limbs, been assigned a dorm room just a few wall racks and chains shy of a torture chamber? Good question, for which I never had time to pursue an answer.

Comparing the PGUs with a real college dorm requires a total suspension of disbelief. Nonetheless, here's what I learned on my official PGU tour.

End to end, walking normally, it is a trip that consumes about 14 seconds. My new housemates line my route distrustingly eyeballing my legs, both of which are the same length and reach the ground.

Unlike theirs.

I had known college would bring life changes, large and small, and I optimistically anticipated the apron-string loosening. But as I contemplate this tableau of the lame and the halt, my spirits plummet. How could I have exchanged the warm comfort of Millie's kitchen for this? And when is the next plane out of Bedlam? The saving grace is that my roommate, Alver Carlson from the south side of Chicago, also walks without metallic or motorized assistance.

Which is why Al and I find ourselves that very morning in charge of the first-down markers as two teams of six players each, 24 wheels replacing 24 legs, engage in a sport less football than it is demolition derby. After each play, Alvie and I forsake sideline chores to lift fallen warriors, brush them off, and check for broken prosthetic devices, then plunk them back in their chairs.

That afternoon at Memorial Stadium, sophomore halfbacks Mickey Bates and J. C. Caroline run wild as the varsity opens its season by trouncing Colgate 41-0, a contest that seems a good deal less violent than the one my new dorm mates had played a few hours earlier.

🍦 🍦 🍦

THE PGUs AND THEIR INHABITANTS

A short history lesson as I continue my freshman year tutorial:

The PGUs were a squat, ugly, sprawling chancre sore on an otherwise handsome, if relentlessly flat, campus in the central Illinois cornfields, 125 miles south of Chicago. Completely enveloped by fraternities, sororities, and actual residence dorms where luckier, ambulatory students lived and walked in relative luxury, the low-slung, single-story military barracks had been constructed in the 1940s to house American soldiers wounded during World War II. Although I never saw it happen, local lore held that a carelessly discarded match could vanish one of those babies in 10 minutes.

After the war, with the student population swollen by returning veterans, the buildings became the centerpiece of the university's unique program for the disabled.

Already equipped with ramps, the barracks were transformed into dorms for special needs students.

A controversial visionary, Tim Nugent, melded classroom work and strict rehab regimens to help prepare handicapped students for the rest of their lives. By the time I arrived a decade later, Illinois was the world's premier university for the disabled, seamlessly incorporating them into campus life.

They attended classes with the ambulatory: Four decades before the Americans with Disabilities Act became federal law, all classrooms, residences, and administrative buildings were wheelchair-accessible, with ramps, handicap-access restrooms, special parking, lifts, and elevators.

My dorm mates irreverently referred to one another as "gimps" and "crips," terms of endearment Alvie and I easily—and with their blessings—appropriated. Able-bodied students around campus grew to admire how our new friends negotiated college life nearly as smoothly, if more slowly, than we. They awakened before dawn and left early for class on the special buses that plied our sprawling campus. So ubiquitous were the lame and halt that they did not warrant even a second glance as their wheelchairs rolled into the classrooms.

For example, one armless young man controlled his motorized wheelchair by blowing through a straw. Barefoot even on the coldest prairie winter days, he took lecture notes with a pencil clenched between the toes of his right foot. Whenever I felt tempted to grumble about life, I'd think of how badly this kid must want a college education.

Three guys from my PGU, Chuck Dahnke, Gene Dreyer, and Bruce Weimer, would become lifelong friends. You will meet them soon, but first …

THE BARRACKS

Like a railroad car, our building was long, squat, narrow. At its center stood the communal bathroom—stalls, sinks, showers. Forget sleeping late. By 6 on weekday mornings, clanking leg braces and clanging wheelchairs were the musical wake-up call you'd never asked for.

On each side of the bathroom area were four bedrooms, two men per. But in our half, two of the four "sleeping rooms" were set aside as a sort of bizarro garage to store spare crutches, braces, and wheelchairs for the entire disabled community. It also was repair central for prosthetics—a "We Never Close" junkyard of spare parts.

Being AB (able-bodied) in a universe of gimps carried responsibilities. I became expert at assisting friends in and out of cars, beds, shower stalls. I could fold and stuff a wheelchair into the trunk of a car in seconds. I learned when to offer help and when to stand aside—but our help never was rejected. In turn, the gimps tried to teach Alvie and me "wheelies"—balancing a chair on its big wheels. It took but one spectacular tumble for me to seek less perilous diversions.

My most memorable barracks-mates:

- Chuck Dahnke was an amiable, Southern Illinoisan who disarmed strangers by sounding like a hick just off the rutabaga truck. In fact, until the auto accident that severed his spinal cord several years earlier, Charlie had been a star high school sprinter. We quickly forged a friendship that lasted 40 years, until his death. I bragged he never would have married Adrienne, a wisecracking AB from the Bronx and Chuck's mirror opposite, had I not chauffeured their dates, allowing them to smooch away in the back seat of his 1947 bucket-of-bolts Ford.

– Bruce Weimer hailed from the flyspeck hamlet of Delavan, in far west-central Illinois. Unlike Charlie, Bruce really was a dad-gum, aw-shucks hick. With his unfailing smile, Bruce was so sweet and gullible that you stayed close lest some city slicker try to con him. His joy was boundless, genuine. He was delirious being with friends, being in college.

Happy, in fact, just being alive.

For Bruce was racing time, spitting in the face of the inevitable. Muscular Dystrophy, insidiously and progressively, saps your strength until you cannot use your lower limbs. Then it creeps up the torso to your chest and neck and head, and now someone must feed you. Then your ability to swallow even tiny bites vanishes. After that, you can't breathe, and you die. Usually by 35. But Bruce, sweet, huggable Bruce, had declared a war on this silent killer that he knew he was doomed to lose. But first, he was determined to earn that accounting degree and get a job.

His roomie was his hero.

– Gene Dreyer was everything Bruce wasn't. Short bristly curls, dashingly (well, as "dashing" as a wheelchair permits) handsome. Urbane and witty. *Hick* not in **his** lexicon. Before polio, a teen tennis star in Kansas City. Beautiful inside and out. Endlessly, effortlessly affable.

Gene dressed snappily.

Not Bruce.

Gene, a huge target for the ladies, would return to Kansas City after graduation and wed the beautiful Thelma. Bruce's fiancée, Barbara, would dump him.

And Bruce Weimer, in return, was Gene's hero.

Bruce had grit and courage. Just extricating himself from bed in the morning and dressing was a heroic act. He refused to let MD purloin his infectious grin, brushing off his disability with "Aw, I've seen people with worse luck." Gene worried about him constantly. We all did. Bruce's condition had left him with Frankenstein legs— knees locked, arms flailing for balance. Any fall, and there were more than a few, rendered him helpless.

One icy winter afternoon, heading back from class, I hear a muffled, familiar voice.

"Help, help!"

"Bruce?" I call.

"Ron! Help me!"

The cries seem to be coming from somewhere near my toes.

"Ron! Under my car!"

I step gingerly on the ice a few feet to where Bruce's shiny turquoise-and-cream Chevy Bel-Air was parked, and peek underneath.

Sure enough, there he is on his back, arms and legs splayed, a perfect snow angel. His toes protrude from under the front bumper—think Evanora, the Wicked Witch of the East creamed by Dorothy's house, her toes twitching and curling.

"Another fine mess you've gotten yourself into, Brucie," I say, grabbing a leg and sliding him out, then picking him up.

I had learned how to pick him up—the only way you could get Bruce upright, given his ramrod legs. Notice I said "pick him up," not "help him up." Bruce was the deadest of dead weights. Get behind, lock your arms under his pits and across his chest, heave him to perpendicular. Don't expect him to help.

Once Bruce and I, again the only residents of our PGU without a date on a Saturday night, drove 30 miles east to a saloon in Danville, near the Indiana border, seeking to drown our solitude in malt beverage.

Bruce is a cheap drunk — one beer, and he is flying. Leaving the tavern around midnight, he executes one of his most spectacular spills in a career of Olympic-class tumbling.

Somehow, he never gets hurt. Again, think *The Wizard of Oz*—except Ray Bolger's Scarecrow bounced up and brushed himself off. Bruce requires unfolding.

But I've had a couple or three beers myself and again it is icy, a meteorological phenomenon occurring in Central Illinois almost any time between Thanksgiving and Easter. I don't want to risk us both sprawled helplessly on the sidewalk, so when a husky patron leaves the gin mill, I intercept him just before he steps on Bruce's predicament.

"Sir, could you please assist me in getting my friend upright? He's had just a touch too much."

The guy amiably sticks his hand out and gives Bruce a yank. Not a chance. Then Good Samaritan grabs both hands, and tugs. I stifle a chuckle; he cannot budge Bruce an inch.

"Let me 'splain," I say, offering a short course in Bruce-lifting 101.

So Mr. Samaritan positions himself behind Bruce, seizes him under the armpits, and tries to follow my tutorial. But Bruce's intoxicated giggle is just one more thing not helping the situation. Having heaved and tugged fruitlessly a full minute and finally suspecting he has been the butt of an especially cruel joke, our volunteer quits.

"You ain't helpin'!" he shouts angrily, and lets Bruce thud back onto the sidewalk. I attempt to explain that there is no way old Bruce can help, but I am weak with laughter. If the guy decides to take a pop at me, *I* will need someone to help me up. Eventually I manage to hoist Bruce, pour him into the passenger seat of his hands-control car, and drive carefully home.

🍦 🍦 🍦

FLUNKING FRENCH

Assisting my new buddies consumed a lot of study time, but I encountered plenty of other distractions en route to academic probation.

I was pleased to discover, while registering for classes, that my three years of high school French qualified me to go right into French IV and satisfy, in one college semester, my language graduation requirement.

For this desultory student, getting credit for high school French was like free jelly beans for life. I had spent three years trying to extricate myself from the doghouse of my stern teacher, Mlle. Thelma (FiFi) Allen (See *"A Toast to FiFi"*).

FiFi had been such a brilliant teacher that, despite my awful high school grades, I found myself "kilometres" ahead of the juniors and seniors in my class.

I aced the first few exams, and my hand always was the first raised in class—FiFi would have been proud (and shocked). Then my Gallic world imploded.

Since kindergarten in 1943, the Brooklyn Dodgers and their yearly post-season collapses had been central to my adolescence. Now, in autumn, 1955, the Dodgers were still seeking their first World Series triumph. And once again against evil incarnate, the New York Yankees.

These days, World Series games are played at night to maximize the TV audience (and sell cars and deodorant). But back in the Pleistocene Age, they played in the afternoons. Alas for my freshman grade point average, the first pitch at Ebbets Field, Brooklyn, precisely coincided with the 1 p.m. start of French IV in Champaign-Urbana.

It may not surprise you that I chose the Dodgers on TV over Victor Hugo, and rejoiced as my "Bums" ended decades of frustration by winning a thrilling seven-game series.

Jubilation was short-lived when I returned to find my classmates reading *Les Miserables*—in the original French. Who would have imagined they could catch and pass me in one crummy week? Dumb but not stupid, I dropped the class and switched to Italian, the language of my heritage. Besides, didn't I already know many juicy cuss words, thanks to Mother Millie and my Italian aunts?

DR. LANDIS AND HIS DAUGHTER

My "*maestra*" in Italian 101 in the spring semester would turn out to be a fetching young woman, Signorina Landis. I fell madly in love . . . with her father.

Professor Paul Landis taught British romantic poetry, and his annual holiday reading of Charles Dickens's *A Christmas Carol* had made him a campus legend.

Tall, erect, with a thatch of snow-white hair. His deep, rich voice was almost a growl. When Landis intoned, "Marley was dead, to begin with," we were magically transported from boring downstate Illinois to exciting Christmastime London.

The semester after discovering this holiday gem, I registered for his class, Introduction to British Romantic Poetry. Three times a week for an hour, Shelley, Byron, and Keats—brilliantly channeled through Paul Landis— transported me back a century to when poetry often actually rhymed.

I inquired of my Italian teacher, his daughter, what it was like to come home every night to the Babe Ruth of poetry. She smiled patiently, accustomed to playing second fiddle to dear old dad. Hard work earned me matching *A's* from the Landises, two big components I needed to escape academic probation.

Actually, probation was a condition expected—nay, encouraged—by university authorities. The transition from carefree high school days to the academic rigors of college exacted a cruel toll. To the 12,000 freshmen gathered in Huff Gym each fall semester for a formal campus orientation, the dean of students issued this "welcome":

"Freshmen, look to your left. Now turn to the right. Two of you will be gone by January."

Hello and welcome. Nice to meet you. Now, cram or scram.

Back then, a diploma from an accredited Illinois high school guaranteed admission to the flagship state university. But it did not guarantee success. The matriculation model was predicated on the mathematical certainty that most of the marginal two-thirds of the incoming freshmen would flunk or drop out in the first semester. Those on the bubble got probation, with most of them gone by summer. The 4,000 still upright in June will be Fighting Illini sophs.

So you would think that the early warning from the dean, that college would not resemble our high school cakewalk, would rivet our attention.

Not all of us were listening.

🍦 🍦 🍦

THE SLIPPERY SLOPE TO ACADEMIC PROBATION

I have many distractions besides helping my handicapped pals. Even with out-of-state tuition a $300 per semester bargain, I need an income if I hoped to indulge in sacred college traditions like pizza and beer.

So I get a job at Kamm's, the campus beer garden, where I earned $1 an hour flipping burgers. Plus nine hours on football Saturdays flipping the caps off thousands of bottles of Falstaff, Bud, and their brethren. A Sunday evening gig checking coats at the Illini Union earns me several free cafeteria meals a week.

Work hours that detracted from study hours? Let's say 30 a week.

Plus my high school sweetheart's letters grow progressively infrequent and considerably less passionate. But earning an "A" for clever, she mailed me the occasional diversionary gift from Douglass College back in New Jersey.

First was a leather-bound volume of Shelley's poetical works. (I still have it.)

Then came a pair of argyle socks, knitted by her very own perfidious fingers. (Years later, with Jill still regarding them with jaundiced eye, I "lost" them.)

Carol's "I will love you forever" pledge of August will translate to "six weeks or October, whichever comes first."

Lovelorn hours stolen from homework? Perhaps a dozen a week.

Then there is basketball. Like many other high school "stars" with profound height, weight, speed, quickness, agility, and accuracy deficiencies, I dream of a pro career.

I am happily stunned on the first day of freshman tryouts to find that the coach is Charlie Kiteoka, a counselor at the Vermont camp I worked at a couple of summers.

What luck! Charlie is well acquainted with my deadly 15-foot jumper, my agility to scoot free for layups, my tenacious defense.

"Charlie!" I shout.

Charlie Kiteoka is just as surprised to see me. Only not nearly so happy. He knows the fool's errand I'm embarking on, and while his voice says, "Hi, Ron," his face chimes in, "I'm really, really sorry, but I am going to be breaking your heart. Very soon."

He knows, and I soon would learn, that I might as well be trying out for the Boston Celtics. Bigger guys than I had ever played against are casually sinking 25 footers and slamming home dunks from heights I couldn't have reached with a ladder. Right then I should have said, "Thanks, Charlie ... Bye, Charlie", and reintroduced myself to my lonely textbooks.

But in basketball, as in love, I am expert in ignoring warnings my brain sends my heart. I refuse to make it easy for Charlie—he is going to have to cut me.

Which he certainly would have had I not saved him the trouble by badly spraining an ankle the second day of practice.

Amazing how hearts can trump brains. The entire Illinois varsity is on full scholarship, the starting five all will graduate into the pros. Manny Jackson will wind up owning the Harlem Globetrotters and be elected to the NBA Hall of Fame. Don Ohl, will become one of the most feared jump -shooters on the planet. Center Johnny "Red" Kerr went on to become one of the most popular Chicago Bulls of all time. And yet I—slow, stocky, 5-11 on my tallest day—dream of wearing orange and blue and performing incredible feats before berserk thousands at Huff Gym. You'd think sitting on Al Lawrence's high school bench because I couldn't find Harry Zingg would have been a strong enough message.

Writhing on the court, ankle throbbing, I finally acknowledge the inevitable: "This is hopeless, Cohen. Go home."

Home now being my bunk in the PGUs, where I nurse the bum ankle until I can limp to class without crutches. What a jerk. Here I am surrounded by people who would never walk again, and I take to my bed in a blue (and orange) funk.

Potential study hours misspent bemoaning the end of my basketball dreams? Maybe 50.

I suspect you are counting lost hours and saying, "With all that heartbreak, he must have flunked out."

Well, you would be wrong. And I haven't even mentioned the marathon poker games.

🍦 🍦 🍦

SPUD-NUTS

Around 8 o'clock on most Friday nights, a bunch of us sit down at a table in the dorm to play stud poker for dimes and quarters, the festivities lasting, on and off, all weekend.

I never had played poker, but I learn fast, parlaying luck and the very questionable skills of most of the other regulars to generally win small amounts. Although drinking in the dorm is forbidden, we make an awful lot of cheap beer disappear.

We also have other regimens. At precisely 4:45 on Saturday mornings we leave cards and money on the table and hustle to Urbana. Spud-Nuts opens at 5.

Ah, Spud-Nuts. The very word (two words?) tickles my salivaries a half-century later. Spud-Nuts are donuts made from potato dough, and at 5 a.m. these beauties emerge blazing hot from a vat of roiling grease and olfactory heaven envelopes the tiny shop like Maine coastal fog.

A couple of those beauties nestled in each hand, plus the anticipated explosion of heat and flavor from the first bite = bliss.

PO' BOYS

The only other thing important enough to interrupt poker is the late-night foray to Po'-Boy's, the closet-sized barbecue joint in Champaign on the undesirable side of the Illinois Central railroad tracks.

Po'-Boys: Xanadu for smoked meat. Ribs, brisket, Polish sausage, zesty sauce. A greasy, smoky, mouth-watering outpost of safety in a neighborhood where only the bravest, craziest, or most desperate dare venture after dark.

The proprietors are Arnie Po'-Boy (we bestowed the alias) and his beauteous wife, "Mrs. Po'-Boy." Lordy, their wares are magnificent—hours of slow smoking rendering meats crusty yet impossibly juicy. As a bonus, the glorious smell clings to your clothing through laundry day, which for most college kids generally is always a week or three away.

In later years my Champaign pal Betsy Hendrick mailed me an occasional bottle of Po'-Boys' sauce. But it was not the same without the Polish.

Nothing beat the Polish, a full 15 inches of tubular Nirvana protruding a prodigious three inches beyond each end of its hot dog bun cradle. How could Arnie possibly make a profit at 75 cents for this gut-busting bliss?

For 50 years, I pester—beg—for his Polish source.

"It is my special recipe," Arnie parries. "I dreamed it up with a butcher in Decatur. He makes them only for me."

"If I drive to Decatur, will he sell me a box? Will he ship it to me every month? Can you sign a letter attesting to my honor and desperation?"

Arnie hems and haws, stammering about how difficult it is even for him to find the butcher shop, and besides the guy keeps crazy hours. Even if you find it, it's probably closed. After a half-century of trying, I finally give up and acknowledge the secret path to Polish heaven will remain Arnie's secret.

Arnie and Mrs. Po'-Boy were wonderful hosts. After graduation it might be 15 years between visits, and although he could never exactly recall my name, he would shout, "I remember you! You covered football for the Daily Illini!"

So profound is my Po'-Boys' obsession that, about once a month, sleep still is interrupted by this recurring dream:

I am visiting Champaign for fun or business. To intensify my enjoyment of Arnie's bounty, I delay my visit until right before leaving. Anticipation grows and grows until it is almost unbearable—then the nightmare! Either Po' Boys is closed or I am summoned home before I can visit. I always wake up in a cold sweat.

One day, 50 years after I had graduated, Betsy sent me a devastating newspaper clipping: Arnie Po'-Boy was banking the hickory in his smoker after a half-century of ministering to the stomachs and souls of needy undergrads, and was trading his apron for a rocker on the porch next to the smoke shack.

Arnie hanging it up? Rocking away the rest of his life? I cannot be the only one who knows how lost he will be minus the 'cue and the camaraderie.

So both of my college-days food palaces are gone. Spud-Nuts had closed years earlier, robbing Urbana of the predawn redolence of freshly fried potato donuts.

And Old Rocking Chair, too soon, claimed Arnie.

Sadly for me, he carried the secret Decatur Polish Sausage Connection to the grave.

🍦 🍦 🍦

PASTEBOARD FOLLIES

End of digression, back to the poker table.

Nobody consciously decides an endless game is the best way to survive final exam week. It just sort of happens.

One of our gang, Jim Davis from Kewanee, Illinois, is everybody's pal. Like a regular guy, he swaps jokes and joins forays to Spud-Nuts and Po'-Boy's. But he is no regular guy. Birth defects have twisted his body into a capital *S*. Every morning his brother Bob straps him into a special body brace, and returns at bedtime to unstrap him.

So tight is the brace that Jim, before can speak must inhale slowly and deeply. Like a pitcher with an elaborate windup. It seems eternity before the exhale, and then, his brain trying to overcome his lungs, the words come tumbling out at warp speed. Until the next inhale.

I really admire Jim. Although most other disabled students' legs have atrophied, they are virtual Arnold Schwarzeneggers from the waist up thanks to thousands of hours of wheelchair acrobatics. Jim is head-to-toe scrawny. Too weak for a chair or crutches, his pretzel body rolls side to side with each painful step.

His only conveyance is a shiny new turquoise-and-white '55 Chevy Bel-Air, with hand controls for the accelerator and brake. Jim loves that beauty, so we are shocked when in a hand of seven-card stud on the third day of our finals-week poker marathon, he contemplates his dwindling cash reserves, re-checks his hole cards, then tosses his car keys into the pot.

He holds the rarest of full houses — three aces and two kings, nothing showing. But poker is not called "gambling" for nothing. My last card, the six of clubs, gives me four of a kind.

I intend to return the car keys, of course—those are Jim's "legs." But first I jerk him around a bit.

"Fair is fair," I declare, raking in the pot and pocketing the keys. To protests from the other players, I reply, "He's a grown-up. I am under no obligation to bail out a sucker."

You'd have thought I was playing Scrooge in Dr. Landis's "*A Christmas Carol*" reading, judging from the howls. But I bide my time until a few hands later when Jim shows two big pair. I make a show of refusing to fold in the face of this power, and my last bet is the car keys. When we turn the cards up, Jim disdainfully regards my small two-pair bluff, huffs a superior sigh to cover his relief, and pulls in four dollars … and the keys. I head off to my biology final.

The night before Christmas holiday break we escalate from beer to stronger stuff. Dispersing in all directions, we will need inner warmth against the bitter Illinois winter that only real alcohol can provide. The game breaks up, we exchange holiday wishes, and I sleep off my hangover on a Greyhound back to Jersey.

Two weeks later, certain my grades had landed me on academic probation, I return to the PGUs. I was correct — but grades turned out the least of my worries.

On my dorm bed sits an ominous envelope. The embossed words, *Dean of Men*, seem about a half-inch high. A brief letter summons me "Immediately."

"What do you know about the drinking orgy at the PGUs the night before Christmas break?" the dean demand when I arrive in his office, conspicuously omitting "Hello, Ron."

"Nothing." As egregious a lie as has ever crossed my lips.

"What do you know about the death of Jim Davis?"

My bones seem to turn liquid, and I grab the corner of his desk to keep from crumbling to the floor. No fibbing my way out of this one.

Jim dead? How? When?

"His body was found the morning when Christmas break began. Acute alcohol poisoning."

Our orgy of poker and booze, innocent if wildly stupid, had turned tragic. I've never been able to erase the thought of poor Jim alone in our frigid barracks, discovered by his brother next morning when he came by for the ride back to Kewanee for the holidays.

I am so distraught it barely registered when the dean discloses that, in addition to academic probation, I will spend second semester on social probation. He will personally be scrutinizing everything I do inside the classroom and out. Screw up and your next Greyhound ticket home will be one-way.

I had hit the jackpot—every kind of probation the University of Illinois offers.

Although I didn't pour booze down Jim's throat, I never, ever, will forget the consequences of our teenage stupidity.

GETTING OFF DOUBLE SECRET PROBATION

I hit the books way more diligently in the second semester, enough to slide off academic probation. With five finals in three days, I study virtually without sleep for 72 hours. When the last one is over, I "zombie" out the classroom door and purchase a 50-cent ticket to the Co-Ed campus theater for the perfect antidote for exhaustion: A double feature, *War and Peace* and *Anna Karenina.* I sleep through five hours and 46 minutes of dark Russian brooding. Twice.

In those Stone Age days, you handed your professor a stamped, self-addressed postcard on the back of which you had printed, "Final Exam ____. Final Grade ____," Then you sweated through excruciating days until the prof deigned to fill in the blanks and the U.S. Postal Service deigned to deliver the postcard. Sweating and studying paid off, a 3.75 grade point average, out of 4.

That took care of the academic half. As for the social component of the not-so-secret double probation, my deportment was beyond reproach. A model citizen. Well, mostly.

I continued to participate in the adventures of my paraplegic buddies, helping where appropriate. I even became the unofficial, unpaid chair pusher and mascot of the Fighting Illini Gizz Kids basketball team.

In the early 1940s, the University of Illinois had had a terrific varsity basketball team, a powerhouse sportswriters dubbed "The Whiz Kids."

Some years later, with the influx of handicapped students, the university decided to field a wheelchair basketball team that quickly became the best of its kind in the world. They adopted the name "The Gizz Kids."

Gizz" is the nickname for the device paraplegics strap around their waists under clothing, for times visiting a bathroom is inconvenient or impossible. Thus, "Gizz Kids."

Wheelchair basketball, unlike wheelchair football which is brute force, is an athletic ballet. My friends controll chairs like able-bodied brethren control their legs, switching directions rapidly, spinning 180 degrees on a dime, running set plays. In their non-ambulatory world, these guys are as athletically gifted as the Whiz Kids had been in theirs. Rules are exactly the same, except a player must dribble or pass after two pushes on the chair's wheels.

One night I am watching from my usual place on the bench—well, technically, there _is_ no bench, since all these guys arrive with their own seats--as the Gizz Kids played a national all-star team. No contest. Midway in the third period, we lead by 40, and my pals decide to break the tedium.

During a timeout, one commands, "Ron, grab a chair. You're going in."

Oh no I'm not. Do you think I am an idiot?

Play or we'll forfeit.

They seem serious, so I reluctantly climb into a spare chair. Public mortification surely will follow.

The game resumes. We miss, the other team rebounds, and nine guys who actually know what they're doing rush down the court as if their chairs are Ferraris. They arrive at the other basket before I can even turn my chair in the right direction. I am 70 feet away, completely out of things, alone near our team's basket.

Then our guy steals a pass and fires the ball half the length of the court, straight and hard as a frozen rope. I catch it before it can maim me, then cradle it in my lap and begin furiously trying to reverse the chair's wheels and "drive" to the hoop.

But changing direction and moving forward are talents exclusive to the nine guys thundering back toward my end of the court. As they get closer and the sound of rubber screeching across hardwood becomes more ominous—total panic. I'll never make it to the hoop before they arrive, so I leap from the chair, dribble once, sink a layup, turn to the stands and shout, "I'm saved! It's a miracle!"

My illegal, immoral, and unnecessary basket is disallowed, of course;, and I earn a technical for "walking with the ball." I slink back to sideline anonymity as the crowd boos and my "teammates" convulse.

Thus are my dreams of Illini basketball glory reduced to playing court jester for a bunch of gimps.

🍦 🍦 🍦

Gene Dreyer and I decide, against all common sense, to celebrate the designation of May as National Tavern Month. We vow to have a beer or two every day of the month.

This is easily accomplished—except for Sundays. Because Champaign County is "dry" on the Lord's Day, we must take Gene's car to surrounding counties. And because that entails fairly lengthy road trips, it seems foolish to restrict ourselves to "one or two." A tough goal, but we prevail — 31 straight days in various Central Illinois saloons.

Somehow these diversions do not prevent escape from the endangered species list. And it turns out freshman year was my lone brush with probation. I graduate, on time, in June 1959, possessor of an acceptable, if not particularly distinguished, academic record.

I keep my diploma in our basement, protected by its nice, faux-leather carrying case.

Orange and blue, of course.

TYING UP LOOSE ENDS

Since then:

The PGUs fell to the wrecking ball soon after I graduated, replaced by tall, modern, thoroughly yawn-inducing modern residence halls.

Although disabled students now are welcomed on campuses everywhere, Illinois remains a prized destination. And the Gizz Kids still rock and roll—and rule the world of wheelchair basketball.

WPGU, our very own radio station, thrives yet today — run by smart undergrads who never saw the structures that gave birth to its call letters.

Charlie Dahnke married his beauteous Adrienne, love conquering the vast cultural chasm between the Bronx and Centralia. They raised two wonderful kids not too far from Champaign until Chuck's death four decades after I had chauffeured their first date. I don't know what became of Charlie's freshman roommate, a guy who quit school after a month because they wouldn't let him smoke in the library.

Gene Dryer returned to Kansas City to the proper life of stock broker and community pillar, wed the lovely Thelma, had two children, and is justifiably adored by a small army of grandkids. After a half-century he and Thelma still seem madly in love, and we remain great friends.

(One month before this book was published, I got a heart-breaking call from Thelma. Gene has died. Goodbye, Gene-Bo. I will miss you every day).

Bruce Weimar obliterated the muscular dystrophy actuarial charts, surviving until age 70. His cheery optimism never faltered, and he found richly deserved happiness in later life in his wonderful nurse/wife, Cheryl, with whom he moved from crossroads Delavan to the bright lights of Peoria. The last time I saw him they were touring Washington with two nurses who bathed and dressed and fed Bruce every morning as he charged, figuratively, into another improbable day of a brave and improbable life.

I returned to campus a number of times over the years — for football games, for Po'-Boy's sausages, to attend the "Overlooked Film Festival" begun by famed movie critic Roger Ebert. One week, I was invited back to spend a week talking to journalism school classes about what to expect in the real world.

Another time I spent a few days interviewing to head the journalism school. Happily, the dean and I agreed real journalism, not fund-raising, was my strong suit.

Fifty years after graduation, I returned for my induction ceremony into the University of Illinois Journalism Hall of Fame. I celebrated by being kidnapped by a bunch of students for a long night of pizza and beer and subversive talk. Just like the old days.

🍦 🍦 🍦

I completed the draft of this chapter in Maine, in late September, 2010 before Shlomo was even born. It has gone through dozens of agonizing revisions, including a couple right at the last minute. It turned out longer than I had anticipated, and what struck me as I rewrote is that although I did a lot of dumb things that first year and didn't study hard as I should have, university isn't all about books and grades. It is about growing up. too.

FRESHMAN YEAR REPORT CARD

Bad things: Good friend dies suddenly, tragically; dreams of basketball fame vaporize; high school sweetheart transfers impossibly rose-red cheeks to a doubtlessly inferior swain (they wind up married forever); I plunge into simultaneous academic and social probation (a Big 10 record?); perpetually broke, I take various jobs, to the detriment of my grades; I drink too much beer, cut too many classes, make too many stupid decisions—one of which forces me to drop French with the finish line in sight. Too many late night/early morning forays in search of unhealthy comestibles.

Wow. That"s some bad pile.

But . . .

Good things: Dodgers at last win the World Series; I make great new friends, some I keep for a lifetime; learn there are many, many things disabled people are "able" to do; get pretty good at poker; survive the loss of Carol, a spectacular plus because I meet Jill in two years; uncover the best barbecue east of Kansas City; somehow don't flunk out; learn that doughnuts can be deliciously made from potatoes; discover I love classical music and Percy Bysshe Shelley; meet my all-time favorite professor and "ace" his class; start four great years working on the *Daily Illini*, where I fiind my life-long niche. I mature, a lot. When I leave campus in June, 1956, I am not the same person that dropped out of the sky into an Illinois cornfield nine months earlier. Will high school friends even recognize me?

School grade: *B* -minus.

Life grade: *A.*

And, at last, no more the burden of "Capable of Doing Better."

🍦 🍦 🍦

Chapter 17

HEY, GIMME FREE BEER!

As an Illinois freshman, despite zero culinary acumen, I fast-talked myself into a job tending grill at Kamm's, the most popular eatery/beer hall on campus.

Never having squared off against a grill before (our kitchen being Millie's unchallenged domain), I was a little disturbed when a waiter picked up my very first burger by the buns and squeezed out a quarter-cup of grease.

Short Order Cooking 101: Before removing burger, flatten with spatula so grease pools on grill, not bun.

But food isn't the attraction at Kamm's on football Saturday home games. Minutes after the final gun, students begin pouring in from Memorial Stadium, dragging their thirsts behind them. By last call at midnight, 500 cases of beer have been demolished.

To avoid falling hopelessly behind while serving the parched and rowdy Drinking Illini, I had to learn the fine art of simultaneously uncapping six bottles, three with each slippery hand, on openers attached to a block of wood behind the counter—another college skill I never was called upon to replicate.

159

One football Saturday a behemoth suddenly appears before me, having flicked aside a gaggle of fellow students like so many milkweed spores.

"Hey, gimme free beer!" he demands in a voice halfway between a roar and an even bigger roar.

I can't believe my ears. Indeed, I wonder whether I ever will be able to use them again. Is this guy serious? Free beer? Why had nobody informed me that Mr. Kaminsky (Kamm's, foreshortened) was the last of the great Midwest philanthropists?

I briefly ponder a snippy retort before sensibly settling on a supplication, delivered in a voice midway between a whine and a whimper. Complying, I explain to him, would certainly end my employment, forcing me to drop out of school and condemn me to a life of selling ill-fitting slipcovers in Hoboken for Imperial Outfielders.

But it is instantly apparent this bruiser, one Ray Nitschke, is not at Illinois to major in logic nor evince even passing acquaintance with the concept of human kindness.

Nitschke was the starting fullback and middle linebacker for the Fighting Illini, and a fearsome presence indeed. After a brilliant college career, he would spend 14 years with the Green Bay Packers, wreaking mayhem on hapless tailbacks and pass receivers who dared venture into his realm, which he considered to be anywhere between the sidelines—and, often, beyond the normal field of play.

Bodily disregard for both himself and enemy quarterbacks would win him unanimous, first-ballot induction into the NFL Hall of Fame, but probably contributed to his death at 61.

Brushing off my tale of woe the way he had shed Michigan State blockers and tacklers earlier that afternoon, Nitschke repeats, more menacingly if possible, his demand.

"Please, Mr. Nitschke," I beg, employing the honorific in the faint hope he might spare my life. "I need this job."

"Hey, gimme free beer!" repeats Mr. Deaf Ears.

As I contemplate whether these four words constitute the entirety of his vocabulary, Mr. Nitschke reaches across the counter, grabs my apron front with a massive paw, and lifts me like a feather.

Even in those days I was not exactly a wraith. Yet as I dangle helplessly a yard off the beer hall floor, self-preservation kicks in. I vow to him that no money will be changing hands for that beer, nor the dozen others he would consume. In fact, please bring your family and all your friends and they will be treated similarly. I quietly enumerate the training rules he is breaking, and wonder whether if he is caught and booted off the team I can be judged complicit for having folded like origami.

Ray's drinking buddy, as always, is his wild-thing compatriot Jack Delveaux, backup fullback and linebacking partner. Mr. Delveaux (I always employ "Mr." with him as well, for I am not a **complete** idiot), also is constructed along the general dimensions of a cement mixer. On any team without Ray Nitschke, this slab of concrete would have been the star. In fact, Jack Delveaux would go on to carve out a great pro career of his own, as a bulldozing running back with the Canadian Football League's Winnipeg Blue Bombers.

Yet on the night I first make their acquaintance, concrete seems the sole material comprising the respective Nitschke-Delveaux occipital ridges.

The real drama begins at closing when the two caballeros stagger onto John Street, fortified with far too many of my "courtesy" beers. Arms linked for moral and physical support, they stumble about four steps before Nitschke is savagely attacked by a parking meter.

That this inanimate object is entirely blameless matters little. Our heroes eye it malevolently, as if it were a quarterback fading to pass.

"Why, you lousy sonofagun!" (or something to that effect) Nitschke shouts. Delveaux, even through his beer-induced fog, senses the retribution Ray contemplates, and shakily nods his blonde buzz-cut.

From opposite sides of the meter, four hairy paws alternately begin tugging and pushing. They are too drunk to guess, or care, that their foe is buried a yard deep in concrete.

Nitschke pulls, Delveaux pushes. Then Delveaux pulls, Nitschke pushes. News of this titanic struggle, immovable forces vs. inanimate object, spreads rapidly. Soon hundreds of students are streaming in assorted bedclothes to join the stragglers leaving Kamm's. For the second time that day, schoolmates are cheering Nitschke and Delveaux to victory.

A couple of campus cops wander by but choose discretion over valor. A solid circle of fans presses closer to the combatants and begin chanting, "Heave, ho! Heave, ho!"

After resisting nearly two hours, the meter groans its surrender. Roaring like jungle beasts over dinner,

Nitschke and Delveaux redouble their efforts, heave a final "ho," and triumphantly hoist the meter skyward, concrete base intact like a sapling awaiting planting.

Then acknowledging the fortitude and endurance of their foe, they tenderly place it against the curb and march down John Street, trailed by hundreds of Cheering Illini.

It remains one of the most astonishing examples of brute strength—and sheer lunacy—I have ever witnessed.

🍦 🍦 🍦

Many years later I happened to spot Nitschke in an aisle seat on a plane from Chicago to Washington. After retiring he had remained in Green Bay, channeling gridiron ferocity into local charities and community projects. Football-crazy Green Bay revered Retirement Ray as much as they did Hall-of-Fame Ray.

He doesn't recognize me, of course, but when I tell him we were fellow Illini he motions to the empty seat beside him. As we swap memories, I find myself straining to capture snatches of his conversation, so thoroughly has the now-gentle giant evolved from the creature who had jeopardized my job—my very existence, actually—at Kamm's a couple of million years ago. I observe, silently but with more than a little pleasure, that he now is even balder than I, with glasses thicker than mine.

How tough was the old Ray Nitschke? Two years into his professional career, a gust of wind felled a steel coaching tower on the Packers' practice field. Legendary coach Vince Lombardi raced over to see if anyone had been hurt. Told the unlucky soul struggling to extricate himself from the tangled mountain of metal was none other than his all-pro middle linebacker, Lombardi responded, "Nothing can hurt Nitschke. Get back to practice."

At another practice, Nitschke threw himself recklessly into a blocking sled. Somehow a steel rod became dislodged and pierced his helmet. Ray emerged unscathed, and the Nitschke legend grew. That helmet, spike still embedded, resides in the Packers museum in Green Bay.

But sitting beside him on the plane I can see Ray's ferocity has been drained by thousands of violent gridiron collisions. He smiles a little sheepishly as I recount our undergraduate encounters.

He does not attempt to blame a difficult childhood for his outsized sense of entitlement at Illinois—his father died in a car accident when he was four, his mother had succumbed to a blood clot when he was 10. His two teen-age brothers raised him to keep the family intact.

No, he does not recall the "Lifting Ron Incident" at Kamm's, but acknowledges that yes, using me as a human barbell sounds about right. Those heady football-star days engendered an elevated sense of his own worth, he recalls, a little ruefully. Then he apologizes with a sincerity that cannot be mistaken.

Emboldened by his remorse, I ask if he recalls a certain late-night parking meter extraction.

He pauses a moment then grins impishly.

"That Delveaux—man, he was really crazy," Ray Nitschke says softly.

🍦 🍦 🍦

Chapter 18

HOW I MET JILL, AND OTHER EXCITING TALES

Jill is fond of saying, "What in the world were Kenny and Beanie thinking?"

Kenny is Ken Broun, my roommate at the University of Illinois. Beanie is Florrie Kogen, Jill's sorority sister and friend from Chicago. I don't know why the "Beanie," but that's who she was when I met her in 1958, and I ain't changing it now.

Kenny and Beanie, who were dating, were unhappy that two of their best friends were not.

So they conspired to set us up on a blind date over Thanksgiving in 1957; I was a junior, Jill a freshman.

Jill, Kenny, and Beanie were all home in Chicago that weekend. I stayed on campus. New Jersey was far too far. I was far too poor. Vacation was far too short.

By noon on Wednesday of Thanksgiving week the 45,000-student campus had magically emptied, save for a few hundred foreign students, an army of ravenous squirrels—and forlornly lonely little me.

Thanksgiving always had been a dazzling feast at the Cohens, a bountiful, multi-cultural repast ranging from lasagna and meatballs to turkey and the trimmin's. Dessert was assorted pies — and cannoli. Every leaf of the dining room table was pressed into service.

So, with frost already dotting the Illinois cornfields, I must attempt to make the best of my plight. I obtain a pound of angel hair pasta and a pathetic jar of ersatz tomato sauce, and call Mom for instructions.

"Boil water in a pan. Don't be stingy with the salt, and throw in the macaroni for eight minutes. Don't forget to stir, or it will stick."

Millie, doubtless, was picturing her own well-stocked kitchen. My entire trove of culinary tools consists of a single-coil electric hot plate with two settings, off and incinerate. It was in a small saucepan upon that hot plate that I heated my main sustenance that semester—a can of Van Camp's baked beans whose vegetarian status I ruined by adding a package of eight cut-up hotdogs.

My second call to Millie, at 11 on Thanksgiving morning, constituted an emergency.

Me: "Help, Ma! What shall I do?"

She: "Whatsamatter?"

Me: "The angel hair is boiling over!"

She: "How can that be? Did you use too much water?"

Me: "Too little pot. Oh my god! It's erupting like Vesuvius! Now it's overflowing onto the floor!"

Mom stifles a guffaw—a couple of years later I discovered that after hanging up she called her three terrific-cook sisters to deliver a blow-by-blow of my predicament, a tale destined to be repeated far too often at family gatherings.

My limp mountain of angel hair having been dumped into a wastebasket, I resign myself to walking to Steak 'n' Shake for fries and a double cheeseburger or three. Rescued at the last moment by my pal Betsy Hendrick, who actually lives in Champaign, I soon find myself at the Hendrick family groaning board.

That took care of Thursday, but I dreaded the remainder of the long holiday weekend. Fate stepped in when the phone rang in my rooming house Friday morning.

Please indulge a slight digression, for I cannot in good conscience brush off 1001 South First Street as a mere "rooming house." Perhaps for the four students who live in "normal" rooms on the second floor. Not for me.

I had spent the entire week before fall classes fruitlessly hunting a place to live. By the time I knocked on Chet Anderson's front door, all his "normal" second-floor bedrooms already are gone. Chet, a sweet and gentle man, regards my fallen crest and offers his attic, for $20 a week.

"Yes!" I blurt, barely even hearing the price. Chet points to the attic door. "Up there."

To get "up there" I must negotiate the stairs—seven steps, a landing, a sharp left turn, and the last four steps on my hands and knees.

I conquer Kilimanjaro to discover that the sole spot I can stand upright is directly in the center of the room where the sharply sloped roof pauses before descending the far side of the house.

A step in either direction from dead center, and I must hunch and duck. Two steps and I must bend at the waist. Three, waddle like a duck.

My furnishings consist of lumpy bed, desk, and a hoary chair with wildly askew legs. The top of the desk doubles as my kitchen. When my single-burner hot plate blows a fuse (frequently), the house plunges into darkness and howls of anguish emanate from the guys studying in relative luxury on Floor Number Two.

Bathroom? Floor Number Two. Telephone? Floor Number One, where Chet and his new wife Cathy reside.

When I get out of bed I invariably clunk my head on the ceiling/roof. There is no closet, no bureau. What there is are two piles of clothes, one filthy, one merely very dirty.

Depart this torture chamber? Drop to all fours and crawl down to the second floor—backwards.

After I met Jill I worried if our courtship could withstand the rigors of "visiting the room." But being short she was able stand erect and walk several steps in any direction before scraping her forehead.

Now return with me to Thanksgiving Friday.

I am alone when I hear the distant phone. The house rule is that the closest person must answer, and since there is nobody else in the house I stumble from bed, crack my skull on the ceiling, scramble backwards down to the second floor, then rush down the next flight to the first floor vestibule. I reach the phone just as Kenny is about to hang up.

"Take the train to Chicago. I'll pick you up at the station. I got you a date for Saturday night."

It has been a number of months since I heard those two unfamiliar and slightly frightening words. "A date."

I have an essay to write, I protest. Kenny isn't buying.

"C'mon. She is really cute."

When I arrive Jill's young sister Marcia, her broken leg in a cast, opens the door. Their mom, Florence, jolly and plump, greets me like a long-lost son-in-law. Smart lady, that Flo.

Kenny hasn't lied. Jill *is* cute. Real cute.

🍦 🍦 🍦

Kenny and Beanie and Jill and I repair to the Ivanhoe, a nightclub of sorts, which turns out to be a faux English Tudor structure containing a faux medieval drinking establishment and a faux elevator that requires several minutes to descend 10 faux feet. (Ivanhoe's next incarnation would be a cheese store.).

When you check your coats they hand you three darts. Toss them accurately at the board a few feet away and win a prize.

Bingo! Jill and I now own matching faux-felt Robin Hood hats, their conical crowns accessorized with a tall feather. This is her first—and last—hint of my athletic prowess.

Jill and Ron, two weeks after the 1958 blind date.

How could I not fall in love?

Terrific first date leads on Sunday night to terrific second date (just the two of us), linguine at romantic

Armando's. I am at the top of my game—a whole meal without knocking over the romantic candle or accessorizing my shirt with gravy stains.

We arrange to meet on the train back to Champaign next morning.

Kenny and I have barely settled into our seats when here comes Jill walking up the aisle, quite dapper in her cheesy Robin Hood hat. Kenny quickly secures another seat, and by the time we pull into Champaign, Jill and I are a couple.

Our campus dates mostly involve hitching a ride with friends to Katsina's, where you can get a pizza and spend hours nursing a couple of 90-cent bottles of dreadful Chianti — it is all I can afford and besides, she has decided to decorate her dorm room with those empty bottles in their cute little wicker baskets.

Our relationship procedes relatively unscathed as I try to ease her justifiable doubts about a half-Italian from Jersey. I begin showing up after her night art classes, telling her how much I love the smell of oil paint and carrying home her bulky art supplies. She is charmed.

One night a biblical rainstorm afforded me another chance to prove my gallantry.

Leaving a movie house, we are forced to wade two blocks through knee-high (almost waist-high in Jill's case) currents overwhelming Champaign's storm drains. We finally reach where we had parked our borrowed car, only to discover Jill is missing a shoe.

I return next morning after the oceans have receded, and there it is, soaked but intact, in the middle of the street near the theater. I place it in a coffin-like shoebox draped with a small American flag and dramatically present it to her. Big points for Mr. Romantic.

Another time she invites me to a dance, shrugging off the glares shot at me by a few of her Phi Sigma Sigma sorority sisters who are unhappy her date is not a frat boy. She doesn't care. Big points for Jill.

One night she invites me to steak night at her sorority. More frowns. Neither of us cares, and steak sure beats weenies and beanies on a hot plate. Before long, we're running out of smiley-face space on our respective scorecards.

But standing in the way of my bid to romance my Phi Sig was one truly formidable obstacle: Aunt Ellie, a prison guard masquerading as sorority house mother and a vigorous enforcer of the immutable 1 a.m. weekend curfew days.

One day Kenny and I decide to retaliate. We enlist the craziest person we know, Ken's fraternity brother Cubby, a John Belushi look-alike and act-alike long before Belushi became the poster child for aberrant behavior. He leaped at the chance to co-conspirit.

The sorority house has double front doors that open dramatically to reveal a quadruple-wide staircase perfect for the sisters to make princess-like grand entrances while mere-mortal swains wait below. At the foot of the stairs, to the left of the front door, is Aunt Ellie's little suite.

I don't ask how Cubby acquired a small, noisy-but-harmless track starter's pistol, but one Saturday night as the clock hands near 1 a.m., we position ourselves at the top of the staircase.

I began the dialogue something like this:

"Keep your filthy hands off my girl! I thought you were my pal!"

"But I love her and can't live without her!"

"Well, if you can't live without her, try this!"

I pull the starter's pistol from my waistband as sorority sisters screech in horror.

"Don't shoot! Don't shoot!" Cubby begs. But I am far too crazed with jealousy to heed. I fire. I fire twice more.

Clutching his chest (to more efficiently smear the plastic bag of ketchup concealed beneath his shirt), Cubby staggers backward.

"I'm hit," he shouts, weaving drunkenly for several seconds, then tumbling heels over head down the entire flight before coming to rest at the feet of a horrified Aunt Ellie, who had been roused by the gunshots. The collective co-ed screaming stops only when Cubby, after a 30-second period of rigor mortis, scrambles to his feet, theatrically checks for broken bones, and waves "Goodnight, ladies." He, Kenny, and I calmly stroll out into the darkness.

Bet they're still talking about it. Maybe there's a historical marker.

♥ ♥ ♥

One weekend, after covering the Big Ten gymnastics championship in Iowa City, I return bearing a tiny silver pin.

Because I am only an "indee," I do not possess a fraternity pin with which to pledge undying love. But I do have that little silver pin which, upon close inspection, turns out to be tiny guy in mid-bounce on a trampoline.

Now getting pinned (going steady) is a big deal in the world of Phi Sig, occasioning a wacky, middle-of-the-night ritual in which coeds are roused from dreamland, throw black robes over their nighties, and are herded into a big room in the attic.

Anticipation is so thick it can be cut only with the knives wielded during Phi Sig's Steak Night as the sisters assemble in a large circle like a coven of witches. Solemnly and silently, they pass a flickering candle hand to hand. When it reaches its destination, the lucky newly pinned girl blows out the flame, igniting shrieks and embraces.

That scene is considerably less joyous at Jill's pinning. When she blows out the flame many of her housemates, feeling duped because the "pin" lacks Greek letters, file grumpily back to bed. Can Phi Sigma Sigma survive the stigma of "Sorority Girl Falls In Love With Mere Indee"?

Jill doesn't care. Which is why I love her.

Our romance survives the long winter, and in March Jill takes me home at spring break for show and tell. Her dad, Sid, seems kind of quiet and a little severe, but everything goes quite smoothly. As we prepare to catch the train back to school, he makes a dramatic grand gesture: He cannot drive because he is recuperating from a heart attack, so he will loan us the family car until June.

I have hit the lottery. The pristine red-and-white beauty is a top-of-the-line 1955 Buick Roadmaster convertible, about a block and a half long. Drive that baby around Champaign with the top down on a sunny day and watch heads swivel like Rosemary's baby.

Sid presses the keys into my hand, then adds the whipped cream and maraschino cherry to this triple-dip, extra fudge sundae: His plastic Union Oil credit card.

At first I am perplexed. Oil company credit cards are in their infancy—I had never even seen one. But boy did I learn quickly! Jill and I utilized every spare moment of every sunny day to drop the top and investigate romantic destinations. The gasoline bills Sid Greenspan received from Union Oil couldn't have done his heart much good.

Meanwhile, Flo launched a brilliant scheme to ensure her daughter's charming new suitor wouldn't slip away.

Every few weeks a package arrives at my rooming house; Chicago Flo has sent a three-foot-long Kosher salami and assorted bagels. I jealously ration this respite from beans and weenies until its replacement arrives. Flo's largesse means I occasionally can scrape together enough quarters to take her daughter to lunch.

So, was it Salami Flo or Roadmaster Sid who convinced me Jill was The One? Probably neither, although they sure didn't hurt.

June 25, 1961.

This covers about the first six months of a relationship now closing in on six decades. Like Jill, I occasionally wonder what our matchmaking friends were thinking that Thanksgiving weekend long ago. But we sure are thankful they persisted.

Marital longevity has taken some work, though. Following are some examples:

- I love sports. Jill would rather have a root canal without Novocain than go to a ballpark or watch a game on TV.
- I read short stories, daily newspapers and am always eight weeks behind on my New Yorker magazines. She is addicted to mysteries.
- So infrequently do our TV tastes intersect that we spend many evenings apart. She is upstairs in the cozy spare bedroom she calls "The Womb,"

watching shows whose British actors speak a dialect I cannot understand. I luxuriate downstairs in a leather recliner with my faithful companion Margo, a 50-inch Panasonic plasma.

— I rarely eat dessert. She has been known to check the back page of the restaurant menu and order dessert first, lest they run out.

— Her back problems mean I no longer have companionship on the long walks I love. She misses them, too.

— Spur-of-the-moment car trips like the ones we used to take in Sid's convertible are my idea of heaven, hers of hell.

While neither ever would request a do-over, when people inquire about our secret formula for matrimonial longevity I know exactly what she will reply:

"What in the world were Kenny and Beanie thinking?"

Kenny and Beanie also have been happily married for years and years.

Just not to each other

🍦 🍦 🍦

Chapter 19

A PINT FOR MY POP

I am relaxing in a recliner, after all these years oblivious to the needle in my right arm and a tube sucking my O-Negative blood into a clear plastic bag on the floor.

A nurse at the local American Red Cross office has verified the pedigree and iron content of my blood and checked my temperature, pulse and pressure before clearing me to donate, a process that takes about 15-20 minutes, depending on the speed of the flow.

Afterwards, I sit 10 minutes in the "Recovery Room," a canteen stocked with drinks, pretzels, and Famous Amos chocolate chip cookies. Volunteers check occasionally to make sure I haven't pitched forward, light-headed, onto the floor.

Having reacquainted myself with the charms of Mr. Famous Amos, I schedule my next appointment for exactly 56 days. I am not eligible to donate until then.

A pint every couple of months adds up to three quarts a year. I did this for almost 50 years before the friendly "vampires" at the Red Cross called it quits—it was getting too hard to locate a strong vein amid the scar tissue. I figure my grand total at about 45 gallons, give or take a pint or three.

I feel a little like Dracula's bride, and my well-worn donor card lauds me as a Red Cross "Hero."

But the real heroes of this story are 150 anonymous souls in Minneapolis who, in the dead of winter of 1958, gave a pint to a man they never would meet.

My dad, Maurie, had contracted rheumatic fever at birth. It ravaged his heart and brought a lifetime of sickness and pain.

For long stretches he was unable to work regularly, and it tore at his soul that his two brothers were "carrying" him at the family business, turning deaf ears when he protested they must at least reduce his salary.

Maurie used "free time" better than anyone I ever knew. A voracious reader, he haunted second-hand book stores and maintained first-name relationships with countless town librarians. He wrote avidly—poems, diaries, short stories, letters-to-the-editor. If never being published hurt, he never let it show. Dad filed away rejection letters as if they were battle ribbons.

He joked that although he sent simultaneous copies of an original short story to only eight magazines, he had received 14 rejection letters.

Dad used to write things for me, and I let him because he could do it so much better. To this day when I read something of his I shake my head and smile a jealous smile.

His most egregious example of ghostwriting my material was when he composed the entire "Today I Am A Man" speech for my Bar Mitzvah. It was simply beautiful, profound far beyond my intellectual and emotional capacity. Its phrasing and cadences shamed my teenage wit and vocabulary.

It ended with a grand flourish, my intoning, in Hebrew, the words "*Next year, God willing, in Jerusalem*—a paean to the Jews' newly minted homeland, the state of Israel.

The plaudits landed on me, but everybody in that temple knew the identity of my muse.

Even more embarrassing was when Hester Switzer, greatest teacher ever, assigned our fourth grade class at Nassau School an original poem.

Dad sprang into action. Poetry was his great love, after all. Two days later, I stood in front of my classmates, plagiarizing his work, "My Sis, Diane."

Oh, it was a beauty! Who could forget its majestic concluding couplet:

"Is it bird, or beast, or man?

No, sir; it's my sis, Diane."

A sensation! Hester Switzer, her kindly, wrinkled visage beaming, shared it at lunch in the teachers' lounge. Its immediate next stop was the desk of the principal, Dr. Boney, who, leaping at the opportunity to show East Orange public school administrators just what sort of geniuses Nassau was harboring, kicked Dad's poem up the educational ladder. In one fell swoop, my literary dad had managed to make BOTH his children (in) famous.

But if good poetry truly is for the ages, "My Sis, Diane" was but a one-week wonder. Hester Switzer's follow-up assignment — a poem about the Easter Bunny, exposed her would-be poet laureate for the fraud he was.

When I had shamelessly sought Dad's "help" for this second poem, I was stunned by the response from a man who fired off letters to the editor every morning before applying a cream cheese shmear to his bagel.

"I showed you how to do it," he said, ignoring my falling crest. "Now, you're on your own."

How could he cruelly yank the ladder out from under his only son just as I was about to scale the poetic summit of Mount Olympus?

Without his "help," my dream of replicating Percy Bysshe Shelley was shattered before I had any idea who the guy was and even before I read this closing stanza to my classmates:

> "So between you and me
> There ain't no Bunny.
> If there is, he can jump in the lake.
> So believe me dear friends,
> If you look through a lens,
> You'll find this whole poem is a fake."

As you might guess, Mrs. Switzer didn't hustle down the hall to the principal's office with this one!

Thirty years after Dad died, I co-authored a book about the downfall of my employer, United Press International, and dedicated it ... "To my father, Maurie, the real writer in the family."

I wrapped my very first copy in heavy plastic to protect it from the elements and placed it on his grave in Lyndhurst, New Jersey. I almost could hear him chortle, "Finally, a Cohen gets published!"

🦉 🦉 🦉

Growing up, I rarely got to do many of the things with Pop that most sons take for granted, like playing catch and shooting hoops. It must have gnawed at him, for one summer day when I was 15, he announced a "father-son adventure."

We would, he told me, drive the family car, a Buick Roadmaster, a couple of hours to the Catskill Mountains in New York where we would go fishing.

I hadn't a clue how to fish, and was quite certain he didn't either. But we bravely rented waders and casting rods from an old general store, solicited tips from the laconic proprietor, and soon were up to our thighs in a picturesque mountain stream. We didn't actually catch anything, but neither did we drown nor embed fishhooks into crucial body parts.

And unsuccessful fishing leaves plenty of time for father-son quality talk. Dad and I, at last, are engaged in a "sport."

After dinner at a diner that had seen better days, we collapse, exhausted, into lumpy beds in our rustic motel cabin, vowing to rise early and try again.

Our idyllic next morning is interrupted — literally — in mid-stream. Dad drops his rod and clutches his chest. I help him to shore, where he gasps an outline for the next several hours of my life, and hopefully his.

"Here are the car keys. We drop off the equipment, and then you have to be the man of the family and drive home."

I am aware of Dad's great faith in Chuck Rosen, his long-time cardiologist, but shouldn't we head to the nearest emergency room?

"No, we're going home."

I play my ace.

"Dad, I have never driven a car in my life, I'll be scared out of my gourd. I have no license, I can't even get a learner's permit for two years. We are two hours from home. You need to be in a hospital right now!"

"Don't worry. I know you can do it."

Arguing not only is hopeless, but also a waste of precious time. Reluctantly I climb behind the steering wheel of the Roadmaster, a beast that looks and handles like a tank (Power steering was still only an inventor's dream). We are both going to die, I am certain, and just as I have begun sinking my patented fall-away jump shot more than twice a week.

As the speedometer inches up—10, 20, 25 miles per hour, my eyes leave the road only for split-second glances to make sure Pop is breathing.

In what to this day seems almost too miraculous to believe, we survive to meet Chuck Rosen in the emergency room at East Orange General. He checks Dad's vitals and announces: No heart attack, just scary, painful arrhythmia. Dad drives home.

In our driveway he presses a conspiratorial forefinger to his lips: Millie must never learn our secret, he warns.

And she never did.

Occasionally, Dad would talk wistfully of a "cure" so he could lead "a normal life." His battered heart soared one day in the mid-1950s with the stunning news that a cardiologist at the University of Minnesota Hospital, Dr. C. Walton Lillehei, had pioneered a surgical technique during which the heart was actually removed from the chest for repair while a magical machine kept the patient alive. Might such "open-heart surgery" be Dad's cure?

He flew to Minneapolis but flunked the physical. Although Lillehei gave him a diet and light exercise regimen to build strength, both realized fixing my dad was the longest of long-shots.

During a couple of years of exchanging letters and phone calls, the bond between them grew. Lillehei became quite fond of this slight, brilliant man so determined to undergo the experimental surgery. Having repeatedly warned about survival odds, Lillehei finally, reluctantly, agreed to be Maurie's last hope.

Two weeks into the new year of 1958, Dad is back in Minneapolis. Not until then did we learn about a huge final hurdle. Surgery might last a dozen hours, and before Lillehei can begin, there must be at least 75 pints of blood in reserve.

And we know not a soul in Minneapolis.

With low hopes for success but willing to try anything, I write the editor of the *Daily Minnesotan*, the campus newspaper, describing the ordeal Dad was facing and our desperate need for donors.

"Please," I wrote, "if you are touched by his plight and can find it in your hearts to donate, my family will never forget your kindness."

My letter, displayed prominently on the front page, strikes a nerve. In a heart-rending outpouring of generosity, in less than one day strangers donate 150 pints.

But the arduous surgery saps what little strength Dad has. He contracts post-operative pneumonia and dies in the hospital a few days later. He was 49.

It took a couple of years to overcome my lifelong aversion to needles, but one afternoon in 1965 I screwed up courage and donated my first pint, at a blood bank in New York City's Greenwich Village. I was so light-headed afterwards that classmates at Columbia University had to assist me home.

That first perilous pint was the down payment on my debt to the citizens of Minneapolis.

My O-Neg is fairly rare—only seven in 100 have it. And it is precious because, regardless of their own blood type, anyone can be a recipient.

My 45 gallons of O-Neg over the years have gone directly to pediatrics wards.

☙ ☙ ☙

Belly filled with chocolate chips, I don my parka to leave the donor center. As soon as the IV had been unhooked, the donor bag marked with a fire-engine red "PEDS," tag, was placed in an iced picnic chest, to be rushed off to save sick newborns.

Another debt payment to the Minneapolis souls who gave blood a half-century ago for a stranger they would never meet; a pint of my blood for newborns I never would meet.

Before leaving the blood bank, I fill out the appointment card for my next donation. Checking the wall calendar, I notice that 56 days takes me to February 14.

Valentine's Day. Perfect.

☙ ☙ ☙

Di and her big brother.

The girls in my life, L-R: Rachel, Jill, cousin Adeena
Fisher (Uncle Sam's daughter), Zen and Diane.

Clockwise, upper right: Zen, Shlomo, Sara Malka and Rivka.

Yukking it up at the deli: Shlomo,
Jill, Malkie, Ron and Rivka.

The early years: Rachel,
Ron, Jill and Jenny.

Circa 2016: Kami, Zen, Rachel, Malkie, Stretch and Rivka.

Chapter 20

ALMOST FIRED DAY 1
(PART 1)

January 15, 1960: First day as a professional journalist.

Very nearly my last.

It happened in Champaign, Illinois, where six months earlier, having ignored warnings from my high school journalism teacher that I possessed zero aptitude for journalism, I earned a communications degree from the University of Illinois.

Then, after six months' active duty at Fort Dix, New Jersey, where I learned enough Morse Code dahs and dits to qualify as a National Guard radio operator, and in need of a real job, I wrote to Harold Holmes, avuncular editor of the Champaign News Gazette.

I remind him I am no stranger—while a reporter for the Daily Illini I had interviewed his son, Harold Jr., a tumbling wizard on the championship Illinois gymnastics team. Young Harold was newsworthy as one of the first to perfect the double-back flip—two complete revolutions of his small but muscular body, sticking his dismount as if landing in wet cement.

"You are hired, $60 a week," came the reply. "Report to City Editor Bill Schmelzle right away,"

Stopping only for gas, I drove my shiny but tiny new Plymouth Valiant 600 miles from New Jersey to the familiar, tediously flat central Illinois fields of corn.

Mr. Schmelzle, on a bright, sunny January morning, issued my first reporting assignment: "Grab lunch, kid, then hustle out to cover the meeting of the sanitary district. One o'clock, sewage treatment plant outside town."

Two years of journalism school and four years on the *Daily Illini* staff had not prepared me for my near-fatal professional initiation.

Blame the pale winter sunlight slanting off a field of fresh snow. Or a blast furnace masquerading as a conference room. Or heavy eyelids, courtesy of a hastily gulped Italian beef sandwich.

Or all three. All I know is that Schmelzle's raw rookie fought unsuccessfully to stay awake as a boring man in a dishwater-gray suit flipped charts and droned about "artist's concepts."

The room was emptying by the time I regained consciousness and made my fateful decision: No news here. Back at the office, I informed both Schmelzle and Executive Editor Ed Borman.

In those days, gone forever as T-Rexes and honorable politicians, our 75,000-population community managed to support two competing afternoon daily newspapers.

Our bitter rival was the Urbana Courier, smaller, feistier and relentlessly hungry for journalistic victory.

At 4:30 p.m. each weekday, a half-dozen copies of the Courier arrived in our newsroom, to be combed for stories we may have missed. Across town, Courier staffers in turn were checking our front page.

At exactly 4:30 that very first afternoon, here comes Borman galloping toward my desk, shouting like a wounded rhino.

"Damn it! Damn it! DAMN IT ALL!!"

Brandishing inches from my schnozz a rolled-up copy of the Courier, its ink barely dry, he screams:

"WHAT THE HELL, COHEN!"

Borman's sclerotic rage terrifies me — I never had seen someone actually stroke out. Slamming the newspaper on my desk, he jabs an index finger at a headline of a size normally reserved for aviation disasters, religious miracles, or the infrequent Illini football success:

"PLANS FOR NEW SEWAGE PLANT." (The words seem to be pulsating.)

By Dudley McAllister, Courier Staff Writer.

I had never formally met Mr. McAllister, but clearly he attended the same meeting and managed to stay awake.

In the ensuing minutes, hours, and days, I will learn more than I wish about Dudley, but in these first panicky moments, I can only cringe and croak, in my best Elmer Fudd imitation: "Never ha-ha-ha-happened! I swear!"

Bad enough to be scooped on a big story, but my disgrace is compounded when Borman informs me, at decibels suggesting he was unaware of the proximity of my eardrums, that the site for this project is currently a golf course—land owned *by my new employer!*

Bill Schmelzle, the no-longer-genial city editor, confines me to my desk as the room explodes in furious activity, with staffers begging anybody remotely qualifying as a news source to shoot down McAllister's "exclusive."

We are dismissed at midnight; the frenzy resumes at dawn. I discover that, although I still am technically (if temporarily) employed, the unspoken message remains: "Stay out from under foot, Cohen. Real journalists at work."

The result that afternoon: Our very own tasteful retaliatory banner headline.

"COURIER SCOOP FLUSHED DOWN SEWER!"

A classic journalism war is launched. The papers trade volleys. Courier exposes on Wednesday, News-Gazette debunks Thursday. Repeat. Repeat again.

The day after the Gazette's oh-so-delicate scoop-flushing headline there is shocking retaliation—a front-page Courier editorial whose gist is:

"The other paper is trying to say their reporter, whom nobody has ever heard of, is more worthy of your trust than Dudley McAllister, who has been covering the Sanitary District and everything else in Champaign-Urbana longer than their reporter has been alive. A 35-year veteran of the Courier, Mr. McAllister is the most respected journalist in the history of this community. The other paper's reporter is a total stranger."

(Well, technically not *total*, since I have been in town four years. But it is not easy to simultaneously quibble and cower).

It concludes with this dart to the heart:

"He drove away from the meeting in a car **WITH NEW JERSEY LICENSE PLATES!**"

Subtle. The Courier is equating my Little Red Valiant with Sonny Corleone's getaway limo. Low blow! And me only half-Italian!

The war rages, and I remain benched. But it is becoming obvious even to casual observers that the Courier has bigger guns, more ammo. My name seems destined to be a verb in journalism's Hall of Shame: "Cohen-ed: The act of being axed before ever typing a word."

Happily for me but most unhappily for Dudley, the Newspaper Gods intervene.

His car windows rolled up tight against howling prairie winds and blinding snow, Dudley McCallister probably never heard the screaming sirens of the fire engine rushing through the red light at the downtown intersection.

That afternoon, both papers printed front-page obituaries for Champaign-Urbana's "legendary reporter," the Courier's melodramatically wreathed in black.

Next morning Bill Schmelzle releases me from Purgatory. Go interview this guy who has invented a unique fishing lure—instead of bait, a package that just *smells* like worms.

My lede:

"Sniff. Strike. Bam! Dinner! Smell-a-fishin'!"

Schmelzle loves it.

I never looked back.

(Postscript: Six decades later, the "new sewage treatment plant on land owned by the News-Gazette," remains an "artist concept.")

🍦 🍦 🍦

Chapter 21

FIRING SQUAD TO BUREAU CHIEF

A few months after the Dudley McAllister tragedy, Bill Schmelzle decided I was not the complete idiot he had originally imagined. So he promoted me.

Instead of working out of a big newsroom in the historic News-Gazette building in downtown Champaign, I would be in charge of the Urbana bureau, a nondescript window-front on the main drag of Champaign's smaller sister city.

On guard at her front desk sat Isabelle, the grandmotherly office manager who answered phones, made sure the rent got paid, and was so miserly with notepads and pencils I was convinced she must have been paying for them herself.

My "staff" consisted of Dick Schwarzlose, a cranky scowler I remembered from journalism school.

Schmelzle had offered words of caution.

"Schwarzlose is not going to be happy he was passed over."

Not happy -- breathtaking understatement.

No matter how friendly I tried to be, Schwarzlose never cracked a smile. After nursing his pique a couple of months, he quit to go back to school. He earned master's and doctorate degrees and became a respected professor at Northwestern University"'s Medill School of Journalism.

In a tasty bit of irony, after I retired I took a job as adjunct professor in Medill's Washington reporting program. That probably drove him nuts, but I never knew for sure because I never saw him again after Urbana, and he died not long after I joined the faculty.

Back then I was far too busy to worry about Schwarzlose. The competition from the Courier, a burly guy named Bill Groninger, while a trace less celebrated than Dudley, nevertheless was a canny veteran who was on a cozy, first-name basis with every newsmaker in Urbana.

I chased his exclusives for several months before I managed to break a few myself.

One of my first was about a proposed vehicular island in front of the post office so drivers could mail letters from their cars. Small potatoes elsewhere, but huge news in little Urbana.

More important, it was the pet project of Police Chief Rex Davis to relieve the downtown *traffic congestion* problem—two words never before seen in the same sentence as *Urbana.* I saw a chance to counteract Groninger's longevity advantage.

It wasn't that my competitor didn't know about the project, which was just around the corner from the Courier building. He simply didn't care. Justifiably so. I, on the other hand, treated it like the Second Coming. It never hurts a young reporter to suck up to the chief of police.

The News-Gazette gave it a huge ride, including my long front-page interview with Rex Davis and an "artist's rendition" of the project— nice symmetry, considering how scant months ago my career nearly ended over an architect's rendering.

I now was Rex's golden boy. Whenever he had a big story he summoned me to his office and, with a conspiratorial wink, would give me an hour's head start— making a dramatic show of "misplacing temporarily" Groninger's phone number.

On a snowy January Saturday in 1961, the day before I was to drive to Connecticut to start a new job, the Urbana police chief tracked me down at the Illinois-Michigan State basketball game.

"Got a big one for you," Davis wheezes as he stuffs his water-buffalo body into a seat that, technically, does not exist.

"Rex, I am leaving town tomorrow. I don't even work at the News-Gazette anymore."

"Sunday's the big paper, pal. Go out with a bang, Ronnie baby."

Davis slips me a scrap of paper that I drop into my shirt pocket. The game is a barn burner—Illinois can't stop the incandescent Johnny Green, and Michigan State can't handle the huge Illini front court.

At halftime my reportorial curiosity gets the best of me, and I pull out Rex's note and read an Urbana address and a name.

Artemis Lampley.

"It's pronounced *Artie Mae,* and Groninger doesn't know about it," Davis whispers conspiratorially.

"And make sure you bring a photographer."

I arrive to find Artie Mae covered with blood. Not her own. She sits, handcuffed, at the kitchen table, calmly answering questions while two cops dust her butcher knife for fingerprints.

On the floor, draped with a sheet, lies her recently alive boyfriend.

My story was bannered across Page 1 of the Sunday News-Gazette, along with pictures of a bloody Artie Mae and her sheet-covered ex. A great going-away present from Rex Davis, who had instructed his cops not to call Bill Groninger for two hours.

Almost six years after I had arrived in the "Little Twin Cities" (Minneapolis and St Paul are the Big Twin Cities) as a scared but hopeful freshman, I at last was saying farewell to Champaign-Urbana.

And with a big splash, thanks to my attentiveness to Rex Davis's mailbox island and to Artemis Lampley, who would be convicted of second-degree murder.

I can't stick around for the glory, however. Well before dawn Sunday, with the front page of the News-Gazette beside me on the front seat, I aim my totally unreliable red Plymouth Valiant and its Jersey Mafia plates toward Connecticut.

I had a date at 6 p.m. with Andy Lyon, managing editor of the Bridgeport Post-Telegram, who had hired me over the phone, sight unseen, when I answered an ad for a reporting job.

Illinois 93, Michigan State 92. I had missed a helluva second half.

🍦 🍦 🍦

Chapter 22

ALMOST FIRED DAY 1 (PART 2)

The long drive from Champaign to Bridgeport afforded time to ponder impending life changes—new job, bigger paper, much bigger city. And in three months I would be bringing my new wife east from Chicago to start our life together.

Bless you, Andy Lyon, for returning me home to the East Coast. Six years in a cornfield can wear on a city guy.

On March 1, 1961, a little before meeting time with my new boss, I park in front of the Post-Telegram building on State Street and ride the elevator up to the city room.

"Andy Lyon, please," I announce to the smallish guy at the first desk in the newsroom.

Puzzled frown.

"Looking for Andy Lyon. I have a 6 o'clock."

The man, who introduces himself as Len Gilbert, city editor and Andy's right-hand man, rolls back his chair and walks around his desk to where I am standing.

He pauses several long moments before saying, almost inaudibly: "I'm very sorry. You won't be able to see Andy."

"But I have an appointment. I've just driven all the way from Illinois."

Another lengthy pause, then Gilbert says quietly, "Andy is dead."

My brain whirrs, but its logic gene is AWOL. All I can manage is, "Impossible!"

Here I am a stranger in town, chump change in my pockets and nothing in the bank, my hungry blonde cocker spaniel in the back seat of my unreliable car, and I am on the precipice of ending bachelorhood. And apparently I am about to remain unemployed. Worse yet, unemployed before actually being employed.

I'm too shaken to appreciate the irony: How much my current plight mirrors my first day at the News-Gazette.

"But, but … I have *an appointment*," I stammer, as if mindlessly repeating non-germane information somehow might resuscitate poor Andy.

"I'm his new reporter."

Gilbert, who I will come to learn is a very deliberate fellow, ponders this unexpected turn of events.

"I know nothing about that," he replies. "Andy died three days ago. He never mentioned you."

Huh? The editor hires a guy and neglects to inform his chief deputy? What kind of joint am I going to work for? Or *not* going to work for, it seems.

"Can we hunt for my application?"

I'm miles beyond nervous. I have nothing in writing, since Andy hired me over the phone. I try to envision how

Jill, the cocker, and I are going to fit in my mom's one-bedroom apartment.

Gilbert shrugs—which I take as assent. I follow him into the former office of the former Andy Lyon.

We rifle through stacks of papers on his desk, but after 15 minutes it becomes depressingly clear that, so far as the editorial brass of the Telegram is concerned, I am just another bug on life's windshield.

With my situation precariously balanced between terrible and hopeless, I offer myself silent encouragement: You didn't survive Dudley McAllister just to see another job disappear before you write a single dependent clause.

Then, aloud: "Look, Mr. Gilbert, I drove 600 miles today. I'm not here to con you out of a job. I've got today's Champaign Gazette in the car, with my byline on the banner story. And you can phone my old boss. He'll tell you I worked there until this morning."

I picture Bill Schmelzle answering the call. Over his head is a thought bubble: "God, Cohen, even now that I'm rid of you I can't get rid of you!"

Gilbert interrupts my reverie.

"How much did Andy offer you?"

I can scarely believe my ears. Is it possible I can get a job and simultaneously give myself a raise? If Gilbert hadn't even heard of me, he isn't aware Andy promised $80 a week.

"A hundred and twenty-five." I hardly recognize my own voice.

Len Gilbert's bemused look fades. This time he is the one uttering, "Impossible!"

"We don't pay **ANY** reporter that much."

"You don't have any reporters as good as me," I reply, a boast as unlikely as it was ungrammatical.

The Bridgeport Telegram turns out to be the worst newspaper ever. In those days, morning papers were almost an afterthought; *The Telegram*'s sister paper in the monopoly market, the afternoon *Post,* was a fat, thick, cash cow. In six months I was permitted to produce a grand total of three stories, and Gilbert always seemed astonished I actually was literate.

A typical shift: Show up at 6 p.m. City editor says, "Things are quiet. Why don't you spend some time in the library?" At first, I think he's referring to the newspaper archives; but, no, he means the actual Bridgeport public library three blocks away. There, my colleagues and I immerse ourselves in best-sellers until 10 p.m. closing time. A quick trip back to the office, where we are told, "Things are still quiet. Get some dinner."

Hot dogs and beer and shop talk at the beach on Long Island Sound, then we return around midnight to check the first edition page proofs for typos. Almost all the stories are from the Associated Press, the rest are cold leftovers from the previous afternoon's Post. The staff of the Telegram, once again, has produced zero stories. Our shifts over, we head home—having stolen another day's wages.

Repeat next day. And the next.

I rented a tiny flat in the basement of a squat and ugly two-story garden apartment building, furnished with castaways from thrift shops. It was there that I performed my hardest labors in Bridgeport—retrieving the stuffing that my lonely cocker spaniel, Kim, furiously extracted from the Salvation Army's former couch while I was at work. Every night he scattered it. Every day I restuffed.

On June 25, 1961, Jill and Ron were married in her mom's backyard at 6204 North Whipple Street in Chicago. When we return to Bridgeport, my co-workers announce they are throwing a wedding party.

"And by the way, can we use your apartment?"

An incident just before deadline one night convinced me to seek alternative employment.

The wailing of nearby sirens sent me and my equally bored compatriots scurrying to the newsroom windows, where we saw fire engines and ambulances clustered around an aging tenement across the street. As flames licked the roof and shot from top-floor windows, firefighters below began unfurling safety nets.

Grabbing notebooks and pencils, we head for the stairwell.

"Where are you guys going?" shouts Len Gilbert.

"There's a fire in the apartment building across the street!"

Gilbert glances at the wall clock then declares, "Too late for the final."

"It's bad, Len. Mamas are getting ready to throw their babies out the windows!"

Mr. Gilbert seems thoroughly unmoved by the image of infants flying through the darkness.

"*The Post* will handle it in the morning."

Even in this citadel of journalistic dyspepsia, I cannot believe my ears.

"The morning? The fire will be out! And what about photos?"

I ignore his shrug and hurry downstairs. But Gilbert was right. Even though I worked quickly and kept my story brief, it never made the morning paper. As he had predicted, Post reporters "handled it" later that morning.

The only photos were of the building's blackened exterior and broken windows and a forlorn portrait of a displaced Hispanic family. Good enough for a monopoly newspaper.

The Bill Groningers and Bill Schmelzles and Ed Bormans in fiercely competitive Champaign-Urbana would have wailed in despair at such monumental indifference.

A few weeks later, I joined United Press International in Hartford, thanks to Bob Lurati, who had quit the Telegram in disgust when Gilbert used an AP story infinitely inferior to his.

"Because it was easier to write a headline for it," our intrepid editor replied to Lurati's anguished keenings.

On my last scheduled night in Bridgeport colleagues threw a farewell pizza and beer party in the newsroom. Unable to face one more second in that soul-crushing place, I played hooky. When they called Jill to see where I was, she told them she had no idea. Then we resumed snuggling with Kim on the ratty couch with the lumpy innards.

Twenty-three years later when I was named UPI's managing editor, the Telegram ran a local-boy-makes-good-story, saying Ron Cohen had "gotten his start in Bridgeport."

Ignored was that I had quit after six months, that I had never warmed to the city of Bridgeport, that I thought the paper's sole utility was to line the bottoms of bird cages, and that I had even skipped my own going-away party.

Another missing factoid:

Six months after prevaricating my way into a $45-a-week raise to get that job, I had happily accepted a $64.50 pay cut to escape.

🍦 🍦 🍦

Chapter 23

ALMOST FIRED DAY 1
(PART 3)

My six months as a non-reporter in Bridgeport mercifully over, I headed to Hartford for a fresh start with UPI.

But—and what are the odds—for the third time in two years, a new job seemed about to evaporate before I could unpack.

The regular night shift guy was on vacation, so almost before I could be introduced to my new colleagues bureau chief Walt McGowan began accelerating my apprenticeship.

Walt sat me beside him for a two-hour crash course, then left me alone in the office with my new "best friend" — a large, loud, daunting collection of bolts, metal and typewriter letters that would carry my deathless prose to UPI's newspaper and broadcast subscribers all over Connecticut.

Perhaps McGowan honestly thought I had learned enough about the teletype machine to muddle through my first night. Perhaps he didn't realize I would be a two-index-finger typist my whole career, with thumbs to nudge the space bar. Or perhaps he was testing the new kid's mettle. No matter. He might as well have left me alone in the cockpit of a 747.

Walt left at 7 p.m. My first scheduled transmission was the Connecticut Zonal Weather Forecast at 8:30. You might think 90 minutes plenty of time to compose a few weather squibs.

You would be dead wrong.

I also had to answer phones. Sometimes it would be a stringer with in a story, a guy who had never heard of Ron Cohen. But then again, I had never heard of Al Fletcher.

One caller wanted to send a package and I had to tell her politely, "Ma'am, we are UPI, not UPS."

Although Connecticut is a small state, the weather bureau divided it into six zones—and unless the forecasts were exactly the same for the whole state, you had to punch (that's what we called operating the teletype keyboard) multiple zonal forecasts. When 8:30 arrives I nervously press the transmission key, having committed about half the weather to the perforated tape that runs through the transmitter. If the transmitter caught up with my typing, the teletype would stop dead.

My index fingers are "flying," so to speak, when the phone interrupts. "UPI, Ron Cohen speaking."

"This is Mims."

I continue searching the keyboard for the letters as I half listen.

"This is Mims," the voice repeated.

No time for small talk. The tape loop I had been preparing for 90 minutes is being consumed by the transmitter at what seems warp speed.

"Look, Mr. Mims, I am really busy right now. Please call back in 10 minutes."

I hang up.

Ring. Ring. Ring.

"Damn it! Don't hang up on me again!"

"I told you to call me in 10 minutes, Mr. Mims. I am swamped."

And I hang up again.

The teletype suddenly stops clackety-clacking; the tape I had punched had run out. The only sound besides some muffled screams of agony from yours truly--yep, the phone again.

When I hear that same pest shouting, I hang up and return to my task. I manage to *almost* get all the zonals out in the allotted 20 minutes (sorry about that, northeast residents of the Nutmeg State) and lean back to catch my breath.

Right now I'm thinking that a quiet couple of hours reading at the Bridgeport public library doesn't sound bad. The phone shatteres that reverie.

I answer, with forced politeness, "Hello again, Mr. Mims. I am free now. How can I help you?"

"Ron, this is Bill Clark." Uh-oh. My big boss. The Connecticut State editor.

"There's no reason why you should know this," he concedes, "but Mims Thomason is the president of UPI, and it seems you just hung up on him. Three times, in fact."

Oh, my god! Here we go again—fired before I can find the men's room.

I mumble cheesy apologies about zonal weather forecasts. Clark, a gentle soul who never got angry when he was sober, which was hardly ever, tries to calm me. Without success.

What the hell kind of name is Mims? And how will I explain to Jill that she is now the only employed Cohen? Maybe I can get back my job driving The Little Red Wagon.

Bill Clark tells me that Mims, who lives in hugely upscale Westport, had been picked up for drunk driving on the Merritt Parkway. It was not exactly his first brush with the Connecticut fuzz while under the influence.

"He phones the bureau so someone can attest to the police what an important man he is," Clark says. "And you just keep hanging up."

I only half-listen. Jockeying in my brain, along with the fears of imminent dismissal, are some random thoughts:

- (a) How unlucky was old Mims to get probably the only staffer in the world who didn't know he was president of UPI?
- II(b) If he was entitled to one phone call, how did he talk the gendarmes into letting him make four, including my three hang-ups?
- 3(c) After I get fired tonight, will any respectable newspaper hire a guy who changes jobs like socks?
- D(4) How am I going to get Clark off the phone? I have only 40 minutes before the next zonals.

— 5(e) Please let Mims be too sloshed to remember my name.

If I don't hear from Mims in the next 24 hours, Clark says, you probably will survive.

I find that less than reassuring, but after a couple of days of silence on the UPI Angry Presidential Front, it appears that against all laws of probability I have escaped the hangman's noose a third time.

🍦 🍦 🍦

About six months later, during a visit to New York, I stop in at the UPI bureau to look around. Managing Editor Roger Tatarian never had heard of me, yet treats me like visiting royalty, showing me around the office and generously introducing me to people whose bylines were familiar even in faraway outposts like Hartford.

My impression that day that Roger Tatarian was one of the most beautiful people ever is shared, I soon learn, by Unipressers everywhere.

The visit to world headquarters—NX, the cable-ese designation for New York—also reinforced my impression that the organization was filled with regular guys, from the very top to the very bottom.

In the men's room on my way out, a man claims the adjoining urinal.

"Hi, I'm Mims Thomason," he says. "Don't believe we've met."

I force myself to stare straight ahead. With my luck, to do otherwise might have resulted in my inadvertently peeing on the shoes of The President.

"Hello sir, nice to meet you. I'm just here to deliver a package."

Journalists are trained to always tell "the whole truth," but a little white lie may have saved my career.

Again.

🍦 🍦 🍦

Chapter 24

FIRST (AND ALMOST LAST) ANNIVERSARY

On June 25, 2016, Jill and I celebrated our Emerald Anniversary, 55 years of (mostly) wedded bliss.

This was no small feat. Being married is hard work. Staying married even harder.

Marriage is a human condition that must be nurtured, mixing love and understanding and forgiveness, and acknowledging you've been an insensitive jerk. Once again.

Little things that matter not a whit in the cosmic scheme—husband forgets to raise the toilet seat, wife purchases yet another easel and one more box of pastels. But devoted couples usually find ways to weather the shoals without capsizing their love boat.

Often when we tell people we have been married more than a half-century, they regard us as they would giant flying reptiles. But we both had parents who doted on each other, so it probably is in our genes.

For instance, a wife learns to adjust to or ignore (or at least not retaliate against) her husband's aberrant concept of humor. Jill does that all the time. Our friends are convinced she is a saint. So am I.

When we began dating in college, I pondered something funny and impossibly romantic for Valentine's Day. So I purchased a cow heart from the butcher and wrapped it in a nice red shoebox festooned with a lovely red bow. As Jill opens it I declare with dramatic flourish, "Now I've *really* given you my heart!"

Okay, so my cocker spaniel seemed much more appreciative of the gift (after I cooked it). That little stunt almost ended things right then. But happily, on our first Valentine's together, I had presented a necklace with a little gold (plated) heart, allowing me to survive the cow heart blunder on residual goodwill.

I had learned a valuable lesson, right?

Sure.

Long after we were married and living in Maryland with Rachel and Tziona, a few days before Easter I saw a supermarket meat counter decorated with sheep heads. I begged the butcher to sell me one and hid it in the downstairs refrigerator. On Saturday I noticed that, despite its chilly surroundings, inexorable deterioration had begun. Am I willing to trash my "romantic" gesture? Need you ask?

By the time I carry the head on a platter into the dining room at Easter Sunday dinner and proclaim, "I Love Ewe," the stench is paint-peeling. All three girls flee the room screaming, leaving behind Me. And Ewe.

But resilient as Jill has proved all these years, we almost didn't make it past our first anniversary. I had made reservations at a German restaurant in Springfield, Massachusetts, a half-hour away to celebrate the momentous day.

Fate (knuckle-headedness) cruelly intervened to destroy our bliss. A few minutes from our destination, we approach the home stadium of the minor league Springfield Giants. The lights are on, we are early, and I sweet-talk sweet Jill into watching an inning or two. She would rue to the grave her reluctant acquiescence.

Now I'm a sucker for ball games—any games, any level of competition. I go to girls' high school basketball games where I don't know any players. I stop for a few innings of a Little League game, or watch a pickup basketball game on an asphalt court and wish I were young enough to join. I will even watch ping-pong and luge and synchronized swimming on TV. And the wrist-wrestling championships from Petaluma, California.

Except auto racing. And cage fighting. Not sports.

So it is entirely in character that I lead Jill into that minor league stadium, fully intending to stay 15 minutes. But the game is a cliff-hanger and the innings mount. One of us (Jill) is aware the clock is ticking away our dinner reservation. Then the crusher: Extra innings.

"We'll leave as soon as it's over, honey," I promise, our dreams of bratwursts and kraut fading almost as fast as her patience.

The game ends in the 12th. The Old Bavarian Wurst House has long ago closed for the night. I try to make amends with stadium hotdogs, their skins wrinkled prune-like from hours soaking in what looks like bathwater (used). Her jaw tightens and her eyes narrow at my pathetic attempt to foist them as anniversary fare.

Then, under the erroneous certitude that my beautiful darling cannot possibly stay mad at my charming self (I since have learned otherwise, once or twice), I compound my sin by ignoring life's basic rule:

When you find yourself in a hole, stop digging.

Thus we wind up staying for the **SECOND GAME OF A STUPID MINOR-LEAGUE DOUBLE-HEADER!**

Ignoring groveling promises to make it up to her, one of us sits absolutely silent on the (barely predawn) ride home. How can she ride 50 miles with her teeth clenched like that, I wonder.

A few years later, fate provided me the rare opportunity to prove that there are, indeed, grooms stupider than I.

At a friend's wedding in Central Park, we watched amazed as the newlyweds, immediately after the "I do's," abandon their guests and a lavish buffet.

David Wolf grabs the hand of his newly minted bride and they sprint across Sheep Meadow, her flying wedding dress resembling the tail of Halley's comet. Before they disappear, David shouts his six-word explanation: "Koufax is pitching in Philly tonight."

Translation: My new wife and I will spend our wedding night in Philadelphia watching Sandy Koufax, not merely the greatest *Jewish* pitcher of all time but *The Greatest Pitcher of Any Race, Religion, Nationality or Ethnic Origin of All Time,* throw for the Dodgers against the Phillies.

For the baseball fanatics in Wolf's wake, no explanation is necessary. For all non-lunatics, no explanation is possible.

At least I waited a year before showing my true colors, I tell Jill. This consoles her. Not.

For although not a baseball fan, she understands this much: At least Dave Wolf spirited away his cutie to a Major League game.

I don't know if Wolf's marriage survived, but somehow mine has. I know I am not doing myself any favors with this chapter, nor on the dozens of occasions I have regaled friends and strangers with my minor-league doubleheader anniversary story.

I am in that hole and still digging, too stupid to accept there is someone—a most important someone—who doesn't consider the story funny. Even when I hastily add that the tale proves I am an idiot and underscores her saintliness, her tight smile seems forced, her teeth clenched as she mulls how to get a lenient judge who understands and condones justifiable homicide.

She won"t watch sports with me anymore, either live or on TV.

Ask her why. Bet you hear her teeth grind.

🍦 🍦 🍦

Chapter 25

NUTMEG DAZE AND KNIGHTS

When it became clear I would survive Le Fiasco Mims, I relaxed and took stock of my new digs: Third floor of a downtown Hartford office building. First floor was a tavern that would play a recurring role in the drama of our little bureau.

Our office was shaped like a very short railroad car, perhaps 25 feet long and 10 feet wide. Noisy, bulky teletypes lined both long walls, leaving scant room to walk. Roll your chair back a little and crack against the chair of the guy at the teletype behind you. A door in the middle of the far wall led to small darkroom.

Near the front of the room, facing on fortuitously named Asylum Street, sat the office of Connecticut state editor Bill Clark, equipped with a washroom and shower stall that appeared to have been purloined from a child's dollhouse.

There were six newsmen—all men— including Bureau Chief Walt McGowan, a small, mustachioed, red-haired bundle of Irish energy; and Bob Lurati, my fellow refugee from Bridgeport whose thumbs-up had gotten me hired without so much as an interview.

The others I dubbed "The Three G's"—Ray Geremia, Larry Grady and Len Granato. Lenny would become a lifelong friend. We played handball at the Y on our days off, and those few times we both could get a half-hour for lunch we rushed to a little Italian hole-in-the-wall and gobbled absolutely orgasmic bowls of shells and sausage. When Len married a few years later, I served as father of the bride—none of Barb Granato's Australian family could make it to the ceremony in New York.

What a fabulous staff! I thought myself pretty good, but McGowan, Lurati, and The Three G's taught me every day.

Two operators transmitted news stories via a more sophisticated version of the basic teletype machine: TTS, shorthand for Teletypesetter. Union rules forbade reporters touching them—ours were more rudimentary transmission machines. Both kinds work similarly: You type on a keyboard, which perforates holes onto a roll of yellow transmission tape—similar to the old "ticker tape" used to send Western Union telegrams. (Google it, kids). Each letter and number produced a distinctive hole pattern in the tape that many reporters—but not I— learned to read.

The punched tape then passed through a transmission box, triggering electrical impulses that sent the story flying across telephone lines and into teletype printers in the newsrooms of UPI newspaper and broadcast subscribers.

Senior TTS operator was Santina Bruno. The second member of the all-Italian telegraph crew was Sal Giuffre, who would graduate to become a full newsman in the UPI Louisville bureau.

Sandy Bruno was very sweet, if a tad too religious for my tastes. Well, okay, a LOT too religious. So religious that she attended Mass before work every morning. Language in the bureau was, by any measure, "colorful." Sandy, beseiged all day with swearing that would have scorched a sailor's ear, quietly retaliated by distributing Mass cards each morning to the previous day's most egregious miscreant.

Poor Sandy. How could she guess we reprobates had a winner-take-all lottery: Thirty bucks each month to the one who amassed the most Mass cards.

One of our biggest stories was the death of 16 people at Hartford Hospital when flames erupted in a laundry chute. Hospitals around the nation soon revamped their methods of delivering soiled linens to the laundry room.

It was the second worst fire in city history: in 1944, a blaze in the Ringling Brothers circus tent claimed 169 lives, spawning the unforgettably dolorous phrase, "The Day the Clowns Cried."

♥ ♥ ♥

Our boss, Bill Clark, who had helped save my butt the night I serially blew off a drunken Mims Thomason, was himself a fierce alcoholic. Although booze binging was by no means unique to journalism, it certainly was substantial hazard. The stereotypical hard-boiled editor who stashed pint bottles in his desk drawers was not just a character in B-movies.

The presence of a saloon two floors below the bureau exacerbated Clark's problem and made life on Asylum

Street quite the circus, in which our smiling, sweet-tempered, bald-as-a-cue-ball boss was the center ring headliner.

Many nights I was alone in the bureau when a ringing phone brought news of another bout of public intoxication. And these had nothing to do with Mims—it was about Clark, a habitué of the downstairs bar. About halfway into his nightly plunge toward oblivion, the bartender phoned the bureau.

"Ron, come collect him." No elaboration was necessary.

Occasionally, the stakes were raised to include "Come right now!", which meant Bill was about to get clocked by a fellow inebriate he had dissed. I lost track of how many times I had to intervene to save his life. Since this was penurious UPI, I could not claim combat pay.

One Sunday, Jill and I were hosting a barbecue for the staff when the phone rang. It was Bob Flynn, newly hired as a replacement for Larry Grady. (If you weren't Italian in that bureau, you were Irish). Come quickly, Flynn pleaded. Bill's really in trouble.

Four not-on-the-clock Unipressers piled into my car and raced downtown, where we found the bartender summoning the cops and poor Bob Flynn wrestling a guy the size of Kansas who is clearly bent on dismembering Clark. We hustled our boss to the elevator just as police poured out of their squad cars and into the bar.

Other occasions Clark simply disappeared. Days passed with no word. When the phone rang we recoiled, fearful of recognizing the familiar, tremulous voice saying, "Bill Clark, please."

"I'm sorry, Bill is out of the bureau and I'm not sure when he'll be back."

We knew it was Bill's long-suffering wife, and we knew that she knew that we knew. The charade never varied. Nor did the denouement.

After four or five days, Clark staggers into the bureau looking like the loser of a death match with a pack of rabid pitbulls, white whisker stubble collecting all the way up to his pink pate. Without a word he stumbles past us and clicks the lock on his office door. We listen for the first sounds of running water: His toy shower.

Soon, a spanking-new Bill Clark emerges. No stagger, no stumble, no stubble. Enough Aqua-Velva to fell an adult giraffe. Shoes polished, gleaming. Clean white shirt, stiffly starched. Trousers creased stiletto-sharp. Jacket buttoned. Tie knotted tightly against Adam's apple. Nuclear submarine tie pin neatly in place. Had he hair, it would have been perfectly combed. Bill Clark, the roaring drunk, has been magically reborn as Bill Clark, highly respected UPI Connecticut State Manager.

Cool as a cucumber, as if he had never been away, he asks:

"What's going on, guys?"

"Your wife called, Bill. A few times."

Thus did things quiet down on the Clark front—until next time.

※ ※ ※

Those were heady days to be a young journalist in Connecticut.

For example, I was assigned to cover the state political nominating conventions in the summer of 1962.

Democrats reigned in Connecticut—the party held the governor's chair, the legislature, and almost every statewide office. Although all the incumbents were unopposed, one congressman was retiring, necessitating a replacement candidate.

"Unopposed" was how Democratic state chairman John Bailey loved elections. And when Boss Bailey wanted smooth, he got it.

Except on that weekend, when there were three hopefuls for the open congressional nomination. Saturday afternoon stretches into Saturday night and then into early Sunday morning. Ballot after ballot fail to break the deadlock, and Bailey's face reflects anger at this rare challenge to his iron rule.

Around 11 p.m., Bailey gavels a recess and disappears. Reporters fan out in the bowels of the Horace Bushnell Memorial Auditorium—we knew Bailey was twisting arms but had no idea where or whose. Delegates mill about, discussing scenarios that grow more preposterous as the clock ticks away the hours.

Shortly before 2 a.m., without warning, Bailey materializes at the lectern, spectacles as always pushed up on his forehead. We take our press seats, anticipating a new roll call, but John Bailey quickly fires the ultimate curve.

"Are there nominations for congressman-at-large?"

Nominations? What the hell! He already has three candidates. Nominees are not his problem —a winner is.

From the floor, a shout.

"I nominate Bernard Grabowski."

"Second!" In stereo, from everywhere.

"Moved and seconded. All in favor say 'aye.'"

"Aye!" scream 2,000 voices.

"Bernard Grabowski is the Democratic nominee for congressman-at-large," Bailey shouts, banging his gavel. "This convention is adjourned!"

It all had taken less than half a minute—my first close-up of raw power wielded by a political master. Bernie Grabowski, who had arrived as a spectator, went home a shoo-in for Congress.

Bailey had "sweet-talked" the other three candidates into stepping aside "for the good of the party," reaching deep into his bag of political chicanery to anoint an unknown.

The Democratic nomination was tantamount to election because of the unwritten rule that reserved the at-large seat for someone whose last name ended in "ski"— a nod to the huge bloc of working-class Poles in central Connecticut. The Boss had found himself a Polish-American, made a few promises to the disappointed losers, and was all set for November. Bernie Grabowski would quietly serve three two-year House terms before slipping back to the obscurity of his Bristol law practice.

I rush back to the empty office to write the story— the only time the UPI bureau was closed was between midnight Saturday and 5 a.m. Sunday. Guess who is scheduled to open it in two hours? So after I transmit the Grabowski story, I return to the most mundane of bureau tasks, punching the Connecticut zonal weather forecasts. A ringing phone shatters my drowsy trance. Oh, no. Please, pul-eeeze don't let this be about Mims. Or Bill Clark.

"Ron, Ron!" cries a frantic voice. "Paul Smith, WPOP. Your building is on fire!"

Actually, Paul is wrong. The whole building isn't on fire—just my bureau.

Even though I am concentrating on the teletype keyboard, the corner of one bleary eye notices flames leaping from the motor of the electric fan in our only window. Do something fast or goodbye zonals, and maybe goodbye Ron. I run into the photo lab, fill a plastic bucket with water, and head toward the fan. Luckily a real fireman rushes in shouting, "Never throw water on an electrical fire!"

I know that, I say under my breath, but it is 5:14 in the morning, I've been up 24 hours, and I'm exhausted. Ditch the safety lecture, please.

How had Paul Smith, in his office several miles away, known about the fire? Well, the Hartford Fire Department had a bell coding system for alarm boxes around the city. When Paul heard the series of five bells, three bells, eight bells, he checked his master list, saw it was 315 Asylum Street, and called me. Good thing, or there might be no memoir.

🍦 🍦 🍦

One 2 a.m. in the spring of 1963, I awakened to a call from Bob Lurati in the bureau.

"Ron, get down to Norwich right away. A dam has burst, the town is flooded, people are dead."

About halfway through the 60-minute drive, I am sufficiently awake to ponder two imponderables: (a) Why the hell am I wearing tennis shoes? And (2) Who drives a convertible to a flood?

I arrive to find that an aging earthen dam has collapsed, transforming placid Spaulding Pond into a raging killer. Its waters had cascaded through the city, swamping houses and cars, collapsing a factory. Muck is everywhere. People in hip boots slog through the darkness, trying to salvage family treasures. Rescue workers, setting up floodlights to aid the search for survivors, inform me seven people had drowned.

A friendly family loaned me their kitchen phone to call the story into my New York bureau—this, of course, being several decades before the magic of cell phones.

After the New York desk guy has taken my dictation, he says, almost accusatorially: "AP has six drowned. We have seven. You'd better be right."

With sneakers rendered unidentifiable as actual footwear, I squish a couple of blocks to a funeral home. Someone there must know.

"How many dead?" I ask the undertaker.

"Six."

Crap. AP is right. And although a relative newcomer, I have learned an immutable law of the wire services: Few things are worse than having to row back — so to speak — on your death count.

I head down the funeral home front steps, framing my excuse to New York, when I spot a shoe sticking out from under the porch.

The shoe is attached to a foot, which is attached to a leg. My heart leaps (although I feel a pinch of sadness for the corpse). Being correct when the dog-assed AP is wrong always brightens the bleakest day.

Returning to the friendly kitchen that serves as the UPI/Norwich communications nerve center, I admonish the grump on the New York desk: "Don't ever doubt me again!"

Flushed with success, I head to the Army-Navy surplus store to buy boots and trash my ruined sneakers. My expense report for gas, breakfast and lunch includes $11 for "disaster boots."

Unaware of, or unmoved by, my heroics, UPI bean-counters say no.

§ § §

On April 9, 1963, six months before I would be transferred to the Montpelier, Vermont, bureau, we got chilling news. The USS *Thresher,* newest class of nuclear submarines, was missing and feared lost off Cape Cod.

Now if anything can get the juices flowing in our bureau, it is any kind of nuclear sub story. Admiral Hyman Rickover was called "The Father of the Nuclear Submarine", but we knew his one-man public relations team was none other than our very own Bill Clark, a genuine sub freak who reports to work every day (when sober) sporting a sleek silver nuclear submarine tie clasp.

America's nerve center of nuclear sub activity is the Electric Boat Division of General Dynamics, in Groton. The christening at Electric Boat in 1954 of the first atomic sub, the *Nautilus*, had provided UPI Hartford with its *raison d'etre*. Nuclear submarines.

Besides the gleaming tie pins he seemed to possess by the gross, distributing to lowly staffers like battlefield commissions, Clark's office walls are plastered with pictures of subs, framed thank-you letters from the Navy brass, a blow-up photo of him shaking hands with

Rickover. Clark attends every launch as an honored guest, taking a lucky Hartford staffer along to do the actual work.

On May 8, 1962, I am that lucky one. First Lady Jackie Kennedy had been chosen to smash the traditional bottle of champagne and launch the nuclear sub USS *Lafayette*. Am I ever pumped! And nervous.

But everything goes smoothly. Jackie did her deed, adroitly sidestepping the shards from the shattering champagne bottle. And the glistening sub, an American flag draping its nose, slid slowly and smoothly into the Thames River. I phone New York to release the advance story, inserting quotes and a description of Jackie's outfit. Then I return to the dining room, where the gala lunch is under way. I hadn't been invited to eat, of course. I am there to write a color story for Connecticut papers.

Bill Clark? At the head table, intently embarked on a red wine buzz.

Soon I feel a tug, and a young ensign asks, "Are you UPI? Call your Washington bureau."

Washington! Oh my goodness! Washington actually knows I exist?

I run for a pay phone.

"Will you accept charges from a Mr. Ron Cohen?" the operator inquires.

"Who?" demands Elsie Holecko, doyenne of the telephone console in the Washington bureau. Ten years later, I would be her boss.

"Mr. Ron Cohen."

Elsie loudly calls out, "Anybody ever heard of a Ron Cohen?"

The silence is mortifying. Please, please, I beg under my breath. Please. Somebody accept the damned call and put me out of my misery!

After what seems eons, a desk editor who apparently had drawn the short straw tells me he needs a quote from Republican Senator Prescott Bush about passage of an important bill. Bush, like his Democratic counterpart, Abe Ribicoff, is at the head table—Senate votes being far less important politically than a photo op in your home state.

My adrenaline level is off the charts. An actual assignment, however measly, from the Gods In Washington! Then my spirits sink. Which one is Bush?

I spot an unsmiling, patrician-looking man at the head table. Must be a Republican.

"Senator Bush, may I ask a question?"

A scowl slowly creases his stone face. Senator Abraham A. Ribicoff, lifelong Democrat, is not even slightly amused.

I slink off to find the real Bush, praying the journalism gods will keep secret my dreadful faux pas.

Supplication stood no chance against Ribicoff, whose reputation for acerbic meanness is legendary and richly deserved. He loudly calls out to Bill Clark, sitting a few seats away:

"Hey, Clarkie. Your rookie thinks I am Bush. Where the hell are you finding these children, in the damned playground?"

By the time I return to the bureau late that afternoon, my thoughtful "friends" have tacked blow-up photos of our two senators on the bureau wall.

With their names switched.

♟ ♟ ♟

Despite that goof, when we got word the *Thresher* was missing Clark sent me from Hartford to the Navy base in New London to try to catch a spot on the search and rescue ship. But I was 10 minutes too late, and so was stuck with the worst reporting assignment of my life: Interview families of the lost sailors.

Intruding on grieving survivors is journalism's most thankless job. It quickly becomes clear that something had caused the *Thresher* to implode, plunging its 129 seamen to their deaths 8,400 feet down, on the ocean's bottom.

I did the dirty work required, but had little stomach for it. I am a far better writer and editor than a reporter, and the *Thresher*'s aftermath clinched my career path.

♟ ♟ ♟

Chapter 26

NOVEMBER 22, 1963

If you were alive that day you will remember every soul-crushing moment from the instant you heard the news.

As years pass and other memories dim, each time someone mentions November 22, 1963, you will describe in perfect detail your personal version of "I'll never forget where I was that day ..."

So, here goes.

I'll never forget where I was that day.

It was early afternoon, and I was preparing for a long nap before my midnight trick at the Hartford UPI bureau.

I flip on the bedroom TV in our new apartment in East Hartford, hoping the usual soap opera pabulum might induce sleep. Instead, there on CBS, is Walter Cronkite, United Press's most famous alum, reading from his old wire service successive flashes (reserved for only the most important news, touching off 10 bells in newrooms around the world): SHOTS FIRED AT KENNEDY MOTORCADE; then, a few minutes later, KENNEDY DEAD.

Jill had our car at work, so I rush to catch the bus to Hartford, fighting an urge to shout the news to fellow passengers. But as I prepare to step off at Asylum Street, I no longer can stifle my reporter's instincts and I call out, "President Kennedy has been assassinated!" Then I jump off the bus.

That was my closest shot at breaking news that awful weekend. Marooned in out-of-the-loop Hartford, we watched with tinges of jealously as Unipressers in Dallas, Washington, New York and overseas exploded into action.

Hartford's responsibilities consisted of collecting reaction. If someone in Connecticut says something memorable (highly unlikely), perhaps UPI's varsity, controlling the wires in New York and Washington, will squeeze a partial quote into a roundup of national reaction. Never happened. Nobody outside Connecticut cares what Gov. John Dempsey has to say. Maybe not even his family.

As the teletype machines clackety-clack at a snail's pace, 60 words a minute, we hunch over them like vultures, drinking in every word of every bulletin and urgent.

From the first gunshot, UPI's coverage was awe-inspiring—poetry in prose—carrying bylines of colleagues we knew only by name.

Merriman Smith, whose brilliance that weekend earned him a Pulitzer Prize; Lou Cassels; Helen Thomas; George Marder. And dozens of others.

We stare transfixed for hours as history pours, word by word, from the bulky black teletypes. "Will I ever be that good?" was everybody's unspoken question.

We dreamed of a day when young wannabes in small bureaus would marvel at **our** brilliant copy from Washington or Moscow or Paris.

Developments unfold all weekend in places far from Connecticut. Then on Sunday morning the unthinkable piles atop the unimaginable.

As Kennedy's suspected assassin, Lee Harvey Oswald, is being led from police headquarters to the county jail, a stocky man leaps from a thicket of cops and shoots him dead, at point-blank range.

Kennedy's avenger would turn out to be Dallas strip club owner Jack Ruby. Authorities swarm him instantly and Ruby is whisked away so quickly that TV viewers ask one another, "Did you *see* that? Will this nightmare ever end?"

That night, alone in an eerily quiet bureau, I answer the phone and hear a woman softly say, "Come to the Route 15 motel in Berlin. I've got a scoop."

"Scoop" —a wonderful word that has joined "Stop the Presses!", and "Sweetheart, Get Me Rewrite," in the pantheon of journalistic anachronisms.

But even though my bureau resembles a morgue, I don't dare leave it unstaffed for what doubtless will prove a wild good chase.

Then come words that dissolve my resolve:

"I used to be a stripper at the Carousel Lounge. I've got dirt on Jack Ruby."

Room 14, she says. I knock 25 minutes later.

Arrayed on her bed, like a stripper's fan, were photos of herself and Ruby at the Carousel Lounge.

As I go over them one by one, the cumulative sadness of a tragic weekend washes over me, and I must fight back tears.

Tears for our country, tears for the whole world. Personal tears, and tears for my family and friends and strangers who long will be mourning the loss of a brilliant young leader taken too soon.

And sorrow, as well, for the young woman sitting next to me, whose closest brush with fame will be grainy photos splayed on an unkempt bed in a nondescript motel in East Nowhere, Connecticut. Sorrow that she is reduced to linking her self-esteem to a man who, that day, had punched his ticket to the Hall of Shame.

Her "dirt" will interest no one, but nevertheless I take a couple of photos back to the bureau to illustrate the 300-word story I will write.

The woman's name is long gone from memory, and nobody used my story. But after days of watching from the sidelines at last I had contributed, however infinitesimally, to my colleagues' historic endeavors.

Two weeks later, I fielded another call, one that changed the trajectory of my career.

☕ ☕ ☕

Chapter 27

BIGFOOT

Vermont takes my breath away. Sub-zero temperatures can do that. Exhale and watch hot vapors mutate into ice crystals. Unless you adore snow and ice, northern New England winters ought be spent much nearer the Equator.

Wait, Vermont? Didn't you just leave us in Hartford? What happened?

What happened is the phone call that closed the previous chapter. It was UPI's Northeast Division Vice President, Cal Thornton in Boston.

Remember how reading the JFK assassination stories by the stars of our Washington bureau had set me dreaming of playing on their team?

Well Thornton's call would prove to be the perfect launching pad for my career, although I could have received astronomical odds had I bet that I'd be playing home games in Washington within a decade.

🍦 🍦 🍦

"Ron, I need you in Montpelier," says Thornton, skipping pleasantries.

Huh? Out of nowhere, he wants to uproot me from a job I love? Our beautiful new apartment? Jill's new teaching position?

Montpelier? What's in Vermont, anyhow? Will I find anything to write about besides cows, maple syrup and snow, snow, and more snow?

"You've got an hour," Cal says. "an emergency."

I phone Jill.

"Do you want it?"

"A lot of responsibility, but they must think I can handle it."

"Okay." It was just one of the six times my wonderful wife would uproot her life for my career.

I call Thornton and accept. After we hang up I realize I have flunked Reporting 101. I didn't ask him to precisely define "It's kind of an emergency."

Thornton's next call is to Jerry Woods in Montpelier, who had committed a fatal blunder: He forgot the rule that reporters cover the news, not make it.

Jerry had sealed his doom at a press conference with the governor. Even in the laid-back Green Mountains, questioning a governor's veracity and the legitimacy of his birth rarely constitute a brilliant career move.

Thornton told me to come to Boston right away for a one-week crash course on how UPI operates in New England, then I would be off to Montpelier.

Mistake No. 2 was not realizing that, at UPI, **nobody** gets a week's training for **anything**. I should have been my own exhibit A, having barely survived *l'affaire* Mims my first day in Hartford.

Sure enough, the "week of training" in the Boston bureau turned out to be three hours. UPI's Vermont clients already were howling for Jerry Woods's scalp.

That's how I find myself riding shotgun as a sweet man named Al Wade aims his car northwest from downtown Boston. I scribble notes furiously on a yellow legal pad as he dazzlingly unveils his encyclopedic knowledge of everything Vermont.

An early December snowstorm that forces us to overnight in New Hampshire doesn't faze my professor. Through dinner and then in our motel room (UPI was too cheap to spring for separate rooms), he continues my emergency tutorial.

"Need anything at Stowe, call Sepp Ruschp and use my name," Alan says, talking about the Austrian who I'd later learn had helped introduce skiing to America. "He'll even give you free lessons."

"The head guy at WDEV in Waterbury is Rusty Parker," he continues, my brain whirring and my head spinning. This Wade changes subjects faster than Sepp can negotiate a giant mogul.

"Write down that name and don't forget it. Rusty runs the best news operation in the state. He needs to be your very first phone call."

I fall asleep dreaming about arcane subjects like what is a "leaf peeper" (the name given tourists who flock to Vermont's gorgeous fall foliage); how Phil Hoff had managed to be elected Vermont's first Democratic governor; and why I must attend a sugar-on-snow party in March. Wade shakes me awake me in the morning for a spot quiz about Ethan Allen and his Green

Mountain Boys, and continues nonstop until we pull into Montpelier.

"Get lunch, and I'll meet you at the bureau at 1. After I fire Jerry I'll stay a couple of days and show you the ropes."

That's the lunch where I informed my sister, Diane, that her big brother—in an impossible coincidence—was being transferred to the same tiny town where she was in college.

To her credit she did not reach for her steak knife. In fact, she masked the despair over the fact she suddenly has a chaperone she doesn't need and wants even less.

Leaving her to digest this cruel turn, I climb three flights to the press room only to find a surly now-ex-staffer still packing his stuff.

Woods is alone. Wade did his dirty deed and fled back to Boston.

He brushes past me with a scowl as if I were the guy who called the governor a lying bastard.

I am now alone in a tiny cubicle with a dozen barely legible pages of Cliff Notes from Al Wade. The phone interrupts my "What do I do now?" moment.

"UPI Hartford, Ron Cohen."

"Rusty Parker. By the way, you're in Vermont. Where the hell is Jerry?"

Gulp. The guy Wade said must be my first call has beaten me to the punch. And I cannot even remember which New England state I'm in!

"Uh, uh … Jerry is gone," I stammer. "He doesn't live—uh, work here anymore."

Silence, then, "Good! Drive over to the station when you get off work, and I'll buy drinks. We have a lot to talk about."

I hurriedly scan the Vermont road map tacked on the cubicle wall. Waterbury, Waterbury ... where the hell is Waterbury? I know Waterbury, Connecticut, but ... I'm in Vermont now. Aren't I?

At last I spot the dot on the map, and luckily it seems only about 15 minutes from Montpelier. But Jill has the convertible, and she is still in Hartford.

Rusty understands. "Never mind. I'll pick you up at 7. God, I'm glad you're here--and I haven't even met you yet."

Over drinks, I sense we will become fast friends. Al Wade was absolutely correct. Rusty's little radio station ran the best news operation in Vermont, and that included the big papers in Burlington and Rutland.

WDEV's weekly Saturday morning feature, "Music to Go to the Dump By," featured wildly aberrant "music" interspersed with interviews of Waterburyans carting trash to the town dump. This is the kind of small-town, quirky, laid-back Vermont I would quickly grow to love.

🍦 🍦 🍦

Another thing Wade had emphasized was the sanctity of my $50-a-month stringer budget. Not a dime more. From it I would pay for the absolute lifeline of my one-person operation, the "stringers" at our radio stations and newspapers who call in news tips. I had to handle them gently and keep them happy—no small feat when I could offer only about a buck per tip. Sometimes 50 cents. My two years in Montpelier, especially as the end of each month approached, would prove a budget-juggling act worthy of John Ringling North.

It didn't take long for my new job to clank loudly against these budget constraints.

Late afternoon on my very first Sunday, ostensibly my one day off a week, I am in the bureau erasing the last vestiges of the previous administration, memorizing stringer names, sticking push-pins into the wall map to show where our radio clients live.

The phone interrupts my geography lesson.

"Bob Smith in Randolph," comes a conspiratorial whisper. "Jerry?"

Scanning the stringer list, I give him the quickie version of why I'm not Jerry. He doesn't care. This is about money, not personalities.

My ledger tells me Bob Smith (his real name!) had received four precious UPI dollars the previous month, a fairly sizable chunk of the stringer budget. So yes, this is someone who might be calling with actual news.

"This is a huge one," he hisses. "I mean huge, huge, HUGE, my boy!"

Over time I will learn Bob Smith is an excitable man who believes every story he stumbles upon deserves a "Stop the Presses!" Sometimes you can calm him, mostly not. Now I am listening, willing to be convinced but suspicious his idea of "huge" in this flyspeck state might be a fox invading a henhouse in St. Albans.

"John Spencer has admitted he is an alcoholic and checked into rehab to dry out."

Who the hell is John Spencer, and why should I care if he is a sot? I wrack my brain. Was he among the 300 must-memorize names from Al Wade's cram course?

Smith realizes he must simplify.

"John Spen-cer, John Spen-cer," emphasizing each syllable as he would for a 2-year-old. "The Democratic state chairman. Brilliant. A big cheese in the national party, too. He made Phil Hoff governor."

Smith proves a treasure. He provides background galore to the newbie—the name of the drying-out spa, quotes from the imbiber himself, the direct phone number to Spencer's room. He hadn't exaggerated. This really *is* huge, huge, HUGE!

"And I'm not settling for a lousy couple of bucks," he says, getting to the money shot before pausing to breathe. "You're brand new, you need to make a big splash. This is going to be front page all over the country. UPI is going to love, love, LOVE you, Big Guy!"

My Boy. Big Guy. He has me, and he knows it.

"Ten dollars," I offer, weakly.

"No way, Jose. I know your stringer budget is 50 bucks. I want it all. *All.* Every damn nickel. Tell the guy who tips you about the car hitting the fawn in St. Johnsbury that he'll have to wait a month for his crummy dollar."

He has me, and now *I* know it.

But there still is a lot to do. Phone Spencer for my own quotes, write the story, get it to Boston for relay to newspapers around the country. But I'm so pumped that I wrap up everything in 45 minutes.

I lock the door of my 4-by-8 cubicle, which is isolated from the rest of the press room by plexiglass privacy partitions reaching within two feet of the ceiling. Leaving the wire copy of my exclusive on a clipboard on my desk, I head across the street to the Tavern Motor Inn.

Amazingly, UPI had splurged on the classiest hotel in town (55 bucks a night), and I don't have to share the room with anyone. The time/temperature sign on the bank next door says 27 below.

I grab a burger and then I'm under four blankets, clueless to the chaos Cohen (Smith, in all fairness) has unleashed.

Because as soon as the UPI stations in Vermont begin breaking into their regular programs to read our story about Spencer, AP's Boston bureau is inundated by irate one-wire stations demanding, "Where the hell is the Spencer story?"

AP rousts the number two guy in its Montpelier bureau, who calls the rehab facility only to learn it's too late for resident phone calls. In fact, the nurse won't even confirm Spencer is there.

Frantic, my competitor breaks journalism's First Commandment: Thou Shalt Not Steal. Clambering onto his desk, he scales the partition and drops into my cubicle.

I lie in wait next morning.

"What time did you guys finally get the Spencer story?" I casually ask as he walks in.

Pause, then recovery. Sort of.

"About 9 o"clock. Nice going. You sure beat us on that one."

I point to a perfectly preserved footprint on my desk.

"Take off your boot, Cinderella. Let's see if it fits."

I could have ratted him out, but there already had been one wire service firing in Montpelier that week, and I wasn't exactly a stranger to youthful indiscretions, either.

And I could afford to be magnanimous. I had arrived that morning to a congratulatory message from Alan Wade on my teletype machine.

"Way to get 'em, Tiger!"

🍦 🍦 🍦

Chapter 28

GREEN MOUNTAIN BOY

Moving from Hartford to Montpelier on short notice shocked both body and soul.

Physically, when the temperature outside the bank says 27 below zero and your breath produces tiny dancing ice crystals almost before passing your lips.

And psychologically because you grew up in the most densely populated state and suddenly find yourself in a place with as many cows as people.

Back then, only Burlington and Rutland had five-figure populations. Montpelier, by far the tiniest state capital, barely nudged 8,000.

But my new job left little time to ponder relative population density.

In vast western states like Montana and North Dakota, UPI one-person managers really were "lonesome cowboys." But from the outset I was too busy being busy to be much concerned about colleagues in Helena and Fargo.

Of the six New England states, two were one-person operations. My next-door neighbor, Alan Prioulx in Concord, New Hampshire, was the other lone ranger.

The only way to get our stories to subscribers was via a telegraph broadcast wire we shared for 20 minutes an hour. The UPI broadcast operation in Chicago took care of the important stuff—news, sports, business, weather, hog markets. Of UPI's 3,700 radio and TV clients, Al and I served 35. So in the broadcasting universe, Concord and Montpelier were dewdrops on a banana leaf.

Few stories were earth-shaking or even New England-shaking — I covered one murder in two years. But to small town radio stations with no reporters, UPI was their lifeline.

Alan and were able to I build a relationship based on mutual isolation. But, occasionally, even friends fight.

If he began sending a story I thought was less important than mine, I could interrupt him by hitting the break key on my teletype machine. He would retaliate, then I would, and … well, you get the idea.

The break key was a sort of tactical nuclear weapon that guaranteed MASD—Mutual Assured Story Destruction.

We unleashed it only in the most desperate instances, after phone calls failed to resolve differences. Because we knew that if angry fingers began toggling those break keys, we would surely squander our 20 precious minutes.

And if Alan and I required further incentive to avoid the nuclear option, it would be Stan Berens.

Stanton J. Berens was our boss, the bureau chief in Boston. You didn't want him picking up the phone and screaming for "you two little jerks" to grow up and play nicely together.

I never met anyone who scared me like Berens. Tall, ghoulishly thin, slight hunchback, 45 degree head-tilt left. One eyeball could look at you straight on, but the other had a mind of its own, careening wildly left, right, up, down. Sometimes it seemed to just disappear.

Even calm, a mood with which he seemed entirely unacquainted, Berens could be terrifying. When angry, he became a kind of strabysmic Ichabod Crane.

Nobody could curse like Stan, who favored machine-gun bursts without finding it necessary to reload (breathe). Once while visiting the Boston bureau, I witnessed what might have been his finest hour.

The unfortunate target was a brand new hire whose only crime was trying to edit a story ... with Stan's favorite pen.

The outburst was violent, immediate, and sustained, a breathtaking cyclone of profanities, during which the ashen-faced youngster murmured, "I have to feed my meter," and disappeared. We never saw him again.

His employment had lasted less than 20 minutes. Even for a wackily run company like UPI, that had to be some kind of world record. I envisioned his resume entry:

"UPI Boston, December 8, 1963; 9 a.m. to 9:18 a.m."

So when Prioulx and I suggest we might coexist more peacefully by hiring someone to help cover the legislature, Berens "suggested" back that perhaps we might wish to seek alternative employment.

🍦 🍦 🍦

That's why I was so pleasantly surprised when this Scrooge, without my asking, forked over $350 for election night, 1964. This allowed me to rent six secretaries and six manual adding machines, plus a Western Union teletype operator. That left $2 unspent; the refreshments were on me.

I padded the work force with Jill and our friend Anne, paying them so little to answer phones that I didn't even have to mention it to Berens.

A reliable teletype operator was crucial, so I drove 35 miles to Burlington to interview the three-person staff at Vermont's only Western Union office. I give each a 200 word election story, held a stopwatch, and inform them I was afflicted with Z-T-T—Zero Typo Tolerance.

The winner is a young man whose fingers are a blur over the keyboard. I am ecstatic! This means I will be able to concentrate on calling winners and pondering twists and turns to add an analytical component to my news stories.

A run-through the afternoon of the election was flawless. The computation ladies practice tabulating phantom test vote totals. Jill and Annie arm themselves with candidate phone numbers. Sandwiches are made, soda pop bathes in a tub of ice.

At 5, Mr. Western Union saunters in like the heavyweight champion of the world and takes a seat at the teletype, exercising his $5-an-hour digits like Duke Ellington before a concert at the Apollo.

The polls close at 6 and I hand him a sheet of paper: Bulletin-UPI. Montpelier—Senator Winston Prouty (R-VT), re-elected.

I had prepared it in advance, because this one is a solid. Vermont, one of the original 13 colonies, never had elected a Democratic senator. Prouty's ancestors had been undefeated in elections since 1908, and Winston, heir to the family "business," had served 30 acceptable if colorless years in Vermont and Washington. He is what Vegas calls "a mortal lock."

I check in on the adding machine ladies sitting at the folding tables outside my cubicle, and wait for the five teletype bells to ring out the Prouty bulletin.

Silence. Where the hell are my bells?

I wheel to find Western Union Whiz (hereafter WUZ) sitting like a statue of Ethan Allen. His digits are frozen inches above the keyboard, his stare catatonic.

"C'mon man! Send the story!" I shout. "This is a wire service, not a monthly magazine!"

Nary a twitch. I suppose I should check for breathing, but I have no time for compassion. I roll his chair into a corner, hoping nobody will trip over him and hurt themselves.

Then I take over the driver's seat and punch the "Prouty wins" bulletin directly on the wire without editing, sending it instantly to radio station newsrooms.

It is a dangerous game to compose directly onto a client wire. Many radio stations are "rip and read" practitioners—ripping the story off their teletype machines and reading it unedited on air. But WUZ's sidelining left me no alternative.

To complicate matters, my added duties mean I cannot pay as close attention to as many things as I would like. For example, after declaring Prouty a winner, I turn my attention to the presidential race and miss that

Prouty's margin is far closer than expected. He will prevail in the end, but his narrow margin should have alerted me that other Republican shoo-ins might be in trouble.

Although Vermont over the next couple of decades would turn reliably Democratic, back then GOP presidential candidate never lost the state.

So complete was the party's domination that Vermont never even tallied votes on election night for down-ballot offices. Towns send totals to Montpelier over the next few weeks, and then GOP winners are certified.

But there never had been a presidential race like 1964. So popular was Lyndon Johnson and so unpopular his opponent Barry Goldwater that by 9 p.m. I was able to write this lede:

MONTPELIER, Vt. (UPI) — Lyndon Johnson burned his LBJ brand on Vermont's Green Mountains Tuesday, becoming the first Democratic presidential candidate ever to carry the state.

Not only that, but Phil Hoff is re-elected governor, and Johnson's coattails help send the state's first Democrat to Congress. As I write these historic firsts, it never occurs that I might be overlooking what would be the night's biggest upset: The races for down-ballot constitutional offices.

🍦 🍦 🍦

After moving the Johnson victory story, I check the far corner of the room. WUZ has not budged, so I shake him alive: Be careful driving, and by the way don't be watching your mailbox for a paycheck. Plus you are paying for your own gas.

The adding machine ladies and Annie and Jill leave at midnight. I tie up the loose ends, and by 2 I am back at our apartment, unwinding with a couple of beers and replaying the election for an analysis story I will write that afternoon.

Around 4 a.m. a light bulb clicks on in the comic-strip balloon over my head.

Democrats had won all the major offices, except the U.S. Senate, and even that had been close. Suppose the party had won the races that were not even slated to be tabulated for several weeks?

Still carrying my beer, I head back to the Capitol building 50 yards from my front door.

Our press room, dubbed The Crow's Nest, is deserted save for post-election detritus—half-eaten sandwiches, empty soda cans, furniture askew.

I dig out the notebook with home phone numbers of all 246 town clerks. While I am certain small towns stayed Republican, I must ascertain to my satisfaction whether LBJ's margin in the cities may have been enough to rewrite Vermont history.

My first call awakens the clerk in Burlington. He hasn't tallied down-ticket votes, but tells me Johnson had routed Goldwater, 4 to 1 in Vermont's biggest city.

Next, Winooski, then St. Albans. Both are near Burlington, both are working-class and reliably Democrat. Johnson, the clerks tell me, won both overwhelmingly.

My hunch seems to be paying off. Those three big victories make me reasonably satisfied that the Democratic sacrificial lambs indeed have all won. I compose four "elected" bulletins, then flip the send key on the teletype. The sound of 20 bells—five per winner—shatters the silence of the empty room.

With those bulletins I am declaring a completely unforeseen Democratic sweep — Harry Cooley will be secretary of state; Jay Gordon will be auditor, Peter Hincks the new treasurer; and John Connarn, the incoming attorney general.

I better be right — I'd never live down such a mistake. Or four. But it's too late to change my mind, so I reach for the phone.

"Hello, Mrs. Cooley? Ron Cohen at UPI. I need to speak to Harry right away."

"Harry can't talk," comes her sleepy reply. "He's where he always is this time of the mornin', in the bahn milkin'."

The perfect venue for a dairy-state state secretary. "Can you get him please, Mrs. Cooley? It's really important."

"He won't be happy. Neither will the cows."

Mrs. Cooley sure knows her man.

"What do you want, you damned idiot?" Harry thunders into the phone.

"Congratulations, Mr. Secretary of State."

Now Harry Cooley is nobody's fool. Few Vermont farmers are. He was talked into running only because Democrats needed a sacrificial name on the ballot. He never dreamed he might win, never suspected he would have to rise earlier to complete his milking chores before driving 30 miles north from Randolph to "The Big City."

That would be Montpelier, whose population barely tops 8,000.

A long pause, then he says softly, "You"re not kiddin', are you." It was not a question.

"I wanted to be first to tell you," I reply. "And I'm sure nobody else knows."

"My God. What the hell do I do now?"

Bingo! Any reporter would give her first-born for a quote like that! Luckily I was childless back then. Thanks, Harry Cooley. And congratulations. The guy you beat had held the job for 15 years.

I hang up and dial Jay Gordon.

All the "winners" are shocked like Cooley, unable to process the unfathomable. Thriftily, they had not even mounted campaigns—why throw money at a job you'll never get? The four Republicans they displaced had held their jobs a cumulative 55 years.

♜ ♜ ♜

Bill Moran, a Downeaster from Portland, Maine, was my AP competitor in Montpelier and a good friend, the pluperfectly laconic New Englander. You never could guess what he was thinking. Hell, you couldn't even be sure he wasn't laughing at you behind his Yankee stone face.

But there could be no mistaking his mood when he arrived in the Crow's Nest soon after, having been yanked awake by AP radio stations screaming for him to match UPI's scoops.

"You bastard," he mutters, passing my cubicle without turning his head to look at me.

(It would not interrupt our Friday afternoon ritual at the Brown Derby — gin martinis, extra extra dry, three olives.)

Propping my feet on a rental chair and sipping what's left of my flat, tepid beer, I indulge a small smirk.

Then a bigger one when I realize my brainstorm had come so early in the morning that I didn't even need to fight Al Prioulx for the wire.

🍦   🍦   🍦

Chapter 29

RASSLIN' THE BEAR

UPI Vermont Bureau Chief, the highfalutin' title I held from late 1963 through the summer of 1965, screams for a couple of asterisks.

* I was earning only $80 a week, and "bureau chief" is less impressive when the only person to boss is yourself.

* At 26, and with a steep learning curve in a new job in an unfamiliar place, there were bound to be screw-ups — and nobody to blame them on.

Yet, that also means the occasional triumph needn't be shared.

Jill and I, married for two years, shared a small, one-bedroom flat in the 10-unit Capitol Apartments with our cocker spaniels, Kim and Knocko. Crowded but cozy, with terrific neighbors.

My "commute" consisted of walking 50 yards to a side entrance of the tiny and beautiful Vermont State Capitol building, up a flight of stairs, then up a second flight via a narrow iron spiral staircase to the UPI bureau a 4-by-8 cubicle under the golden dome.

I shared this lofty aerie, dubbed "The Crow's Nest," with the Associated Press and the Vermont News Bureau, whose two reporters wrote exclusively for the state's biggest papers, in Rutland and Burlington.

Although we all competed, especially UPI against AP's three staffers, we all socialized as well. It would have been impossible not to, in a tiny remote outpost like Montpelier.

Lunch, when the work pace allowed, was with other reporters at a table in the Capitol cafeteria. Or a two-minute walk home for a sandwich with Jill. After work, it was across State Street to the Tavern Motor Inn to schmooze over strong libations with legislative leaders, in hopes of snaring a news morsel or two.

But one lawmaker, Richard Snelling, heavyset and tall with hair like steel wool, seemed immune to the world of cocktails and confidences. He was smart, wealthy and very ambitious, and for a dozen years had wielded clout in the House of Representatives while representing the Lake Champlain hamlet of Shelburne.

Political ambition carried him to a 1964 race for lieutenant governor, a mostly ceremonial post that in the past had been a stepping stone for bigger prizes like governor or senator.

His game plan was solid and seemed likely to succeed, since Vermont back then was so intensely Republican that Democrats often couldn't even recruit candidates willing to run and lose. But two years earlier, in 1962, voters had chosen the state's first Democratic governor, Phil Hoff, a setback that still rankled the Republicans.

Vermont governors serve two-year terms, and the Republicans were trying to unseat Hoff with Ralph Foote, the lieutenant governor. Snelling would be Foote's running mate.

Snelling's campaign strategy was brilliant, if cynical. Late every afternoon an aide delivered a press release to the Crows' Nest containing quotes from that evening's campaign speech. Busy reporters became unwitting co-conspirators, taking the easy route by writing stories off Snelling's prepared remarks.

I was uncomfortable with this, even though working from an advance certainly made my job easier. Snelling's speeches, models of moderation and inclusiveness, seemed out of place with his conservative reputation.

Could Snelling really be outlining a sensible-sounding bipartisan agenda? Or might he be a textual deviate? I had to check it out.

He scheduled a 6 p.m. speech at the Grange hall in Randolph, about a half hour south of Montpelier. When the text arrives in late afternoon, I stuff it into my pocket and head off to Randolph.

I choose a seat in the back row, and tried to make myself even more inconspicuous by slouching behind a stoutish farmer. Suspicions confirmed. Snelling tosses his text and slips comfortably back into his old, hard-right self.

My story next morning revealing his chicanery ignites controversy; Vermont adores political intrigue.

The following night I head to Burlington, where I am a frequent panelist on a weekly political roundtable on WCAX, Vermont's only TV station.

By delicious coincidence the guest is Richard Snelling.

Eschewing pleasantries, I immediately swing for the fences.

"Why are you lying to the people of Vermont?"

Snelling is caught off guard, and sputters as he attempts to recover his smug superiority.

"What are you talking about?"

"Well, what you peddle in your press releases to us is entirely different than your actual spiel at campaign rallies. And I call that lying."

"Not true!"

"Is too!"

Watching his show deteriorate into a playground sandbox, Charlie Lewis, the gentle moderator, tries to intervene. We ignore him.

"Are you calling me a liar?"

"I am, sir, because you are!"

"Nobody calls *me* a liar!"

Snelling rises, menacingly shuffling his considerable girth in my direction.

He may be bigger but I possess the powerful journalistic weapons of truth and moral rectitude. Although a committed pacifist whose one and only fistfight had been in seventh grade, I rise to meet Snelling, center ring.

"We'll be right back after this word from our sponsor!" cries Charlie Lewis, frantic to salvage any shred of his show's dignity.

But his producer, loathe to risk missing actual fisticuffs and lose those viewer eyeballs, keeps the cameras rolling.

Round 1, Snelling vs. Cohen, for the unofficial Heavyweight Championship of Vermont. Dancing Bears immediately fall into a clinch. Pushing and shoving ensue, accompanied by language frowned on for live TV.

Luckily for both no actual punches are exchanged, and we wriggle out of a Sumo-like clinch. Short of breath, we can muster only baleful glares.

Draw. Rround Two 2 canceled. Cut to commercial.

Snelling and I spend the rest of the show vacillating between semi-cordial and half-contrite. We are more embarrassed than angry, and mourn dignity squandered.

In November Snelling and his fellow Republicans are buried in the Johnson landslide. My scoop and our one-minute TV waltz had precisely nothing to do with his loss.

Richard Arkwright Snelling, wiry curls grown gray, took time off from his successful business career 13 years later to mount a political comeback.

In 1977, he was elected governor, the first of a record five terms. He turned out to be a terrific chief executive, pushing a moderately progressive agenda to unite voters of both parties.

In fact, as a measure of how highly regarded my erstwhile sparring partner had become, his colleagues elected him chairman of the National Governors' Association, a job that frequently brought him to Washington to lobby for issues important to the states.

He called me one day at the UPI bureau, the first time we had spoken since our mixed martial arts fiasco. We spent a pleasant lunch revisiting "The Fight of the Century."

It would be the first of several such meetings, and it was with considerable sadness that I learned in 1992 Snelling had died, seven months into his fifth term. He is widely considered one of Vermont's finest governors.

The morning after our televised confrontation, on my weekly Saturday morning visit to the meat market on Main Street in Montpelier, the butcher/owner removed a blood-stained apron, raised my right hand in mock victory, and called out:

"Let's hear it for the guy who beat up Snelling last night on TV!"

Another smidgeon of glory the chief of a one-man bureau doesn't have to share.

🍦 🍦 🍦

Chapter 30

A TOAST TO FIFI ALLEN

Every July 14, on Bastille Day, I raise a glass of vin rouge to Thelma V. Allen.

"FiFi" Allen was my West Orange High School French teacher in the early '50s. Her greatness did not register on my hormone-clouded brain until after I left her classroom, having compiled a perfect D average in three years of behaving like a jerk.

Mlle. Allen was a passionate Francophile. Each summer, as soon as school was out, she and her sister flew to Paris to recharge batteries sapped by her valiant but oft-futile efforts to pound idiomatic expressions into behaviorally challenged teens.

FiFi was a walking *haricot vert*, a veritable *Tour d'Eiffel* — 6 feet plus, prodigiously skinny, a demeanor stern and serious. Yet, in those rare moments she wasn't hissing *"tessez-vous"* (shut up) to the class stinkers (me), traces of a smile could crinkle the corners of her mouth.

Speak English in her class and be slapped with a nickel fine—a fortune in the days of $5 weekly allowances, 5-cent Juicy Fruit gum, and 19.9/gallon gas.

At year's end, she cracked the kitty and introduced us Philistines to the wonders of pate, baguettes, gâteaux.

Over the years, it became clear how deeply into my subconscious Mlle. Allen had managed to stamp her imprint.

I didn't have to wait long for my first inkling. Upon arrival at the University of Illinois to begin freshman year, I learned that passing just one semester of college-level French would satisfy my entire foreign language requirement.

The very first day of class, tossed in with a pack of upperclassmen with three semesters of college French under their belts, I discover to my surprise that this lowly freshman measures up very well. Their classes had been taught by young assistants who couldn't hold a "bougie" (candle) to Thelma V. Allen.

"Awright, FiFi!" I exult to myself. Can't wait 'till I get back home at Thanksgiving and tell you.

Happiness proved fleeting.

That was the autumn my beloved Brooklyn Dodgers would win their only World Series, skunking the hated Yankees in seven games. Back then all games were afternoon contests. Catch the 2 p.m. French class, or catch my boys on TV?

No contest.

I returned a week later to discover everyone had caught and passed me; they are reading "*Les Miserables*" in Hugo's original French. With yet another "D" looming, I make the cowardly but sensible decision to abandon French. A wise move, for I replaced it with Italian and sailed through with perfect grades.

A decade later on holiday in Europe, I was delighted to discover I understood Parisian French better than London

English. I could order *escargots, gigot d'agneau, pommes frites*--and stand a decent shot the waiter wouldn't collapse in hysterics.

The European vacation was actually a long-delayed honeymoon. After two years with UPI in Vermont, my bosses gave me a one year leave of absence to obtain a master's degree at Columbia University's Graduate School of Journalism. I would then resume my UPI career in world headquarters, the New York bureau.

But back to FiFi. Despite my minor successes with the French language that summer on the continent, it wasn't until 1970, a full 15 years after I walked out of her classroom the last time, that I truly learned how lucky I had been.

I was on weekend assignment in the Montreal bureau, where our staffers, overwhelmed from covering a huge story round-the-clock for two straight weeks, badly needed a rest.

The FLQ, a band of separatists determined to split French-speaking Quebec from Canada, had kidnapped the senior British diplomat in Montreal, James Cross. Then Pierre LaPorte, the Quebec labor minister, disappeared amid ransom demands that included a half-million in gold and safe passage to Cuba.

It was a first-magnitude story, not just for Canada but for the world. Prime Minister Pierre Trudeau, invoking Canada's Emergency War Measures Act, had declared his nation in an "extreme crisis."

I had sent the Montreal Unipressers home for the weekend and was alone in the bureau early Sunday morning. The little desk radio was tuned to a classical station—Bizet, as I recall—when the music abruptly turned solemn, funereal.

Oh, shit. This is it.

I dig out the list of contacts that bureau chief Terry McGarry had left for me, and dial Quebec Provincial Police Headquarters.

"*Parlez-vous Anglais?*" which pretty much exhausted my French vocabulary.

"*Non, monsieur.*"

Crap. Sunk. No choice but to summon my straight-D high school French.

"*Monsieur Cross? Monsieur LaPorte?*" I plead, mangling my best imitation of FiFi's nasal whine.

"*LaPorte e mort,*" she replies, in poetical sing-song, then unleashes the cascade of rapid-fire French I have been dreading.

Furiously scribbling in English in my notebook, I slowly realize that I am keeping up almost word for word. LaPorte's body had been found in the trunk of the abandoned kidnap car, she says. He had been strangled with the chain of his religious necklace. No arrests. No sign of Cross. The manhunt continues.

With enough in hand to file the breaking news story, I cry "*Merci! Merci, bien!*", hang up, spin my chair to the teletype machine, and bang out the bulletin on one of the year's biggest stories.

For hours, UPI is exclusive. Only when I had filed several updates, thanks to my new best friend, the "*jeune fille*" at police headquarters, did I phone for reinforcements—the Montreal staffers who actually were fluent in French.

We pound out the copy in French (the Montreal staff) for our Quebec clients; in English (me) for the rest of the world. It was nearly noon before I slow enough to find the water fountain and the men's room. Basking in UPI's scoop, I know who deserves credit for my linguistic heroics.

So I sit down to type a thank-you letter to Mlle. Allen, describing how her old nemesis had learned French *"malgre lui"*—in spite of himself. I mail it to West Orange High asking that it be forwarded. If, in fact, Mlle. Allen still is alive.

♀ ♀ ♀

A few weeks later, I answered the phone at home and was greeted by a familiar nasal twang:

"Monsieur Cohen? C'est FiFi."

So she had known of her sobriquet all along. Of course. How self-absorbed we must have been to think we had invented it. She had, after all, been teaching more than three decades.

She told me she had retired years ago and lived alone—her sister had been dead a long time.

Don't move, I tell her.

Fifteen minutes later I knock on her apartment door, and even the dark hallway cannot conceal our tears as we fall into each other's arms.

After that reunion we talked by phone frequently-- mostly in French, in fact. Occasionally I visited, climbing the stairs to her tiny third-floor flat in East Orange. Her apartment walls, dotted with inexpensive but colorful prints of Paris landmarks, were testament to penurious teacher pensions and a lifetime spent wishing she were somewhere else.

Over *vin rouge* and *fromage,* I apologize for having been such a jerk. She shrugs. "Well, you weren't the worst I ever had"—and somehow I find small consolation in that.

One day I venture gingerly onto a precipice. A few days after our class had graduated in 1955, Mlle. Allen attempted suicide by jumping from her second floor classroom window. I had never been able to shake the dreadful feeling that my comportment in class had been a factor.

She scoffs, attributing her act to the loneliness of spinsterhood, the failing health of her sister, the realization that fast-approaching retirement would end her sweet Paris summers. That all these crushing sorrows collided in my senior year—happenstance.

"But no surprise that you blamed yourself. You always were a bit self-centered!"

FiFi says she knew all along I was not really a D student.

'If you had studied harder and not been such a *'fou'* (fool) in class, you could have easily climbed to a C minus," she says, familiar crinkles reappearing.

Nor had my language heroics in Montreal surprised her. After all, who would know better what a terrific French teacher I'd had?

When our family moved to Washington in 1972, FiFi and I mainly kept in touch through holiday cards.

One Christmas my card was returned unopened, and I knew I had lost her.

So each Bastille Day, this toast, with the best Bordeaux I can afford:

"*Merci, FiFi. Je t'aime.*"

🍦 🍦 🍦

Chapter 31

BABY RACHEL

Sometimes the best stories are born when best laid plans go awry. Thus this tale:

"The Day Rachel Was Born."

As soon as Jill told me we were going to be parents for the first time, like most dads-to-be I began plotting the logistics of how I would prepare to flawlessly whisk her off to the hospital for the babe's coming-out party.

As D(elivery)-Day reached single digits, I took stock one last time. Small, hospital stay suitcase. Temperamental French car tuned like a Swiss watch, tank full. Alternate routes mapped for the 10-minute ride to the hospital, in the event of traffic. Delivery swift and uncomplicated. Celebratory cheap cigars and bright balloons ready for deployment. Practicing, in front of the bathroom mirror, my nod of modest agreement as friends and family swear they never had encountered so magnificent a creature.

Yeah, sure.

As the delivery date approached, late summer of 1967, Jill's mom Florence arrived from Chicago to stay in our one-bedroom garden apartment in Montclair.

She could help Jill up the flight of stairs to our flat, and, because I worked the midnight shift for UPI in New York, Flo would be there if the baby chose an inconvenient time to debut.

Which, of course, she did.

Only in retrospect do I say "she." Unlike modern times, most parents were clueless whether to prepare for a boy or a girl. Sonograms were in their infancy, so to speak.

So we had no idea whether this would be a "Rachel" or a "Shlomo." Like many fathers-to-be, I dreamed of teaching my son to shoot baskets, how to make a batter cringe helplessly at an untouchable curve ball, how to pull together a scrumptious meatballs and gravy dinner for Italian Sundays. But to hit a golf ball or a nail cleanly, he would require a tutor with different, better skills.

No way this first kid would be a girl. Never even acknowledged the possibility. Hadn't my parents' first-born been me?

But I fell in love immediately, hopelessly, forever. (Kami, don''t tell your mommy. She still thinks I regret she wasn''t a boy!) I would race home from work every morning, driving like a madman along traffic-free westbound Route 3, lording it over the eastbound working-class stiffs headed bumper-to-bumper for the Lincoln Tunnel and Manhattan.

Mere minutes after leaving my office, I could revel in my gorgeous little girl's gorgeous little smile as she greeted her pop.

But I am way ahead of myself. All that baby bliss came in the aftermath of the difficult day Rachel made her grand appearance.

It was 2 a.m. on August 15, 1967, when the phone rang at my desk at UPI. Florence, slightly frantic, says a taxi is coming to take them to East Orange General.

"I'll leave work as soon as possible, and meet you there," I promise.

"As soon as possible" turns out to be very delayed indeed. I was smack in the middle of writing a huge story — grizzly bears had killed two 19-year-old college girls in separate incidents in Glacier National Park, Montana. Our Washington reporters fed me the latest from the Interior Department, and our bureau in Montana sent quotes from park rangers.

As I type with my two fingers, the wall clock seems to be racing at triple time. I am an emotional basket case, torn by the fact that this story will be on front pages across America at the very moment my first child is agitating for a look-see at her new world.

I finished at 4:40 a.m. Will I make it on time?

Down the elevator to the street. In the car, turn the key. A good sign—the engine fires up immediately. Almost unprecedented—my Simca likely is the least reliable vehicle ever to roll off an assembly line. I shifted to drive, then heard a familiar "thump, thump, thump."

The right front tire is a pancake.

Although we only have owned the Simca a couple of months, already we have endured every indignity a lemon car can inflict. The very first time I drove "Simca the Sorrowful" we suffered a flat on one of the most dangerous roads in the world, the Pulaski Skyway near Newark, which did not have even the hint of a breakdown lane. Then I discover the jack is a flimsy joke, the pathetically tiny wrench cannot even budge the lug nuts, and the instructions are too small to read.

And are written in French.

Over the next five years we regaled many a dinner party with the foibles of our imported junkster. Rachel wasted much of her childhood in the waiting room of the Chrysler dealer. Every week brought new disaster— something different broke. Or just plain refused. We frequently lacked transportation for days, awaiting replacement parts from Paris.

And on Rachel's big day, in midtown Manhattan before dawn, here I am again, vigorously cursing a hopelessly flat tire. Back at my desk on the 12th floor of the Daily News building, I begin dialing and finally find a gas station guy willing to help. (amazing what sweet talk and fifty bucks can buy, even in New York.).

I arrive at the hospital at 7:30, only to discover I not only am not late, I am far too early.

"Your wife isn't nearly ready," her doctor says. "Go home and get some sleep. I'll call when it's getting closer."

When the phone rouses me at noon, I learn his liberal definition of "getting closer."

"It's a girl. She and Jill are fine."

All that rushing and I still miss the grand arrival. But when I peer into Rachel's bassinet in the nursery at East Orange General, I don't care.

Had there ever been such a gorgeous creature?

Nah.

Well, at least not until Jennifer Michelle Cohen (Zen/ Tziona) arrived five years later, same hospital, same nursery—far less aggravation for Dad.

Thus was "The World's Most Beautiful Daughter" contest deadlocked.

Forever.

🍦 🍦 🍦

Chapter 32

RACHEL, SHAUN, AND THE GOALIE

It was an occasion for the kind of parental dues paid by generations of predecessor dads: Endure personal pain for the social and cultural enrichment of your kid.

A pistol pressed to my temple, I might ignore. But the soulful eyes of my daughter?

In spring of 1977 I spot a newspaper ad: Due to (totally inexplicable) popular demand, a matinee has been added to Shaun Cassidy's sold-out Saturday evening show at the Baltimore Civic Center.

Rachel, 10, has joined the legion of Shaun freaks sprouting across America like 'shrooms in a rain forest. She also had just won a report card in which only a hereditary deficiency in penmanship had robbed her of straight As.

A better report card than her dad ever got in 17 years of elementary school, junior and senior high, college and grad school. Dare I dream that, at last, a Cohen might apply to Yale without the admissions office collapsing in gales of laughter?

I call Ticketron.

On Saturday morning, chest swelled with parental pride and hope, casually as possible I inform Rachel we are headed for "something special." In Baltimore, we dally at the Lexington Market over Polish sausage, clams and oysters (me), and fried chicken (she). Rachel is having fun, of course, but her eyes question whether a succession of lunch counters really constitute "something special."

"Here comes the second half of the surprise, honey," I announce when we spy the marquee in front of the Civic Center.

"Shaun!" she squeals, eyes flashing with happiness. "I knew it would be something I'd like and you wouldn't!"

Listening, Yale?

Then come the hawkers. Programs with a smiling, barely pubescent Cassidy. Shaun Posters, $3. T-Shirts, $6. "I Love Shaun" banners, $3.50. Heaven knows what they would ask (and probably fetch a thousand times over) for an authentic Cassidy forelock.

At our seats, 3 bucks poorer and a rolled-up poster richer), I contemplate my surroundings—other parents also dutifully suffering for their broodlings. Stuffed inside the old arena are more than 12,000 barely post-pubescent screaming teeny-boppers. Lord, how they can scream.

At 3 o'clock, a nasty little group smuttily calling itself "Virgin" appears on stage as "Shaun's Special Guests."

Fingers in my ears in a futile effort to preserve sanity, I lean to Rachel and shout, "You owe me!" I could have saved my breath. She cannot not hear over the din.

Five dreary, ear-splitting, numbers later (the whole act seems to consist of exhorting kids to scream ever louder), she leans over. "Daddy, I'm really tired of 'Shaun's Special Guests.'" What took her so long?

Virgin drones achingly for nearly an hour. I cannot watch. Worse, I cannot sleep for the thousands of strobe lights flashing every instant. And me with no Kodak or GE stock.

Mercifully, Virgin leaves at last. Even the most hard-core of these little girls have had quite enough, thank you, of these hoodlums that only their mothers—if even—could love. A disembodied voice intones the only words I have understood in the past hour. Naturally they involve commerce.

"This is now intermission. You have 20 minutes to get soda pop and cotton candy and Shaun Cassidy T-shirts."

"We want Shaun!" scream 12,000 sopranos.

I start to tell Rachel of my ancient, unrequited love for Shaun's mother, Shirley Jones, whose sweet smile and voice had brightened "Oklahoma," "Carousel," and "The Music Man", musicals whose lyrics you actually could understand, memorize and sing along with. I catch myself in time. This is her day, not mine.

When the big moment finally arrives, it seems clear that Master Shaun's legacy would include a generation of deaf teenagers.

The screams grow even more feverish when when he wiggles his butt. Why are little girls barely out of diapers so crazed by a young man's backside? "You owe me!" I yell again, but Rachel is singing along.

Three songs in I reach my absolute outer limits of parental tolerance. "I must leave for a few minutes," I announce. She barely nods.

I stumble up the aisle to the deserted mezzanine and wander aimlessly for what seems eternity. Then, rounding a turn, I spot some abandoned hockey nets, rusting relics of the defunct Baltimore Clippers.

Anything to shut out the noise, still at jet-engine decibels even outside the actual arena, I equip myself with an imaginary goalie's stick and take up position in front of the cage, gliding across an imaginary crease in balletic slow-mo. Kick-save. Poke-check. Somehow snare with my trusty catching glove a slap shot traveling too fast to see.

Puck after puck ricochets off my pads and mask, and my net is still a "Virgin." Barely muffled screams and cheers for from the arena (thank you, Shaun!). Celebrating yet another Montreal Canadiens championship, I slowly navigate the rink's perimeter, MVP trophy in one hand, Lord Stanley's ancient cup hoisted high in the other hand.

It matters naught that I had always hated ice-skating, whose only rewards were aching feet and purple bruises. For today at least, I am Baryshnikov in the Nutcracker.

My reverie is shattered by a smattering of applause. A half-dozen other Shaun-shocked parents had abandoned their charges, only to stumble upon the Walter Mitty of the NHL.

"You play much better than he sings," one mom says with a grin. I skate away, mortified at the thought that there had been an audience for my foolishness.

I return to my seat just as Shaun launches into his big hit, "The Do Ron Ron." My agony must be nearing its long-overdue conclusion.

"He's singing the song about you, Daddy," Rachel says with a nudge. "'Do Ron Ron.' Get it?"

Song over. Lights on. She turns, beaming. "See, Daddy? See how cute he is, and how talented, and how cute he is?"

Long pause.

"I love you, Daddy."

She doesn't owe me a thing.

Chapter 33

"LOOSEN UP, SANDY BABY"

In 40-plus years as a journalist I have written about wars, assassinations, elections, floods, tornadoes, plane crashes, fires, volcanoes, moonwalks. I interviewed presidents, wannabe presidents, movie stars, two extraordinary women who ran their world-renown family wineries in the south of France and the north of California, Rothschild and Wente; several governors who wound up wearing orange prison jump suits, best-selling authors, Hall-of-Fame sports figures.

Not to mention a dark-haired woman who had regularly been smuggled into the White House, under Jackie Kennedy's very nose, for middle-of-the-night dalliances with the president of the United States.

But the story that caused the biggest sensation, I must acknowledge with more than a touch of chagrin: John Riggins and Sandra Day O'Connor.

Google the words "Loosen up, Sandy Baby" and you will find several hundred references to the night of February 1, 1985, when John Riggins, star running back for the Washington Redskins, and Sandra Day O'Connor, first woman Supreme Court justice, found themselves at the same table at a formal dinner.

I was an organizer of the Washington Press Club's annual dinner, which honors members of Congress—even if they haven't done anything particularly honorable, which these days is most of the time.

The dinner, held that year in the vast ballroom of the Washington Sheraton Hotel, is a big event on Washington's always-crowded social calendar. Journalists and members of Congress, women dressed in long evening gowns and men in tuxedos like strutting penguins, mingle at an hour-long schmooze-fest masquerading as a cocktail party. Then, after consumption of the usual dreary banquet fare, several newly elected members of Congress chosen for their supposed wit attempt to entertain the crowd. Occasionally one actually does.

Here's what happened that night:

John Riggins, a hero in Redskins-crazed Washington, is the guest of Time magazine. Others at the Time table include Justice O'Connor and her husband, John.

Sandra Day O'Connor: A role model for women clawing to break through the "glass ceiling" of jobs historically reserved for men. One of the world's most respected women. Reserved and proper. Tight lips, tight smile. Prim, formal, aloof. Nary a blonde curl awry.

Tight.

John Riggins: Outgoing, outspoken, outrageous. Funny, profane, brutish. Motorcycles his preferred mode of transportation. The hairdos under his football helmet run the gamut from Mohawk to ballooning Afro. At

6-foot-4 and 245 pounds, he'd rather flatten tacklers than evade them. Toothy grin fairly tickles his earlobes.

Loosey-goosey.

Placing these two at the same table is a prescription for combustion. Riggins having knocked back more than a few before dinner is a prescription for disaster.

Riggins stumbles into the dining room clad in tux and calf-high cowboy boots. As he half-heartedly hunts for his seat in a vast sea of identical tables, guests bounce off him like undersized defensive backs.

Jill and I are at the UPI table, right next to the one where *Time* magazine execs are entertaining their guests. We had the perfect vantage point for the drama that was about to ensue.

Riggins and O'Connor sit across from each other at the table, which is round. Riggins tries to engage her in somewhat long-distance conversation in a room abuzz with hundreds of chattering guests. She cannot hear him or chooses not to.

He grows frustrated by her repeated failure/refusal to acknowledge his egotistic self. Finally his bleary eyes narrow, and in a voice that could have been heard in an adjacent time zone, he utters the fateful words:

"Loosen up, Sandy Baby! You're too tight!"

"Sandy Baby" reacts as if she had been dipped into a vat of primordial ooze. But in a valiant attempt to regain the composure befitting a Supreme Court justice, she purses her lips even more tightly and continues to talk to her husband sitting beside her.

The *Time* execs seem too stupefied to intervene.

Riggins, still tossing down tumblers of what my old UPI friend Leon Daniel liked to call "Loudmouth Soup," is feeling absolutely no pain.

Then, as armies of waitresses are clearing the salad plates, he rises with considerable difficulty, mumbles something incoherent, takes a couple of shaky steps, crouches on his haunches—then slides to the floor almost in slow motion, coming to rest, outstretched, under Jill"s chair. Then, quite noisily, he falls asleep.

"Had I'd known I was going to be sleeping with John Riggins I'd have worn my nightgown," Jill joked afterwards.

And the next day she would tell a reporter calling from *the Los Angeles Times*:

"Then he squatted and was staring off into space. He was really out of it. Then he dropped to one elbow, and then he was flat on the floor. I knew he was under my chair when his cowboy boots hit my shoes."

As Vice President George H.W. Bush rises to deliver the evening's closing remarks, the football star's snores and belches are audible several tables away.

I find a pay phone outside the ballroom to call the office, and I dictate a story to Lori Santos, its lede featuring the fabulous "Loosen up, Sandy Baby" quote. Lori wondering whether I also had had too much to drink, didn't believe me. But I was her boss, so …

Surprisingly exclusive in a room filled with journalists, my story splashed on front pages the next morning. Radio and TV stations quoted it in an endless loop.

Competitors scrambled to catch up, including the rival Associated Press.

An AP reporter made follow-up calls to guests at the UPI table, only to be told, "The AP? Are you kidding?"

Jill had a "Loosen up, Sandy Baby" T-shirt made for me.

The T-shirt that women in O'Connor's morning exercise class presented her with said, "Loosen Up With the Supremes."

That fateful night would forever entwine the lives of Supreme Court Legend Sandra Day O'Connor and Gridiron Legend John Riggins.

When he was inducted into the NFL Hall of Fame seven years later, news stories gave Riggins's infamous dinner antics nearly as much ink as his gridiron exploits.

And when O'Connor retired in 2005, reporters normally more familiar with the judicial system than the sports world wrote about "Loosen up, Sandy Baby."

Riggins launched a short-lived acting career after his gridiron days. In the audience for his Broadway opening night was Sandra Day O'Connor.

In his dressing room backstage after the show she handed him a Sharpie and a shiny new football.

His smile as he autographed it nearly tickled his earlobes.

And she grinned a "loosened up" grin right back.

🍦 🍦 🍦

Chapter 34

LUNCHEON WITH MITZI

When strangers hear what I do for a living, their response tends to be, "Oh, you must meet so many interesting people!"

The most honest reply would be, "Yes, and most of them are journalists." But I bite my tongue.

Mostly my career involved supervising and editing reporters, who perform the really hard work of journalism. But there was no shortage of memorable characters along my way. They included:

– Joseph Heller, author of the classic war novel *"Catch 22"*, with whom I chatted for three hours in his room at the Madison Hotel during the national promotional tour for his novel, *"Good As Gold"*. I was to have been first in a series of 30-minute interviews, but we got along so well that he canceled his five subsequent appointments to continue chatting through the room service lunch he ordered for us.

- Rose Elizabeth Bird, former chief justice of the California Supreme Court, one of the most delightful and brilliant people I have ever known. We maintained a close cross-country friendship for 20 years until she died of breast cancer. In my file cabinet are dozens of special-occasion greeting cards, her favored method of correspondence even on non-special occasions.
- Christine Jorgensen, among the first Americans to undergo sex-change surgery — whom I "interviewed" long before I ever decided to go into the news business. Check the chapter with her name in the title.
- George W. Bush in 2000, a few months before he was elected president, in an interview at the governor's mansion in Austin, Texas. For two hours he seemed disinterested, almost dyspeptic, until at the end when the subject shifted from politics to baseball. Then his eyes brightened as he described a crafty southpaw curve-baller on his daughters' high school baseball team. His real calling may have been commissioner of baseball. Perhaps we would not have invaded Iraq.
- Benazir Bhutto, a poised and brilliant woman deeply wounded by self-imposed exile from her beloved Pakistan, whom I interviewed in a Washington hotel in 2003. Four years later the only woman to lead a Muslim country would return home, heavily favored to win a third term as prime minister. Her dream died at an assassin's hands.
- In 1977, in a room at the Hotel Washington, a block from the White House, I listened as Judith

Exner described in excruciating detail a series of late-night assignations with President Kennedy consummated mere steps from where his wife Jackie was asleep. It took me four days of pumping Kennedy family intimates to satisfy myself Exner was credible, then I wrote a story that landed on front pages everywhere.

– In the visitors' locker room after a heartbreaking last-second loss to the Washington Redskins in 1976, New York Giants football coach Bill Arnsbarger took such umbrage at my pointed question that he aimed a kick at me. I acrobatically (?) dodged, which seem to further enrage him. Uncorking a stream of obscenities that still may be hanging in the ozone layer over RFK Stadium, he chased me through the locker room bent on murder. I beat a hasty retreat, only to be demoted in the Washington Post's account of the incident to "local radio reporter."

Far more pleasurable than *l'affaire* Arnsbarger was:

🍦 🍦 🍦

MY LUNCH WITH MITZI

The voice on the phone that morning introduced himself as Jack Bean, and would I care to have lunch with his wife?

Only someone infatuated since boyhood with Mitzi Gaynor could have known that the Mr. Bean who was calling was her publicist. And her husband.

My reply was a quick "yes." And a second yes when he asked if Jill and I would be like to watch his actress-singer-dancer wife's one-woman show that evening--from the front row.

At lunch I sharp-elbowed other invited scribes and snared the chair next to my 20-year-long crush. I heard myself spouting inane stuff like how I was her biggest fan, and how wonderful she had been in the movie version of "*South Pacific*." I even told Jack Bean what a lucky guy he was. He pretended it was the first time he'd heard that conversation-killer.

In short, I comported myself like a complete ass.

"See ya' tonight," Mitzi whispered to me as lunch broke up. Three little words that made the rest of the afternoon seem endless.

At the Shady Grove theater-in-the-round that evening, Jill and her star-struck husband slipped into our prime seats. Mitzi dazzled in a two-hour tour de force—endless costume changes, clusters of muscular males tossing her skyward and catching her inches from disaster. Mitzi was a high-energy, huge-talent blur, and despite the packed theater, it felt like she was performing in my living room.

After her last encore, the applause still ringing loud, Mitzi slowly circled 360 degrees of stage, smiling and bowing and waving. Her finish line was our seats.

She crouches, and her face is inches from my mine. And that's when Mitzi Damn Gaynor blew me a kiss.

Jill has grown quite weary of this story, which I recount as often as I can.

🍦 🍦 🍦

Chapter 35

A BALLAD OF IRONS AND STEEL

Perfect day for golf. I gaze longingly from the wrong side of my 10th-floor office windows when the phone interrupts dreams of prodigious drives and laser putts.

My version of "hope springs eternal" consists each spring of dismissing an unsullied career of ineptitude to dare dream this will be the year my golf game will flourish.

TV promos for the Masters and the golf journals arrive in late winter, cruelly feeding my hopeless fantasy. Amnesia erases the piles of cash squandered in quest of what has never brought even modest improvement. Yet I continue to believe I am only a single miracle club from golf greatness.

"Yes, I can!" is my midwinter battle cry. "Farewell, double and triple bogies. Hello, birdies and pars. My first hole-in-one surely is a mere VISA swipe away!"

This year's object of misguided affection is a new set of irons—but how to justify spending $800 of daughter Zen's college tuition on a game that provides nothing but heartache?

My caller identifies herself as a booker of speakers for business meetings and conventions.

This turns out to be my first contact with Washington's high-powered world of "speechifying for cash." Until now, my public appearances had been confined to non-paying gigs at college j-schools. Nevertheless, after exchanging a few pleasantries, I hear her proffer a chance to speak at Sharon Steel Co. in Western Pennsylvania.

Steel? What the heck do I know about steel? That it is manufactured in sprawling plants, in huge smoke-and-fire-belching furnaces generating hundreds of degrees of heat. And the result of all this is miraculously transformed into skyscrapers and other modern atrocities. My speech will last approximately 9 seconds.

Now it is a well-known fact that Washington is the gas-bag capital of the universe. Upon leaving office, for example, a president of the United States can make more in two weeks on the rubber chicken circuit than in eight years in the Oval Office.

In 2012, just for example, a dozen years after he left office, Bill Clinton raked in speaking fees of $17 million. That is not a misprint.

His wife, Hillary, after retiring as secretary of state in 2013, pocketed a cool $200,000 each time she flew on some private jet to some Valhalla to share a few words of wisdom and pose for photos that bigwigs could brag about to their friends. And their enemies. Those big payday speeches would play a role in her presidential campaign defeat in 2016 to Donald Trump.

In Washington's grand scheme, Ron Cohen is a nobody. Surely my caller had exhausted her entire Rolodex before shrugging and dialing me. I prepare to tell her I have no intention of trying to speak authoritatively on a subject I know absolutely nothing about..

"It pays $1,500, plus travel and expenses," she interjects.

She says 15 grand. I hear "New Set of Irons."

"Of course," someone with a voice much like mine replies. Fifteen hundred bucks might be chump change to the Clintons, but it represented my first step on the path to links respectability.

"I'll send a messenger over with all the details," she says, before I can come to my senses. "It is in two weeks--just polish up your regular speech."

My Regular Speech? This Loony Tunes is under the delusion I have done this before.

"Hello, new clubs!" I croon gleefully a few days later as I head into the office of the Commerce Department's resident expert on domestic steel. He loads me up with more pamphlets and surveys than I can digest in a lifetime, then states the painfully obvious:

"Making steel sexy and glamorous ain't gonna' be easy, Ron."

Next I meet with a State Department expert to learn why foreign-produced steel is making folks in Sharon miserable. The unrelievedly bleak future she paints suggests that I should counsel my audience to substantially adjust their career arcs.

On Speech Day I board a cramped commuter jet for the one-hour flight to Erie, Pennsylvania, where I will be met at the airport and driven to Sharon. Aloft, as I silently rehearse my speech, it is crystal clear this is the most tedious essay on the most boring topic ever cooked up by humankind. These guys are going to be slapping their foreheads, wishing they had ponied up another $73,500 for Dan Quayle.

As I panic over looming disaster, the question nags: "Why the hell are you doing this?"

Honest answer? New Irons.

Irons. Steel. Even someone as petrified as I can appreciate the humor—the "irony", if you will—in all this.

Deep introspection is interrupted by a man waiting in the terminal carrying a sign: "Mr. Cohen."

That's me, I declare, mustering phony cheerfulness in the face of impending doom. As he opens the back door of a sleek black limo, I wonder if the steel industry isn't healthier than the State Department thinks.

Luxuriating in the soft, richly red Corinthian leather seats, I extract a cold Iron City from the on-board fridge and regard the passing countryside through smoky privacy windows.

When the driver stops, I climb out of this condominium on wheels and scan for towering stacks belching black smoke. But this place in no way resembles a grungy steel mill town. In fact, it seems to be doing a darned good imitation of yet another dreary suburban strip mall.

Which it certainly is.

Several official-looking suits rush to greet me. "Mr. Cohen, welcome to Youngstown!" one cries, shooting out his right hand while clasping in his left the largest pair of plastic scissors in the free world.

"Edward Scissorhands," I quip, so transfixed by his weapon that his "Welcome to Youngstown" flies right past my consciousness.

He thrusts the scissors toward me. I leap back two steps. This thrust-and-parry ballet is interrupted only when a ratty-looking Ford pulls into the parking lot, brakes squealing, horn honking, windows rattling.

Out pops a guy who seems on the precipice of apoplectic combustion. He grabs the scissors and the nightcap of my thrust-and-parry doubleheader begins.

"Who are you?" he thrusts.

"Mr. Cohen," I parry, again moving out of scissors range.

"The hell you are, I am Mr. Cohen—*the* Mr. Cohen!"

"Then I guess I must be *that* Mr. Cohen."

It turns out he is a New York developer, and is responsible for this eyesore of a strip mall. The guy driving the ratty Ford had taken him to Sharon Steel at the same time the hapless limo driver had transported me to the mall.

The Mr. Cohen, paying me no further mind, employs his weapon as scissors, not sabre, and snips the ribbon on yet another unnecessary mall in a country up to its Asian fingernail salons in unnecessary malls.

🍦 🍦 🍦

That evening after an exciting, up-close primer on how steel is forged, I stand onstage and discard my Horrible-But-Well-Researched speech.

Instead, I recount the morning's drama of the reversible Cohens, and wittily quip that I had negotiated the far better deal.

Then I tell them what they clearly had hired me for—down-and-dirty horror stories about their down-and-dirty federal government, at work and at play.

To sustained laughter and applause, I disclose Washington indeed is even more dysfunctional than it appears from downtown Sharon, Pennsylvania.

And I answer a bunch of questions that, blessedly, have absolutely nothing to do with steel.

They love it.

In case you're curious, the new irons elevated my game from putrid to merely crappy.

Chapter 36

CHICAGO FLO

Florence Greenspan, world's best mother-in-law. A character for the ages.

A grade school teacher, Flo was smart and proud and witty, and everybody loved her. When she died at 91, she had lived 42 years longer than Jill's father, Sid. Coincidentally, they shared the same last name—Greenspan.

They met on a blind date in college, set up by Sid's sister. Flo and Sylvia had adjoining desks in a class that, happily for all concerned, was seated in alphabetical order.

Florence Greenspan.
Circa early 1970s.

Flo and Sid Greenspan, Jill's
parents. Circa late 1940s.

So Flo was the only person I ever knew who didn't have to decide whether to take her new husband's name. But she missed out on a good joke by not choosing Florence Greenspan-Greenspan.

She possessed inner beauty, outer charm, and a bountifully generous spirit that put the lie to all those crummy mother-in-law jokes.

I think we fell in love the night I picked up Jill for our first date at their home in Chicago. After that she cleverly nourished the courtship by mailing bagels and three-foot Kosher salamis to me in Champaign every few weeks so I could save my pennies and afford to take her daughter on pizza and cheap Chianti dates.

Flo lived nearly all her life in Chicago. When Jill and I would return for a visit, we took her to Arlington Park, where she loved wagering a couple of bucks on horses she selected solely for their names.

That random handicapping worked beautifully once when, on a visit east, we took her to Aqueduct. Thumbing the program for catchy names, Flo found one in a late race — but wouldn't tell us anything. Since we only planned to stay for a few races, all three of us secretly placed advance bets.

On the way home I switched on the car radio just in time for the late results from Aqueduct.

Ninth race: Chicago Flo. $58 for a $2 bet. We rocked the car with our cheers, for each had secretly bet on that perfectly named winner.

Flo also loved it when we took her to Wrigley Field to see the Cubs. Even when she was in assisted living near us in Maryland, she grinned with anticipation when

I promised to take her to a ballgame as soon as she was feeling better.

But in the last six months of her life, Florence Greenspan, sweet and kind and everyone's friend, endured shameful indignities beyond comprehension.

Her sin? Living a full and long life in a country that has become proficient in keeping people alive but is failing to fill those extra years with dignity.

Until her late 80s, Florence was in relatively good health for someone whose birth date was one one one one—January 1, 1911. She's always ready for a convertible ride for movies and ice cream.

Sure, her short-term memory was failing—she would ask the same questions over and over. But she compensated by obliterating you in quick-quip contests. Confronting a box of fancy chocolates, she breaks out in song: "Nobody knows the truffles I've seen ..."

One afternoon I took her to see "The English Patient," a complicated, interminable movie. If the flashbacks and flash forwards were giving me a headache, I wondered what poor Florence must be enduring.

No worry. Plot twists don't matter when you can't remember 20 seconds ago. She just is delighted to be out and about on a date with her son-in-law.

If she occasionally groused about feeling lousy, just bring in a doctor or a nurse and watch Flo dial up the charm. She could mask her aches and pains with wisecracks and flirts, hoodwinking her caregivers.

"There's nothing really wrong with this old broad," they would assure us, time and again. Then, as soon as they left, she flipped on the complaints switch.

Her nightmare descent into hell began when a private-duty aide in her assisted-living apartment wasn't paying close attention, and Flo fell in the bathroom. She broke her femur, but we weren't notified for hours. Then it took more than a full day before anybody ordered an X-ray, and 48 hours until she finally reached a hospital, in excruciating pain.

Waiting for a room, she was left unattended in a hallway outside the emergency room and fell four feet from her gurney to the unyielding hospital floor.

The horrors continued. At the rehab and physical therapy nursing home she was sent to, nurses failed to recognize that she had become dehydrated. Despite the fact her kidneys were on the verge of shutting down, our pleas that Flo receive emergency attention went unacknowledged.

Finally Jill, frantic watching her mom suffer, demanded an ambulance be called. EMS workers arrived to find Flo close to total renal failure, and rushed her back to the hospital. Again, no bed is available. In a horrifying case of déjà vu, Flo spends the night on a gurney in the same E.R. hallway she had fallen a week earlier.

But she was, indeed, a tough old broad, and a few days later found herself in another, different, nursing facility.

When she continued to show scant improvement, an orthopedist suggested surgery on her broken leg. Although operating on a 90-year-old woman seemed cruel, he said it was her only hope for a relatively normal life. Jill reluctantly gave consent, and the operation was scheduled.

Further disaster. The driver of the medical van transporting her to the hospital had neglected to strap Flo into her wheelchair. When he swerved to the shoulder of Interstate 270 to avoid a sudden traffic jam, Flo went ricocheting around in the back like a deranged pinball.

Following the van a half-mile back, Jill spotted the driver, without a mobile phone or emergency radio, waving for help on the shoulder.

She called 911 on her cell, but it took rescuers 20 minutes to extricate Flo and place her in the ambulance. Her doctor had to delay surgery. Thank you, short-term memory loss—luckily, Flo quickly forgot it all.

She survived that operation, but had to wear a torturous post-surgery ankle-to-chest brace. And her dignity was given its last rites by a Rube Goldberg-like hydraulic contraption employed to hoist her, like a container-ship crate, from bed to wheelchair.

A few weeks later, during to a gastroenterology appointment, she fell while being helped onto the doctor's exam table. Emergency responders arrived and—curtain up! The flirty jokes began to fly.

Such calamities, piling up cruelly and rapidly, finally proved too much for Florence's sunny disposition.

"Nobody should have to live like this," she told us, still alert enough to realize there now was little medical professionals could—or would—do for someone her age.

Too proud to be pitched onto antiquity's scrap heap, she began refusing food. But she never lost her ability to trade jokes. Right up to the moment she lost consciousness, Flo was bantering with her nurses.

The day after she died, we encountered in her room a handsome young male nurse who often had been on the receiving end of Flo's flirtatious jokes.

"I will miss her," he said, staring at the empty bed and fighting back tears.

A couple of weeks later, I dreamed I snared a Sammy Sosa homer in the bleachers at Wrigley.

I glanced at the ball. The stamped autograph of baseball commissioner Bud Selig had been replaced by a familiar handwriting in bold cursive:

"Chicago Flo."

♚ ♚ ♚

Chapter 37

OF BRATWURST AND BRIEFS

I am a world-class dreamer,. Not the daytime kind, lost in gauzy visions of desert isles, movie starlets, throwing a last-second TD pass to clinch the Super Bowl.

No, the jerk-your-head-off-the-pillow-at-3-a.m.-in-a-cold-sweat-just-before-your-nightmare-gets-REALLY-bad variety.

Sometimes, my dreams are cruel—I wake up just before my glue factory nag crosses the wire at 100-1, or right when Doris Day is about to croon undying love into my ear.

But mostly they are embarrassing, all too frequently centering around being in public in underwear. Or less.

Each scenario is different: I am on campus heading for a final exam, or at the South Pole dressed even less sensibly than the penguins.

One time it is a strange city, where I am moderating a weighty discussion on journalism ethics. This is especially embarrassing because one panelist is my new boss—who hired me only because *her* boss told her she had to.

Disciples of that most famous dream dissector, Sigmund Freud, will assure you that mortifying dreams are universal. And yes, I always force myself awake before things get really dicey. But just suppose that one time it isn't a dream?

Yep, I've had one of those.

It was when I had traveled from Washington late in winter 1976 to help the UPI bureau in Milwaukee cover the Wisconsin presidential primary.

The night before Election Day, I awakened in a panic in my room at the Pfister, grande dame of Milwaukee hotels. Suppose my bratwursts spoil?

Jill will tell you that this was hardly the only time my slumber was interrupted by bratwurst. One night in Munich a decade earlier, I had wandered the streets in a fruitless (meatless?) search for an all-night wurst wagon.

But I digress. Back to Milwaukee.

I had purchased the wursts in question at Usinger''s sausage emporium, perhaps the single blithest spot on planet Earth.

If the Hope Diamond is Nirvana for gemologists, and praying at the Western Wall the dream of observant Jews, Usinger's is Mecca for the sausage stricken. My treasure embodied a carnival of charcuterie—smoky brats, knockwurst, bockwurst, liverwurst, garlic sausage, Polish sausage, kielbasa. A hundred bucks worth, which in 1976 currency represented a heckuva lot of tubular meat.

The dream that awakens me at 3 a.m.: My bounty is spoiling because my room lacks one of those miniature refrigerators.

I realize this is absurd, because it is February and I already have transformed the room into my personal Antarctica. The box of smoked meats sits on the ledge of the window, which is open all the way. The air conditioner right beneath it is going full blast. The meat cannot possibly spoil, because the snowy, frigid Milwaukee outdoors has been replicated right inside my room.

But even as I personally shiver under a pile of extra blankets, I fear the worst for my wurst. So I grab a bucket and head for the seventh-floor ice machine, leaving my door slightly ajar. One step into the hallway, I hear "BANG!"—as an Arctic gust slams my door shut.

Stay calm and rational, whispers my subconscious. This is only a dream, force yourself awake. But honestly, how laid back can anyone be clad only in Jockey shorts and carrying an empty ice bucket in a hotel hallway? I head toward the elevators, certain I will find there a small table bearing a house phone. All old hotels have them.

Not the Pfister.

I ponder my options. None. At least nothing particularly good.

When my elevator door opens at the lobby, I look carefully in each direction and strategically position the ice bucket for maximum coverage. The one good thing I have going for me is the time. It is 3 a.m. Tuesday morning. Surely I will have the lobby to myself.

How many times can a guy be wrong in five minutes?

The cavernous room is a rabbit's warren of old-fashioned high-backed chairs—many of which appear to be occupied by little old ladies!

As unconcernedly as a nearly naked man possibly can, I zig-zag through this obstacle course, avoiding eye contact with fellow insomniacs as I head for the relative safety of the front desk.

I am third in line. Can you believe it? At 3 a.m.?

Clamping my knees together in a pathetic stab at modesty, all I can do is hope the young women ahead of me don't turn around.

After five numbing minutes, I finally am face-to-face with the world's slowest hotel clerk.

"Help!" I whisper hoarsely. "Duplicate key! Room 712! Hurry! Please!"

Slowly, she eyes me head to toe, then toe to head, then back down again, savoring my predicament and memorizing every bit of this picture that she will repaint for friends forever.

Then a sweet yet slightly snarky smile creases her face as she delivers a most deliciously evil question:

"May I please see some ID?"

Chapter 38

FOR YOUR GRANDCHILDREN

UPI's Washington bureau, where I worked for 15 years in the 1970s and 1980s, was journalism's Broadway and 42nd Street, its Hollywood and Vine.

Countless Unipressers in Lubbock or Reno or Cheyenne or Montpelier dreamed of covering a big story, getting "discovered" by the Keepers of the Transfer, and being whisked on a magic carpet (expenses paid) from the bush leagues to the majors.

The Washington bureau. WA in cable-ese shorthand.

It was easy to see why. During its glory years, UPI/WA was home to upwards of 100 staffers, among the best and brightest the wire service could muster. Washington staffers regularly had bylines that the AAA wire distributed worldwide, or shot dramatic photos gracing front pages around the globe. Lawmakers and presidents were on first-name relationships with our reporters, who were invited to fancy parties where they rubbed elbows with the elite, cultivating sources that could be crucial on a big story.

I knew first-hand of the hunger for Ascension to the Big Leagues. I had been one of those starving dreamers.

I joined UPI in Hartford, Connecticut, in 1961, and after a two-year stint as bureau manager in Montpelier, Vermont and a year's leave of absence to obtain a master's degree at Columbia University, I began working in New York, UPI's world headquarters and the only bureau rivaling Washington in importance.

My first day I told the boss, managing editor H. L. Stevenson, that I would be treating New York as a temporary layover before a transfer to Washington.

"Get in line," he replied, his smile tinged with a hint of sympathy. "Three-quarters of UPI wants a transfer to Washington."

"I'm better than any of them," I lied.

Within two years, in the summer of 1968, I had worked my way up the responsibility ladder to be assistant editor preparing UPI's report for afternoon newspapers.

One morning Steve corraled me.

"I'm sending you to the Republican convention in Miami next month to run the report for PM papers. Temporary loan to Washington. Don't screw up. It's only your career on the line."

This was big, I knew. Maybe unprecedented. Covering the conventions, where the political parties select their presidential candidates, always had been the province of the Washington bureau. Now the big boss was sending an unknown from New York to supervise some of UPI's most talented staffers.

Stevenson was not just testing my journalism chops--he already had seen me deal with big news stories. Now he wanted to find out how I would deal with the distrust an intruder from New York surely would encounter among the WA pros.

Who is this guy ordering us around? Hell, he's never even BEEN to a political convention! The office gossip would be brutal; some Washington staffers had progeny older than I.

"You're putting me in charge of people who have been my idols, Steve. What's gonna happen when some punk kid starts telling them what to do?"

"Simple. I''ve told Jay Frandsen (Washington vice president and manager) and Grant Dillman (Washington news editor) that I have big plans for you."

Simple, he says. A rookie pitcher starting the seventh game of the World Series?

Actually, it did prove simple. Really simple. Dillman assigned me some of his best writers: Mike Feinsilber, John Hall, Lou Cassels, George Marder, Bill Meade, Ray Lahr. Giants of the UPI wires.

About all their "editor" had to do was mark the paragraphs and draw three little lines to signify a capital letter. I could have edited these poets from a cabana on South Beach. And, perhaps sensing I soon might be more than a "loaner", after our shifts my "staff" dragged me along on forays to Miami's funkiest bars.

A few weeks later, when Democrats held their convention in Chicago, I edited from our headquarters in New York. That getting-to-know-you time in Miami proved crucial when my new Washington friends found themselves smack in the middle of the wildest, perhaps ugliest political convention ever.

Opposition to the Vietnam War was tearing America apart, having forced President Lyndon Johnson to step down after one term. The darling of the antiwar movement, Minnesota Senator Eugene McCarthy, had been eclipsed in the late stages of the Democratic primaries by Senator Bobby Kennedy, who had been attorney general when his brother Jack was assassinated in Dallas.

On a June night in 1968, having all but clinched the Democratic nomination by winning the California primary, Bobby Kennedy delivered his victory speech at the Ambassador Hotel in Los Angeles—then was shot to death by a lone gunman in the hotel's kitchen. That left a clear path for Vice President Hubert Humphrey, once a liberal hero but now stained by Johnson's bloody war.

The Democratic Party was in shambles by the time the delegates got to Chicago, but not even the most prescient could have foreseen the four-day "perfect storm" awaiting in the Windy City.

In a brutal and ugly display, police fired teargas and clubbed thousands of unarmed antiwar protesters. Chicago Mayor Richard Daley flailed out with overwhelming force in a desperate effort to save his city's image. He failed spectacularly.

TV viewers, watching in horror the unprovoked violence against America's children, punished Humphrey and the Democrats on Election Day by handing Richard Nixon a narrow victory.

🍦 🍦 🍦

A couple of months after the election, I boarded a chartered bus in Manhattan for inauguration weekend in Washington, where I joined thousands of protesters as the much-despised Nixon rode a bulletproof black limo down Pennsylvania Avenue to the White House. I wore a white Nixon death mask, providing D.C. police officers ample excuse to shove me into a clump of bushes when I didn't move back from the curb as fast as they had suggested.

Afterwards I strolled a few blocks to the UPI bureau to say hello to "old friends" Frandsen and Dillman.

Jay Frandsen, an angular, old-fashioned stickler for detail and protocol, made zero effort to conceal his distaste for this ragamuffin carrying a Nixon death mask. Was this really the guy for whom H. L. Stevenson had "big plans?" Mr. Frandsen was not amused.

Fast forward to January 20, 1972. Jill and I have moved to Washington with Rachel, now 5, and Jennifer (Zen, Tziona,), our brand-new baby. Frandsen had retired, Dillman was in charge, and I had realized my dream: Newest recruit at UPI/WA.

My first assignment: supervise UPI's coverage of Nixon's second-term inaugural parade, the event I had protested four years earlier. That irony was not lost on the Washington staff.

A few months later I was named Washington news editor, now in charge of supervising my long-time journalism heroes. The task was formidable: Convince the men and women who had been my idols that their new boss was worthy of their trust and respect.

It didn't take long for the poop to hit the fan. Six months earlier, June 17, 1972, burglars had been caught inside Democratic National Committee headquarters at the Watergate Hotel. Nobody could have dreamed that this seemingly insignificant event, derided by the White

House as "a third-rate burglary," would blossom into the scandal that forced Nixon to resign in disgrace.

Like other news organizations, UPI could not match the Pulitzer Prize-winning Watergate coverage by Washington Post rookies Carl Bernstein and Bob Woodward. But nevertheless we managed to break a few stories, and our reporting was swift and sure-footed throughout this historic tale's amazing twists and turns.

In the summer of 1974, the House voted articles of impeachment against the president. Any ensuing Senate trial would surely result in Nixon's conviction and removal from office. In the lull before the trial, Jill and I drove our girls to Chicago for the wedding of Jill's sister, Marcia.

We were driving on Lakeshore Drive when we heard the radio report that sealed Nixon's fate. Conversations secretly recorded in the Oval Office, which Nixon had fought to keep secret, were ordered released by the Supreme Court. One, dubbed the "smoking gun" tape, proved the president had known about the burglary and approved it—then lied repeatedly to cover it up. The White House announced Nixon would address the nation at 9 p.m. the following night.

I knew I must get back to Washington. After two years and countless 20-hour days of all-consuming Watergate coverage, I could not let this guy resign without me.

Disobeying every speed limit from Illinois to Maryland, I pulled into our driveway at 8:25 p.m. the night of August 8, 1974. Barely stopping the car, I toss family and luggage onto the lawn, head downtown, and burst into the bureau with loads of time to spare. A full 90 seconds, in fact.

A few minutes later, when Nixon declares "I shall resign the presidency, effective at noon tomorrow," I push a button on my computer and transmit the words that sets off 10 bells ringing in newspaper offices and broadcast stations around the world:

FLASH —WASHINGTON--NIXON RESIGNS.

It took several days for the enormity of this to sink in. Even though I was only 37, I suspected I never would cover a more important, more complicated story. And I was correct. My career would include covering three presidential assassination attempts, numerous national elections, the terrorist attacks on Washington and New York on September 11, 2001 that would forever be recognizable by the simple shorthand "9/11." Even another attempt to impeach a president, Bill Clinton. Nothing ever compared with Watergate for complexity and longevity.

For 25 years, as close to Nixon's August 9 resignation date as possible, Jill and I hosted a "Watergate Wallow," inviting friends and the UPI staff, many who arrived costumed as their favorite Watergate characters. Even Rachel and Zen dressed up, and loved to help dad decorate the house and yard with pictures, newspaper articles, posters—anything we could dig up with a Watergate connection. It was an invitation everyone wanted and nobody refused.

After the 25th anniversary party, in 1999, Jill ended the tradition with these words:

"That man has suffered long enough. And so have I."

🍦 🍦 🍦

With Watergate over, the big story became the 1976 presidential election, my first as news editor. Our election night blueprint was tried and true; no need for me to even tinker. But I was nervous nonetheless—my first election in charge must be faultless.

Our strategy was to rely on the manager at each UPI state capital bureau to declare when a candidate had carried their state, with the running electoral vote tallied in Washington. First candidate to reach the magic number, 270, would clinch.

Although occasionally during the evening we prodded a few states we suspected were being overly timid, Washington never forced the issue. I had to trust that their proximity and experience made them far more knowledgeable than I about their state's voting idiosyncrasies.

Our other major tool was something called the News Election Service, established and funded by UPI, the Associated Press, NBC, CBS, and ABC. NES stationed workers in each precinct across the country, reporting raw vote totals the instant they were available. Computers compiled these numbers state by state and made them available instantaneously to all five consortium members.

NES didn't decide winners; that was up to each news organization. Competition was fierce; careers could be made or destroyed.

Small wonder I had been an insomniac for weeks.

The Republican incumbent was Gerald Ford, a respected, easy-going congressman who had represented his district of Grand Rapids, Michigan, for a quarter-century. His route to the White House had been fortuitous, indeed. Ford became vice president in 1973 with the resignation of scandal-plagued Spiro Agnew. When Nixon quit over Watergate the following year,

Ford moved into the Oval Office. If ever there was an accidental president, it was affable Jerry Ford.

His opponent was Georgia Governor Jimmy Carter, a peanut farmer who had sprung from political obscurity to best far better-known Democratic hopefuls. Carter's fresh face consisted mainly of a huge smile that revealed preternaturally enormous white teeth.

Incumbents generally can boast built-in advantages, but Ford had big problems. Soaring inflation was dragging down the economy, and perhaps even more damaging, he was the very definition of an accidental president.

Many voters still were furious that Ford, soon after being sworn in, had pardoned Nixon. Although weary of Watergate, most Americans believed the former president should not be spared the criminal proceedings that had sent many of his closest aides to prison.

National polls were close, and we knew we likely were in for a long election night. The day before I had sent a memo to all the state managers, reminding them of UPI's long-standing motto: "Get it first, but first get it right." I had a personal stake in their performance—if we called the race incorrectly or even very late the lion's share of the blame would fall not upon the managers in each state, but on the Washington news editor. Me.

That night I concentrated on our most important task: Declare a presidential winner. As the clock slid past midnight, it was even closer than pollsters had expected. Although we had crackerjack journalists in Washington and the state capitals, UPI was in its familiarly historic position—huge underdog. The AP, which boasted more staffers and lots more money, had hired outside political experts to provide a depth of expertise far beyond what our meagre financial resources permitted.

In turn, the TV networks had far outspent AP. Their glistening, expensive election night stage sets crawled with experts opining on everything—why Ford was doing better than expected in Maryland; why Carter was cutting into Republican territory in the south. The networks' resources were intimidating; how could tiny, financially strapped UPI even hope to compete?

Network experts and anchors blathered and decreed on the TV screens around our narrow quarters in the National Press Building, even more cramped than usual that night because reporters who worked on Capitol Hill and the federal agencies crammed into the downtown bureau.

We seemed to be holding our own, although occasionally the networks' sophisticated computer capabilities enabled them to call a state first.

I was pretty much resigned to the fact that one or all the networks would beat us in calling the next president, but the AP was a different story entirely.

That was outright warfare—the heavyweight boxing championship, the Super Bowl, the World Series all rolled into one. Army vs. Navy, Michigan vs. Ohio State, Moscow vs. Washington—all paled alongside UPI vs. AP.

Neither wire service had access to the other's stories, so I did not know how close AP might be to declaring a victor. Reminding myself that they were in the same boat brought scant comfort.

No Republican had ever won the presidency without carrying Ohio, and I felt pretty good about our chances there. Especially when veteran political reporter Lee

Leonard called Ohio for Carter around 11 p.m., well before his AP counterpart and even before the networks.

The fact that Leonard's call came with fewer than half the votes counted unnerved me a bit, but we had our unbendable rule: go with the state expert. So we sent a bulletin that Carter had won Ohio, and I placed the Buckeye state's fat batch of 25 electoral votes into the Democratic column.

By 2:30 a.m., Carter by our count was closing in on 270. I looked at the percentage of the votes still unreported in the states we had not called, including Hawaii and Mississippi, whose combined nine electoral votes would put Carter over the top.

Hawaii was reliably Democratic, and Carter was practically a favorite son in neighboring Mississippi, so I got on the horn. Could we call Carter, I asked Honolulu? A long pause, then "Okay"—even though the polls had just closed there. I had fudged our rules by applying gentle pressure, but I was convinced no Republican could carry Hawaii.

Now Carter stood just four electoral votes from the Oval Office. Andy Reese, our man in Jackson, Mississippi, was one of our most knowledgeable political veterans. He was holding off until he could analyze the next batch of votes.

I wasn't about to pressure Andy Reese. He had forgotten more about Mississippi politics than I could ever know.

Slowly, slowly the minutes ticked. Bureau clocks seemed to march in reverse. Finally, at 2:55 a.m., Andy Reese sent his bulletin:

"Carter carries Mississippi. Give Carter six electoral votes."

This was it. Dave Wiessler, an old friend from New York days whom I had transferred to Washington, was the night editor in the "slot," filing our stories directly to the wire. Dave, the prepared-in-advance flash on his screen, waited for my final go-ahead.

I turned to Grant Dillman, my boss.

"Grant, we're calling Carter. Andy Reese just gave him Mississippi."

Dillman's thin lips pursed ever tighter until they vanished entirely, and his face was chalky-white like a street mime. Although our desks were just inches apart, he seemed in a trance.

"Grant!" I yell. "We have to do it!"

Silence. I count to three under my breath, giving him a last opportunity to intervene. Nothing.

"Go!" I shout to Wiessler.

Dave's right index finger jabbed the "send" button amd 10 bells instantly began ringing like gunshots in newsrooms around the world.

FLASH

WASHINGTON—CARTER WINS PRESIDENCY.

UPI 257aes.

At precisely 2:57 a.m., Eastern Standard Time, UPI had informed the universe that Jimmy Carter was America's president-elect.

We had beaten everybody.

The Associated Press, with its fat wallet and far bigger staff.

The networks, with their hired-gun political experts and gazillion-dollar dazzling studio sets.

Yep. Little old UPI had just creamed ***ab-so-lute-ly everybody***.

Dillman's countenance remains impassive as ever, but doubt bordering on fear is evident in his eyes. He, after all, had been my predecessor, the man who had written the UPI playbook on political coverage. Now this whippersnapper had just shouldered him aside. Two days later, he would invite me for a celebratory lunch and confess—after a couple or three Manhattans:

"When I heard those bells and saw the flash, I knew I had lost control of my bureau forever."

It was quite the hyperbolic statement, and wildly untrue. But that was two days later. In the here and now we had to pray that Andy Reese—and Lee Leonard—were correct.

The bells from our flash still echoed when CBS anchor Walter Cronkite, the planet's most respected journalist, held up the "flash" torn from his newsroom's UPI teletype and began upbraiding two of the network's stars, Diane Sawyer and Mike Wallace, assigned to call Hawaii and Mississippi.

Cronkite had began his career in the 1930s in the Kansas City bureau with UPI's predecessor, the United Press. He became a wire service star in Europe during World War II before being lured to CBS by the fascinating potential of a fledgling medium—television.

Cronkite always retained a soft spot for his old shop. Without his UP training, he loved to say (it didn't become UPI until a 1958 merger with International News Service, long after he had departed), he never would have evolved into "Uncle Walter," America's most beloved, most trusted, newsman.

But right now, at 3 a.m. on November 3, 1976, Uncle Walter's feelings toward his old stomping grounds were anger and disgust, not nostalgia.

UPI has called Hawaii and Mississippi, and CBS has not, he demanded on camera. What's holding us up? It wasn't a question, and Sawyer and Wallace, highly respected correspondents, had no response. Their computer terminals could spit out vote totals, but only a human could declare a winner. And neither Sawyer nor Wallace had the Mississippi chops of Handy Andy Reese.

I wished Cronkite could hear the cheers in our bureau as he acknowledged, without congratulations, that his old company had whupped his current one.

At 3:30 a.m., 33 minutes behind us, ABC called it for Carter. CBS and NBC followed quickly. AP limped in last, more than an hour after our flash. At that time of the morning, every minute was crucial. Two-service newspapers on deadline had little choice but to use our story. And exclusive UPI radio stations were destroying their AP-only crosstown rivals.

UPI's rout seems total, but my euphoria is short-lived. Minute by minute, votes straggling in show Ford slowly chewing away at Carter's lead in Ohio, the state we had called for the Georgia governor five hours earlier. Carter's lead was eroding in Wisconsin, as well. Should he blew both I will go down in history as a journalistic goat—my mortification rivaling the infamous *Chicago Tribune's* "Dewey Beats Truman" headline in 1948.

The recesses of my mind are fertile ground for the evisceration strategies I picture for the body of poor Lee Leonard—scenarios even my Italian ancestors would have applauded.

But there is scant time for sinister daydreams. Every few seconds I push a computer button and refresh Ohio vote totals. Our victory flash has been on the wire for more than an hour and I watch Dillman peering nervously into his computer terminal at Carter's narrowing margin in Ohio, my boss's home state.

Since we declared him the winner, Carter's 35,000-vote Ohio advantage had been sliced in half. Refresh button. Refresh again. Damn. 15,000. 14,800. Now 13,900. Refresh. Refresh. Refresh until my right index finger is officially numb. And Dillman clearly is contemplating doing unto Cohen what Cohen is contemplating doing unto Lee Leonard.

But by 6 a.m. the bleeding has stopped. Carter's final Ohio margin was 11,000 votes, a hair's-breadth difference of 0.27 percent. Never a doubt, right Lee?

Wisconsin also held firm. And my hero of the night, Andy Reese, had been right on the money.

Our unanticipated election night rout so pleased the UPI brass that Managing Editor H. L. Stevenson, who had transferred me to Washington four years earlier, ordered thousands of flyers printed to shout our success to the world.

He sent me the very first one, with this note:

"Ron. For Your Grandchildren. Steve."

So my darlings, here it is. Forty years later.

🍦 🍦 🍦

A victory for UPI too!

```
A007
      F W
           AM-ELECTION 11-2
FLASH
WASHINGTON -- CARTER WINS PRESIDENCY.
UPI 11-03 02:57 AES
```

"All three networks trailed United Press International, which declared Carter the winner at exactly 2:57 a.m."

TIME, November 15, 1976

FLASH! Carter wins presidency.

🍦 🍦 🍦

Chapter 39

CUSH AT 90

Apart from my dad probably nobody had a more profound effect on my life than Uncle Cush, my mom's brother. You may be wondering why this man with the funny name keeps popping up.

Hard to say. Cush defied precise definition. Friends and family employed words like sweet, funny, honest, curious, opinionated, charismatic, relentlessly loyal, relentlessly honorable, relentlessly kind.

All accurate, but each fetches competing memories. So I have stopped trying to define his essence, and hope that recounting some of our adventures in a number of chapters will, in some small way, do justice to why he was so important to me and to everyone whose life he touched.

🍦 🍦 🍦

I knew how Cush felt about me, and I knew he knew how I felt about him, although we took pains to conceal "unmanly" emotions.

But here was Uncle Cush about to begin his 90th year, and I knew it was well past time to put into writing my love and respect. Although I knew before I started that it, too, would be inadequate, I enclosed this in a birthday card:

Dear Uncle Cush:

I can remember back before I even could walk when you would pick me up in your huge hands (before your fingers got all gnarled from playing the ukulele . . . badly), and I would feel safe and loved. And I have never stopped feeling that way.

You always have been there whenever I needed a hug, a lift, a laugh, my ego boosted, a little man-to-man talking to. I know whenever I come to a room where you are that I will feel loved. Despite the fact you already are ancient and I am just approaching that state, we are soul brothers, cut from the same cloth. People like you, married for 60 years, help me understand how I have been able to avoid contributing to the obscene divorce statistics. You married for life, like people are supposed to. And you worked hard and made it work, like people are supposed to. You raised three of the most terrific daughters anybody ever had, so of course, I had to follow my hero and raise two of the most terrific daughters anybody ever had.

I am really glad you are turning 90. I can't even begin to imagine life without you.

Happy birthday.

I love you.

"Bucky" (His generic nickname for guys).

I don't hear back, hadn't expected to. A few months later, I drive four hours from Maryland to New Jersey, up to the old house on Washington Valley Road in Martinsville where he has been living alone since the death of his beloved Vi.

We go to his favorite restaurant, an all-you-can eat Asian buffet in Somerville with an otherworldly array of options. Cush heads unerringly to his favorites; I stumble around indecisively, brain-numbed by the multitude of decisions that face me. I finally return to our table to find him pushing back his chair for Round 2.

I try to keep up, really I do, even though I knew he will love boasting to his cronies how he out-ate his kid nephew. But I come in a badly beaten second. Cush has home field advantage and is treating this like The Last Supper. That happens, apparently, when you hit your tenth decade and never are sure which meal will be your last.

Back home, MSG oozing from every pore, we slump into facing easy chairs and doze off.

Cush doesn't notice when I open my eyes, for he is busy unfolding a single sheet of paper which he begins reading by the dim light of the table lamp next to his chair. Soon silent tears are sliding down his craggy cheeks.

"What's wrong, Unc?"

He looks up startled, trying to regain his composure. When he cannot he just gives up and gently waves my birthday note.

"I keep it on this little table," he says, voice cracking. "I read it every day. I love you, Bucky."

I can't trust myself to respond. But he knows.

🍦 🍦 🍦

Chapter 40

"THE PRESIDENT HAS BEEN SHOT!"

In 40-plus years in journalism, I heard these terrible words twice. The first was November 22, 1963, and nobody alive back then ever will forget exactly where they were and what they were doing when John F. Kennedy was assassinated while riding in a presidential motorcade in Dallas.

As a junior staffer in UPI's small Hartford bureau, I was scarcely more than a spectator as our national reporters monopolized the wires for four days with stories covering every angle of his assassination.

The distance between Connecticut and Washington is but 400 miles, but my bureau might as well have been on Mars that weekend. For hours I was hunched, mesmerized, over our clackety-clacking teletype machines, reading one riveting story after another carrying bylines of UPI colleagues I knew only by their names on the wire.

For his brilliant coverage of the murder of the young president, UPI White House reporter Merriman Smith would win a Pulitzer Prize, journalism's highest award. But that weekend in Hartford, as I marveled at the skills of Smitty and his colleagues, I could only dream that someday I might win a transfer to Washington to "play with the big boys."

A decade later I joined UPI's most important reporting bureau, but not just as a teammate to a roomful of established stars.

I would be their boss.

🍦 🍦 🍦

On March 30, 1981, just a couple of months after Ronald Reagan was sworn in as America's 40th president, I heard the horrible words for the second time. The president has been shot.

Reagan was targeted by John Warnock Hinckley, a young man haplessly, hopelessly lovesick over an actress he never could possibly have. And I found myself not a few hundred miles away in some small bureau but right smack in the middle of a story as difficult to corral as Jell-O.

It was Monday after Gridiron Club weekend. No, that has nothing to do with football. Gridiron members are journalists who cannot throw a tight spiral but can throw a wonderful annual white-tie-and-tails dinner to poke fun at "Official Washington."

Guests, usually including the president, must at least act as if they enjoy four hours of speeches, skits, and song parodies lampooning ridiculously easy targets—the politicians, the pundits, and the journalists themselves.

Attending his first Gridiron as president, Reagan was surprised and delighted to discover that his wife,

Nancy, target of merciless criticism for imperial taste as she put her fashion stamp on White House drapes and china patterns, had slipped from her head table seat to reappear on stage in tattered rags, singing amusing new lyrics to the old Roaring Twenties hit, "Second-Hand Rose." Her parody, "Second-Hand Clothes", delighted her husband, charmed detractors, captured front-page encomiums, and brilliantly melted her ice queen image. Less than 48 hours later her husband, the president, would be fighting for his life at George Washington University Hospital.

I had come to work that Monday morning with a big-time headache. It also was *my* first Gridiron show, and I had sung silly lyrics on stage with my fellow hams. Plus, I had seen my lyrics from Nancy Reagan's show-stopping "Second-Hand Clothes" lauded on the front pages of newspapers across the country. My aching head was the result of too much "party hearty."

Things were quiet in the newsroom early Monday afternoon, so I told night desk editor David Wiessler I was going to return my rental tux, then take the bus home. But with a few minutes to kill before the bus came I decided to run back upstairs to the office just to make sure everything still was under control.

It wasn't. The lazy tableau I had left 20 minutes ago was bedlam: teletype bells clanging out bulletins, staffers barking into phones. Relief creases Wiessler's face with the discovery that I am not actually on a bus going home, and he shouts to me, "The President's been shot!"

I rush to a computer to lead a legion of rewrite deskers who will serve as UPI's nerve center the next 12 hours. I begin assembling a preliminary story based on bits and pieces of information from our White House reporters, especially Dean Reynolds, who had been UPI's man on the scene at the Washington Hilton Hotel.

In the dozen hours following the fateful shots, the frenzy never abated. Lead writers churned out dozens of updated versions of the main story, every word under Dean's byline. Reynolds had been inches from the presidential limousine, which was idling outside the hotel when Hinckley fired six shots that wounded Reagan; his press secretary, Jim Brady; a D.C. police officer; and a Secret Service agent.

Reynolds raced the wrong way up a hotel escalator and dashed across the lobby to the check-in desk where he grabbed the phone from a startled clerk and dictated UPI's bulletin.

Thirty-five years later and now a widely admired network television correspondent, Reynolds recalls:

"I remember that day like it was yesterday. My first call was answered by Eliot Brenner, who was on the desk. And my first words, I believe, were, 'Shots were fired at President Reagan as he left a Washington hotel.'

"Eliot was calm and collected as I went on describing the scene. I remember momentarily losing my composure at the enormity of what I was dictating.

"'Get back! Get back!' yelled the Secret Service agents. Eliot could hear the emotion in my voice and just said, 'Steady, partner.' I will always remember those words and the underlying meaning—that we were all partners, every day, at UPI."

His recollection brilliantly summed up the ethos that carried United Press International through 80 years of competition at the pinnacle of the journalism world.

"We were all partners, every day, at UPI."

❦ ❦ ❦

My computer screen is just a few steps from where Wiessler sits in "the slot." All of our stories will flow to him for final approval before he pushes a computer button and sends them flying out on the wire to UPI subscribers all over the world. I position reporter Pat Koza at my side, to be my eyes and ears. She clutches the TV remote for dear life.

Of course, this being UPI, we had only one television set.

Like Siamese twins, we are inseparable for what will seem like forever. No need for instructions—Pat knows exactly what I will be needing: Keep clicking the remote and changing the channels. I must know exactly what the networks are reporting at every second.

Across the city, our reporters scramble for tidbits. Secretary of State Alexander Haig takes the podium in the White House briefing room and proclaims, grandiloquently: "As of now, I am in control here, in the White House …"

Haig, a retired Army general accustomed to delivering orders obeyed swiftly and absolutely, has blithely ignored the Constitution's order of presidential succession. When the president is incapacitated, the vice president, in this case George H. W. Bush, takes over. After that come the speaker of the House and the Senate president, respectively. Secretary of State is fifth, so Alexander Haig isn't even close to being "in control here." That careless burst of bravado will make a man who had devoted his entire adult life to his country the butt of cruel jokes forever.

On Capitol Hill, UPI staffers buttonhole everyone, furiously hunting any nugget. We transmit everything we can quickly confirm—reaction, analyses, a history of attacks on presidents, how the country will be governed until Reagan recovers.

If he recovers.

Several reporters are working from a makeshift briefing room at George Washington University Hospital, where the president is in surgery. In a nearby operating room, Press Secretary Jim Brady lies unconscious as a neurosurgical team races to control his brain hemorrhaging. Brady's prognosis is beyond grim. Any moment, we are certain, we will be reporting that Jim Brady has died.

This stuff is the meat and potatoes of a wire service, its very *raison d'être*. Using our internal message wire, we implore bureaus around the country to unearth anything, however insignificant it may seem, on John Hinckley and Jodie Foster, the young actress who was the unwitting muse behind his rampage.

Our reporters react with alacrity. The Denver bureau tracks down the gunman's family in suburban Evergreen. John Hinckley Sr., chairman of Vanderbilt Energy Corp., had contributed big bucks to George Bush's unsuccessful presidential challenge to Reagan in 1980. In fact, Hinckley's older brother, Scott, has a dinner date the following night with Bush's son, Neil. Interesting, if not crucial. It goes into our story.

Sixteen minutes after the shooting, our Dallas bureau reports that the Federal Bureau of Alcohol, Tobacco, and

Firearms has learned that Hinckley purchased a $47 handgun at Rocky's Pawn Shop in Dallas. Plus, Hinckley had been an inconsistent and vaguely intermittent student at Texas Tech University in Lubbock. Into the story it goes.

The six illegal and almost always fatal "Devastator" bullets Hinckley fired are specifically configured to explode on impact. The first two hit Brady and the D.C. cop; the third a building across the street; the fourth the Secret Service agent and the fifth bounces off the bullet-resistant window of the presidential limo. The final one ricochets off the limo and through Reagan's left rib cage, settling in his lung. Luckily none exploded, or four men likely would be dead. Into the story this goes.

UPI staffers in Nashville report that Hinckley had been arrested on gun charges in 1980 for stalking Reagan's predecessor, Jimmy Carter.

My old bureau chips in. Hartford staffers get in touch with Jodie Foster, who is a student at Yale. She has no idea this deranged young man has shot the president in an inconceivably aberrant effort to impress her. Jodie Foster, famous actress and now Ivy League coed. Into our story.

From UPI's Vernon Scott in Los Angeles comes word that Hinckley's infatuation with Foster began a few years earlier when he saw the film *"Taxi Driver"* for the first of at least 15 times. Hinckley apparently identified with Robert De Niro's character, Travis Bickle, a cabbie who befriended a 12-year-old prostitute played by Foster. Toward the end of the film, to impress her, Bickle attempted to assassinate a senator running for president.

Bickle. Hinckley. Could this possibly get more bizarre?

As Hinckley's obsession with Foster grew, he followed her around the country, even enrolling in a creative writing course at Yale in 1980. He began writing and phoning her, refusing to take no for an answer. At her wit's end, reports our Hartford gang, she turned the matter over to New Haven police.

But Hinckley fled before authorities could investigate. Appropriating the film's narrative, he decides to kill a politician to impress Foster, who many years later would, ironically, reveal she is a lesbian. Muttering "You couldn't make this stuff up," I fold in Vernon Scott's contributions.

In mid-afternoon our wire service competitors, the Associated Press and Reuters, report that the shambling Brady, whom reporters adore and endearingly call "The Bear," has died on the operating room table. UPI-only subscribers on deadline jam our switchboard with frantic calls, and are told UPI hasn't been able to confirm Brady's death. My mood darkens. We are getting creamed on an important piece of the biggest news story in years.

When reporter Peter Brown phones in from GW, I tell him, "Find out if Brady is dead. I don't care how—steal scrubs and burst into the operating room."

We cannot get back into this crucial competition without confirmation on Brady. I don't try to sugarcoat our dismal predicament.

"Peter, dammit, FIND OUT IF BRADY'S DEAD!"

Clicking her clicker, Pat Koza lands on ABC as veteran anchorman Frank Reynolds is informing viewers Brady is dead, quoting both AP and Reuters. The pressure on us mounts.

From Capitol Hill, veteran reporter Steve Gerstel calls to say he has just been told by Tennessee Senator Howard Baker that Brady is dead. I've never trusted any reporter more than the peerless Gerstel, and I know he and Baker are great pals. But I tell Steve no—it must come from a responsible source at the hospital.

Suddenly Peter Brown is on my line.

"Brady's alive!" he shouts.

"Who says?"

"Nofziger!"

Lyn Nofziger. At Reagan's side from the back lots at Warner Bros. movie studios in Hollywood, to the governor's mansion in Sacramento, and now to the pinnacle, the White House. Nofziger's word is plenty good enough for me.

We rush out a bulletin. Everyone else is wrong, UPI is right. Brady is alive. Stay tuned.

Frank Reynolds, eyes flashing angrily as he reads our bulletin, dramatically pounds his desk and thunders, "This is a man's life we're talking about!"

I raise my eyes briefly from my computer keyboard to shout at the TV: "Believe the UPI story, you idiot—the one that's **GOT YOUR SON'S NAME ON IT!!**" Of course he can't hear me—but it's true. Frank Reynolds is Dean's dad.

Brady's continued presence on the planet goes immediately into our story. Thank you, Lyn Nofziger. Great job, Peter Brown.

That's how it works at UPI: The reporter at the scene gets the byline and glory, the vital supporting cast labors in anonymity. Some of the best rewrite men and women spent entire careers crafting brilliant stories under somebody else's byline. Teammates selflessly subjugating ego for the greater good is just one reason UPI was the best damned job I ever had. By miles.

When the last loose ends are finally tied up, about 2 a.m., I glance at the stack of stories spilling crazy-quilt off oversized clip-boards. Tens of thousands of words from dozens of reporters, crafted by brilliant writers under excruciatingly competitive deadlines. Never a false step. Nary a correction. Flawless contributions from bureaus from Atlantic to Pacific, and points in between. I have been a Unipresser for 20 years and I still only know some of that day's biggest heroes by their bylines on the wire. Thinking of that day still gives me goose bumps. Goose bumps writing this chapter, too.

Merriman Smith, who committed suicide in 1969, would have been proud.

🍦 🍦 🍦

Pat Koza had missed her last bus hours ago, so I drive miles out of my way to take her home. We quietly replay the dozen hours we just had spent as a makeshift tag-team.

Pat opens the car door and steps into the darkness in front of her house—then leans back in through the window.

"That was the most amazing day I've ever spent," she says. "Thanks for letting me be part of it."

I love you, Pat Koza. I will always love you for that day, and now you and everybody else know it.

🍦 🍦 🍦

A year later, on April 5, 1982, UPI Managing Editor H. L. Stevenson phones from New York. In a few minutes the Pulitzer Prizes will be announced by my journalism alma mater, Columbia University.

"I just got a call from the Pulitzer board," Steve tells me. "You guys are runner-up in the national reporting category."

I am stunned. What could possibly have beaten out our coverage of the attempted murder of the president of the United States?

Soon I found out. It was Rick Atkinson of the Kansas City Star for "a series of national articles" about problems in the water supply of greater Kansas City. Now I have never met Atkinson, and I am sure he is a very fine fellow. But c'mon Pulitzer jurors, you are the cream of our profession. Drinking water in Kansas City versus "The President Has Been Shot?"

Atkinson would also share a Pulitzer in 1999 as a reporter for the Washington Post, and won another four years later for the first of a trilogy of bestsellers about World War II.

Pulitzer scoreboard: Rick Atkinson, three; Ron Cohen, none.

🎭 🎭 🎭

Jim Brady spent 10 harrowing hours on the operating table and was still unconscious when they wheeled him, after midnight, into his room in GW Hospital's intensive care unit. A nurse sits with him through the night, periodically moistening his lips and watching the tiny lights on his respirator, blinking eerily green in the ICU blackness. Her weary eyes suddenly snap open. Have I nodded off? Am I hallucinating?

Or had Jim Brady's right hand really moved?

She stares hard at that hand and sure enough, a half-minute later —"He's doing it again!"

Painfully, slowly, the Bear's claw reaches toward his nightstand, pulls a single sheet of Kleenex from its dispenser, crumples it and tosses it, super slo-mo, toward the trashcan.

Dr. Arthur Kobrine, still asleep after performing a dozen hours of surgery, groggily picks up the phone that is ringing on his bedside night table.

Not only is Jim Brady alive, Kobrine hears the ICU nurse say, he is conscious.

"AND HE IS SHOOTING HOOPS!"

Kobrine, a renowned neurosurgeon, is a brusque, no-nonsense, seemingly unsentimental man. Whoever coined the praise-phrase "good bedside manner" probably never met Arthur Kobrine. Yet his heart leaps. Against overwhelming odds, he had saved Jim Brady's life. Maybe he is the only person on the planet who could have.

When he looks into Brady's room a short time later, Kobrine sees the proof for himself: Wadded-up balls of Kleenex littering the perimeter of his patient's wastebasket.

Now it just so happens that Dr. Kobrine in later years would perform three back surgeries on my wife, Jill. I've never seen a better doctor.

🍦 🍦 🍦

Brady's speech and brain functions were badly compromised, but he would survive for 33 years, largely confined to a wheelchair. He and his wife, Sarah, became tireless advocates for handgun control, and in 1993 Congress passed "The Brady Law" requiring federal background checks for handgun purchases. Sarah Brady died early in 2015, eight months after her husband.

Nine months after the shooting, in my capacity of chairman of the Washington Press Club's annual "Salute to Congress" dinner, we secretly invite Jim and Sarah Brady.

Eight hundred formally dressed diners barely are settled into their seats in the dark ballroom of the Shoreham Hotel when a huge spotlight leaps to life and zeroes in on the two large double doors being pushed open.

And there is Sarah Brady wheeling her husband into the room and up the head table ramp, his first public appearance since that fateful afternoon last March. Crusty journalists shrug off their carefully nurtured cynicism and leap to their feet, whistling, shouting, stomping. And shedding tears of happiness.

At the head table, UPI's chief political reporter, Clay Richards, greets his fraternity brother with the Sigma Chi handshake and a "Hi, Brother Bear."

Brady, eyes moist, haltingly rasps his reply.

"Thank you, UPI, for not killing me."

Rick Atkinson, congratulations on your Pulitzers.

Because Jim Brady's "thank you" is prize enough for me.

🌑 🌑 🌑

Chapter 41

GOING HOME

Can you ever really "go home again"?

Although we have lived near Washington for almost a half-century, "home" is where your heart is—and mine is, and always will be, 225 miles north of the nation's capital.

I'm a proud Jersey guy from the very heart of what the outside world now knows, thanks to HBO's hit series about Mafia hits, as "Soprano-Land": East Orange, West Orange, Montclair, Verona, Bloomfield, Cedar Grove, Belleville, Nutley, the Caldwells. I grew up actually knowing guys who looked and talked like the goombas in "*The Sopranos*": "Big Pussy" Bompensiero, Paulie Walnuts, Bobby "Baccala" Baccalieri.

In one memorable episode after Tony Soprano's outrageous mother Livia finally dies, he and his sister are in the basement culling the detritus of their childhoods. His Old Country scowl suddenly turning soft and dreamy, Tony's hairy hands begin caressing a small item from a cardboard box. Slowly, ever so slowly, the camera crawls in for a close-up.

There, dwarfed in his huge paws, is a maroon and white West Orange High School varsity letter, the "W" and the "O" intertwined. It is an archaeological curio of eons past, recognizable only perhaps to the few still-surviving "Cowboy" alums of the massive Gothic structure standing sentinel on Northfield Avenue.

A few years after I graduated, a sudden growth spurt in my home town caused a new, bigger, breathtakingly nondescript concrete penitentiary to materialize way farther up the mountain, christened West Orange Mountain High. Our beloved maroon and white ("Maroon and White, Maroon and White, Fight Team, Fight Team. Fight! Fight! Fight!") battle colors were heartlessly abandoned, dumped for unsatisfying and unsatisfactory blue and white. They didn't bother to survey the class of '55 (1955, that is) about those colors, you can be damn sure.

The abandoned building, whose panache is far too costly to reproduce in these days of austerity and minimalism, became home to interlopers—a private Catholic prep school whose all-boy student body wouldn't in a million years recognize the old maroon-and-white varsity letter with its interlocking WO, being caressed so tenderly, in his hands and in my heart, by Tony Soprano.

🍦 🍦 🍦

The Grove Street Oval sat a few blocks from where I attended grammar school in East Orange. It is now called simply Oval Park, although it still sits on Grove Street. It was there that I spent summer weekend days nurturing what would become my lifelong love, baseball.

And it was there that I grew up watching a bunch of guys named Satchel Paige, Leon Day, Bingo DeMoss, and "Cool Papa" Bell cavorting like happy children in uniforms that read Kansas City Monarchs, Homestead Grays, Pittsburgh Crawfords, Newark Eagles, Baltimore Elite Giants, Birmingham Black Barons.

I was pretty little, so young that my dad had to help me cross busy Main Street. So young that although it was clear these were supremely talented athletes playing exciting baseball, I had no inkling I was a party to history. For within 25 miles of the old and shabby Grove Street Oval stood Ebbets Field, the Polo Grounds and Yankee Stadium, storied edifices where the Bingos and Cool Papas could only dream of playing.

Because they were black. Back then, the only way Satchel Paige could get into a Major League ballpark would be to purchase a ticket.

A few years later, two stupendously courageous men, Branch Rickey and Jackie Robinson, would team to breach baseball's despicable "color barrier." Within a few years Satch, well past his salad days, would join the Larry Dobys and Don Newcombes and Roy Campanellas in "The Show." The Majors. The big leagues. At last.

Major League Baseball ultimately would hatch the ill-concealed palliative of inducting some of the old-time Negro League stars into the Hall of Fame in Cooperstown. Too little, far too late.

Imagine what baseball would look like in the 21st century were blacks and Latinos still excluded.

And how's this for irony: Ebbets Field, the Polo Grounds and the original Yankee Stadium have all been gone for years.

🍦 🍦 🍦

After I retired from the news business, I made my way one day back to check out my old neighborhood, 18 South Munn in East Orange, where I lived until I started junior high. It was there, when I was about 8 and returning from school one afternoon, that I had heard a scream and looked up to see a form hurtling toward the concrete driveway.

A woman had jumped from the fifth-floor roof, for reasons I've never known, and landed 15 feet from where I stood. For weeks my parents struggled to console me, but even the passage of seven decades has not quite scrubbed away the horror.

Bsck on our block years later, I discover the driveway of my many nightmares is gone. In fact, what had been an unprepossessing apartment building on a lovely, tree-shaded street, apparently had fallen into such disrepair that it, and its identical twins, 14 and 22 South Munn, also were razed.

A few doors away, on the corner of Main and South Munn, stood the gorgeous, ivy-covered building that had housed the town library. I was such a regular visitor that if I had not arrived by 3:30 on a school day, the librarians phoned my mom to see if I was okay.

My precious childhood sanctuary has been seized as a home for the municipal courts; the replacement library a block away is squat and so thunderously ugly that city planners were surely bent on discouraging young minds from uncovering the magic of reading.

A library for a municipal court. Lousy swap.

🍦 🍦 🍦

Eagle Rock Reservation, atop the Watchung First Mountain in West Orange, is a densely wooded 408-acre tract laid out a century ago by Frederick Law Olmstead, founding genius of American landscape architecture. Olmstead's designs include the grounds of the U.S. Capitol and the White House, Acadia and Yosemite national parks, Manhattan's Central Park, and even Great Falls National Park near our home in Potomac, Maryland.

The best thing about Eagle Rock is an unfettered view of the Manhattan skyline. In my high school days I would drive there in my Chrysler Town and Country "woodie" convertible, accompanied by my best gal and a sketchily obtained quart of Miller High Life. Nursing the beer, we would gaze across the Hudson River at Manhattan's shimmering lights and try to guess what our futures might hold (not each other, it turned out).

When I married and moved back to North Jersey, I showed off my old hometown to my new best gals, Jill and little Rachel. We would *ooh* and *aah* at the skyscrapers, which now included the spectacular twin towers of The World Trade Center.

Eagle Rock still offers glorious views, but the skyline's most arresting feature was obliterated by an unimaginably despicable act of human cruelty. On September 11, 2001, the 101-story Twin Towers buckled then crumbled in an avalanche of twisted steel and screaming bodies. Religious terrorists had deliberately piloted hijacked jets into the side-by-side buildings, killing almost 3,000 innocents whose only crime had been the daily grind of going to work. This unspeakable act was instantly memorialized by the shorthand "9/11." No elaboration ever would be necessary.

In its immediate aftermath, Eagle Rock's observation wall blazed to life with a jaw-dropping display of retaliatory patriotism ... American flags, photos of loved ones lost, mournful memorial poetry encased in plastic sleeves against autumn's rain and winter's snow.

Essex County subsequently replaced this haphazard outpouring of grief with a lovely permanent memorial that cost $1 million, much of it the dimes and quarters and dollars of broken-hearted mourners.

But the tributes keep arriving, the pictures and the bunting and the poetry and the flowers, all bittersweet reminders of a brilliantly sunny Indian summer day in 2001 when hateful murderers, in the name of a deity who surely would never have approved, shattered forever America's innocence.

In a bold display of defiance, a replacement tower, the biggest in the Western hemisphere, is the centerpiece of a series of skyscrapers that opened for business 15 years later near the footprint of its departed predecessors.

Yes, Tom Wolfe, you can go home again. But it never is quite the same.

🐾 🐾 🐾

Chapter 42

WONDROUS, WONDERFUL AMERICA

Perfect excuse for a cross-country adventure: Deliver to my daughter the larger, more reliable car she needs now that she is about to present my first grandchild.

So on Tuesday, September. 30, 2003, I aim our '97 Honda wagon westward on a leisurely, meandering journey, needing only to arrive in San Francisco before Rachel's due date, October 16. And smart people tell me first-borns always are late, so there's wiggle room should I care to tarry.

Day 1: Buzzing along I-70 west at 80 mph near Newark, Ohio, windows are rolled up as I listen to John Updike's four-volume Rabbit Angstrom epic on tape. I have read and reread all the Rabbits, but this is the first time they are being read to me. I love Updike, especially the way he can make a pure diamond leap unexpectedly from straightforward, often Spartan, prose. I glance out my side window and spot a guy on a motorcycle with his gal sitting behind, bundled like Eskimos against 40 degree temperatures. She hugs him with one arm and flips the pages of a soft-cover novel with her opposite hand, as if snuggling in front of a fireplace. I hope she is loving hers as much as I am loving Updike describe The Rabbit.

Day 2: Fort Wayne, Indiana, with Connie, save for me the oldest of the 14 Fig cousins. I love Connie. She is smart and savvy and fun, and it doesn't hurt a bit that our politics and philosophies and love of life and family mesh precisely. Delicious lasagna, festooned with assorted pork products and splashed down with red wine; our reunion is sweet pleasure.

Day 3: Shun the interstates to spool leisurely through the rolling hills and flyspeck hamlets of central Indiana farm country. How picturesque are the fields of withering cornstalks, remnants of just-departed summer. How stark is their contrast with the lush green vines dappled with Halloween pumpkins, fat and juicy and orange. Meet up with Betsy Hendrick, who still lives in Champaign-Urbana, a great and loyal friend since college days. I stroll the oh-so-familiar quadrangle, nostalgically conjuring lovely memories—Illinois was the lone institute of higher learning willing to overlook my lousy high school grades a half-century ago. I will remember that kindness forever and keep loyally rooting for its lousy football team.

Day 4: Kansas City is America's best-kept urban secret, a wonderfully livable big city. As a judge officially certified by the hallowed Kansas City Barbecue Society, I am here for the annual two-day American Royale barbecue contest. Judges are warned to sample just enough to assign each entry a grade; cleaning your plate each time would mean consuming, in just two hours, four pounds of ribs, sausage, beef brisket, and chicken. I am not the only judge who simply cannot play by the rules, and besides, who says four pounds of barbecue is too much? Witty team names abound: Slabba Dabba Doo (This Bone's for You); Roadkill Redeemers (If It Tastes Too Strong, It's Been Dead Too Long); and Midwest Gastroenterology Center (Guts and Butts Our Specialty). Spent two nights with another old college pal, Gene Dreyer, and his very special wife Thelma. Friends who beyond all reason never seem to consider my antics tedious.

Day 6: Kansas is endless. Fight boredom by reading road signs and nibbling leftover smoked meats purloined from the contest. Each exit on I-70 seems to trumpet ads for a different adult bookstore. Never would have guessed Flyover Country concealed such a smutty underbelly. In Abilene, spied this message on a dull gray barn: "No God, No Peace. Know God, Know Peace." Rest stop in Russell, hometown of former senator and '96 presidential loser Bob Dole. Surprised to discover this tiny town also is the boyhood home of Pennsylvania Senator Arlen Specter. Ponder those odds!

Back on the interstate from hell, I reach the hamlet of Oakley and surrender to the billboards I have been reading for hours that tout "World's Largest Prairie Dog." Hard by Twister Treat, a drive-in shaped like a giant soft ice cream cone, is Prairie Dog Town. Only after forking over six bucks are my suspicions confirmed: The "World's Largest Prairie Dog" actually is quite immobile, not especially surprising since it is a four-ton concrete sculpture. But Larry Farmer, 63, who conjured this sideshow on the Kansas flatlands 35 years ago, proves so affable that I cannot stay angry for having been hoodwinked like thousands of rubes before me. Besides, dozens of real (normal-sized) prairie dogs constantly pop from holes to peer at the latest sucker, and I find further comfort that my money was well spent when Larry introduces me to the six-legged cow and the five-legged steer (both real).

Day 7: First of two days in Denver with Jim and Barbara Eschen. Barb, Connie's younger sister, is my soulmate. Our affection long has been a family joke, other cousins acknowledging our perpetual love fest with cries of "There go Ron and Barb again!" I could spend a lifetime with Barb, but two days seems a pretty good alternative.

Day 9: Stop for several hours north of Denver to traverse Rocky Mountain National Park's dark, remote and stunningly beautiful trails. Still farther north, in search of the last remnants of the old Wild West, I am disappointed to find that, despite its euphonious name, Cheyenne, Wyoming, lacks the cowboy boots, bucking broncos, and swinging saloon doors I had expected. Low spirits quickly dissipated by a glance in the rear view mirror. I wheel the car to the shoulder and pop my body through the moon roof like a (real) prairie dog from its burrow. There I snap photo after photo of a setting sun that is brush-stroking the heavens inferno red.

Day 10: Yellowstone National Park, and my first "Bison Crossing" sign. The main road weaves through the charred, twisted remnants of hundreds of thousands of evergreens consumed by the wildfires of summer, 1988. But I am delighted to see that, at the feet of these ghostly sentinels, sprout millions of healthy offspring, new generation inexorably replacing old. Just like my soon-to-be-born grandchild someday will be taking over for this relic of a grandpa.

Day 11: Very few sights rival the eruption of Old Faithful under a harvest moon at 3 a.m.--right on time to the minute, as always.

Day 12: First "Elk Crossing" sign, near Cataldo, Idaho. Wonder whatever became of my old high school classmate, Phil Cataldo?

Day 13: Overnight with old friends in Buncom, Oregon, a Gold Rush ghost town they purchased in 1989. Reeve Hennion is mayor for life;, Lyn is Baroness of Buncom. For five bucks, I join the Buncom Historical Society. (www.buncom.org), and elect myself Court Jester. Ran unopposed.

Days 13-15: From a bluff at Lyn and Reeve's weekend retreat in the hamlet of Smith River, California, just south of the Oregon border, we watch the violent, storm-tossed Pacific pound the rocks below. My home ocean is the Atlantic, and I marvel at the beautiful dissimilarity of America's coasts.

Day 16: South on California 101 in gorgeous Humboldt County. Spy a "Scenic Route" sign and exit, wondering how anything could possibly best the 101. Discover that the words "Scenic Route" don't even begin to describe the grandeur of the *"Avenue of the Giants,"* 32 miles long and containing 17,000 acres of ancient redwoods, some well over 300 feet tall and 20 centuries old. Only the strongest, most determined of the sun's rays can penetrate to the dank forest floor. I snap a picture of *"The Immortal Tree,"* *(address: 28101 Avenue of the Giants, Humboldt Redwood State Park, California).* It is immortal because, though a mere stripling at age 1,000 it has survived lighting strikes, forest fires, woodsmen's axes. A sign proclaimed that its 104,389 board feet could build several houses. That such a glorious sentinel is even vaguely connected with the idea of a few more ticky-tacky houses or another load of picnic tables saddens me deeply, and I press on to reach my destination tonight, even if that gets me to San Francisco a few days early for the main event. Greeting me in Marin County, hot tub-and-chardonnay capital of America, is my favorite creature-crossing sign: "Red-Legged Frog Crossing." Arrive at Rachel's after dark. She is off teaching a class, but my marvelous daughter has left me a hot meal.

Day 18: Rachel rousts me from a deep slumber at 5 a.m., with "Good thing you didn't drive more slowly, Dad." For in only a few hours, Kamille Sue Peralta will burst into the world: 8 pounds, 3 ounces, 21 inches. She already has far more hair than Grandpa.

Astonishingly long fingers and toes.

Basketball star? Concert pianist? Both?

Why not? Everything is possible in wondrous, wonderful America.

Chapter 43

THE ROAD NOT TAKEN

Chance can profoundly influence our lives in ways perhaps not apparent for years. Or ever.

A job offer rejected because you decide to wait for something better. A friend offers you the opportunity to "meet someone special," but you lamely claim you are tired.

A kiss lost when resolve wavers, inches away from heaven.

Such are "Roads Not Taken."

This is the story of mine.

❦ ❦ ❦

The dreamy loveliness that was Helene Anne Jefferson had not floated across my consciousness for, oh, maybe four decades—until a drive down East Daniel Street in my college town of Champaign, Illinois. That's when I spot "The Porch."

It surprised me that the drama on that very porch could still entice a wry smile almost a half-century later.

The background: Second semester 1956, freshman year, University of Illinois, British Romantic Poetry. Only a heart calcified and sere could resist the love songs of Shelley, Keats, Byron. And it certainly seems that Helene Anne, tall and lissome and sitting across the aisle, shares my thrall.

I screw up enough courage to suggest a date. She declines, rather lamely I thought. Second request, different excuse — no less lame. Percy Bysshe Shelley might be piercing Helene's concrete heart, but I quit trying before she can say "strike three."

The last day of class, I inform her it had been swell, but I am transferring to the University of Florida. My parents and sis Diane had moved from New Jersey in hopes a more temperate climate could magically restore Dad's health.

I am beyond surprised next morning to discover Helene waiting for me at the Greyhound terminal. She engulfs me in a paralyzing hug and whispers huskily, "Are you sure you can't come back?"

"Where have you been the last three months?" I hiss.

The bus ride south is spent plotting how to tell my folks—without revealing the not-so-subtle promise implicit in Helene's farewell—that I really didn't want to transfer. But preparations prove unnecessary. My folks inform me as I step off the bus that they hate Florida and are moving back to Jersey.

Like a condemned man given an 11th-hour reprieve, I begin envisioning scenarios awaiting our autumn reunion. The stuff of poesy.

But not even the most romantic poet could have supplied the backdrop for my reunion with Helene

Anne: A huge, fiery-orange harvest moon suspended motionless over miles of withering central Illinois cornstalks.

Returning to Kamm's, where I had been a short-order cook only months ago, we leisurely consumed a double sausage/triple garlic pizza (my old pal Guido, pieman extraordinaire in Kamm's basement, hasn't lost his touch) and a couple of pitchers of cold Falstaff.

We barely can keep our eyes off one another; surely, the long wait for this nymph of my dreams is proving time well spent.

Afterwards we stroll hand-in-hand, savoring the night and the companionship, to her old wooden rooming house at 406 East Daniel — the one with the old-fashioned, wrap-around porch.

We settle into a glider and let the unique thrill of budding love wash over us like the glow of that inconceivable moon. Perfection.

Well, for a few moments anyhow.

Our mood and serenity suddenly are shattered by a racket on the steps. Santa's entire reindeer gang? Reality is slightly more prosaic.

A short (okay, squat) young man is tearing to the top steps, then he skids to a halt and drops theatrically to one knee directly in front of my date. From his pocket, he extracts a small, rectangular box that looks like it could hold a ring. Which it certainly does.

He is proposing! (To Helene, not to me.).

Galloping ghosts of Byron and Shelley! This scene two centuries earlier would have provoked whole libraries of romantic verse.

I sit, bemused, awaiting Canto 2. Helene, improbably still clutching my hand, glances slowly from him to me. Then back to him. Then back to me. Then back to him. Am I prisoner in a deranged badminton video? Time seems suspended, like that harvest moon, with nary an autumn zephyr to encourage it along.

Finally, Helene's sweet whisper, so recently reserved for my left ear:

"Yes. Yes. Oh, **YE-SSSS**!"

Strike three. Game over. I extricate my damp fingers from her now slack ones, rise, and descend The Porch stairs, summoning as much aplomb as history's most harshly jilted swain can muster.

"Have a nice life, kids," I generously call over my shoulder to the clinched lovebirds. They ignore me.

Never saw Helene Anne again.

Driving slowly down East Daniel 40 years later, my mood turns philosophical.

How different things might have been had I not chosen that poetry class, or had I transferred colleges. Or had that squat little toad not bounded up the steps of The Porch.

Or if Helene had told that twerp "No!"

Two years after the porch fiasco, I began to court, on that very campus, the wonderful woman I would marry. Without Jill, there never could have been a Rachel and Zen, never would have been the four sensational grandchildren to whom this volume is dedicated.

I certainly wouldn't have been driving through Champaign that day headed for San Francisco and the debut of the first grandkid, Kamille Sue Peralta.

Perhaps I would have wound up a lawyer or a druggist or a matinee idol. Or a stock manipulator.

Here's how Robert Frost, America's answer to Byron, Keats, and Shelley, put it in his classic poem, *"The Road Not Taken"*:

"I shall be telling this with a sigh
Somewhere ages and ages hence:
Two roads diverged in a wood, and I—
Took the one less traveled by
And that has made all the difference."

🍦 🍦 🍦

My "Road Not Taken" was Helene Anne Jefferson.
My sweet grandchildren, you will have your own roads.
May those journeys be wonderful as mine.

🍦 🍦 🍦

Chapter 44

UNCLE CUSH

I am in the doorway of Uncle Cush's room at Overlook Hospital in Summit.

Hadn't known he was back in the hospital. I wouldn't even have been in New Jersey that day, except that I had driven my sister Diane to the hospital for outpatient surgery.

Cush is angry, agitated, his signature infectious grin missing in action. It was the first time I had ever walked into a room without seeing his face light up.

"What's wrong, Unc?"

"I asked the damned nurse to shave me, but she disappeared."

Here is this beautiful man—my idol, my soulmate, my hero—who absolutely knows he will never leave this hospital bed. And all he can think of is a shave.

No need to ask why.

"The girls are coming," his voice softens and drops an octave.

His beloved daughters, Connie, Helen, and Barbara. Coming. To say goodbye.

"I'll do it," I say, finding his razor and a small can of shaving cream and carrying the plastic hospital wash basin to his bedside.

I never have shaved anybody but myself, never contemplated it. In truth, Cush doesn't even need a shave.

But his girls are coming.

Extra carefully, I get down to business. When I finish and rinse the extraneous dots of cream from his cheeks, I survey my handiwork. No blood. Not even a nick. Not bad.

He rubs his cheeks, and now I can see his whole body visibly relax. Finally, here comes the crooked-tooth grin.

"Smooth as a baby's bottom," he says, with unconcealed glee.

For his girls are coming, and when they kiss him hello and goodbye, his beard will not chafe them.

His final gift in a lifetime of giving.

Cush as a young man.

Early next morning, Connie calls to give us the news—inevitable yet still inconceivable. Cush is dead.

Constantine Figlio--"Jack" to his friends and co-workers, Cush to his sisters and brothers, Pop to the fabulous daughters, Uncle Cush to 11 nieces and nephews. Pal to everyone whose heart he ever touched. Gone at 93.

Even having known it was imminent, I could not process the loss — everyone's loss was my ***personal*** loss. I was eldest of 14 cousins, and in the eyes of Cush and his brothers and sisters I could do no wrong. Even when I did wrong, and I did wrong plenty, I could do no wrong,. Except for one sister. Millie, my mom and sternest task-mistress.

My aunts and uncles, though, forever believed I hung the moon. Filomena Figliuolo, in her charming mish-mash of broken English and Neopolitan Italian, had christened me "Bay-bee Pair-fect."

But nobody had spoiled me like Cush. He and Millie were closest in age and closest in looks of the Figliuolo kids. To him I was the son he never had — although he wouldn't for an instant have traded any of his daughters for all the world's riches. After I became an adult, Cush was "The brother I never had."

The Cush of my early years was tall, erect, strong, stunningly handsome. He played semi-pro football in Northern New Jersey, and an occasional teammate was his younger brother Rudy, even taller and stronger. What a pair they were—walking between them was like holding hands with Everest and Kilimanjaro. It was the safest I would ever feel—safe and invulnerable.

An early memory, maybe I was 4: Cush taking me to his games. When I fell behind his long strides he would lift me like a toy with one hand and nestle me in the crook of his arm like a football. He always was in battlefield regalia—as much hand-me-down equipment as he could cobble together. There were no locker rooms so he donned his uniform at home and we walked—well, mostly he walked and I rode—a couple of miles to Branch Brook Park in Newark. He would plop me down on the sideline; when I toddled onto the field, he would call, "Time out for Ronnie!" and redeposit me in my "reserved seat" in the grass.

God, but he was strapping and handsome! He looked just like Burt Lancaster. And since I looked like Cush, by extension, I also was Burt! I never stood taller than returning home with Cush after a game, his uniform grassy, muddy, a little bloody. Win or lose, to his tiny nephew he was the conquering hero. And so it would be all my life.

Reality intruded on my nostalgia when Connie reminded me that Cush had wanted me to deliver his eulogy.

I was honored, but nervous. How, in only one day, would I ever find the words to memorialize this most towering presence in my life?

But it turned out okay, so I think I'll sprinkle in some of what I said that day. You will recognize them by the *italics*.

"How could even someone who earns his livelihood with words possibly do justice? My uncle spent 93 bountiful years spreading joy and happiness wherever he ventured, touching the lives

of every soul whose path he crossed. Adult and child, great and ordinary, man and woman, relative and stranger -- once you were captured in Jack Figlio's force field, you could never escape. And why would you ever want to?"

I had been hanging with Cush for 70 years. My pal. Father and brother combined.

He took me everywhere. I wouldn't be surprised if someone told me I had been along on his first date with Violet, his wife for more than 60 years. No man ever loved a woman more than Cush loved Vi, and she returned that a hundredfold throughout her long, courageous struggle against cancer.

"Cush was the giant figure in my life, the moral and spiritual compass I lost when my dad died a half-century ago. Whenever I face a dilemma, I ask myself, 'What would Cush do?' Because nobody ever had a better mentor. What supreme irony that heart failure finally stilled the man with the biggest heart I ever knew."

In a delicious role reversal, when I got to high school and played varsity basketball, Cush and Rudy would come to my games.

A couple of years before Cush died, I became president of the Gridiron Club, a group of Washington journalists who toss a lavish, white-tie-and-tails dinner every spring in which we entertain our country's leaders with skits and songs. The big-wigs, usually including the president, endure good-naturedly our amateurish lampooning.

In the tight little circles of official Washington, the Gridiron dinner is a big deal that has endured more than 125 years. By tradition, the conductor of the U.S. Marine

Corps Band serves as music director of the Gridiron—the very first, in the 1880s, being none other than John Philip Sousa.

Being Gridiron president is a really big deal, too. You ascend by virtue of seniority, and you have to wait in line years before making it to the top. It took me two. Decades, that is. And there is no re-election. One year and gone.

The Gridiron president gets to sit front and center at the head table next to the real president, in my case, George W. Bush; gets to turn off the lights in the ballroom and deliver a (hopefully) humorous speech to 700 people dressed like penguins and princesses; gets to eat fabulous food (by hotel banquet standards) that he himself has selected; and gets to invite three dozen friends/family to bask in his fleeting importance.

So how could my Gridiron dinner not include Cush, a still spry 91? It couldn't. I explained it would be a long and tiring weekend, but promised to sure he got plenty of rest. I told him he would meet the president and Laura Bush, and the vice president and Lynn Cheney, at an oh-so-private cocktail party before dinner.

"So, Unc, will you come? Please?"

What a question. He soon was bragging to every ear how he was going to Washington "for this big political dinner where I will meet the president, and the big star will be my Jewish nephew."

I never quite understood why my uncle always introduced me that way, as though being half-Jewish made me an exotic rather than just the product of mixed-heritage young lovers.

But he was wrong about one thing. The Gridiron weekend's "big star" unquestionably was Uncle Cush.

The words of Jimmy Pelusio, my cousin Elaine's stepson, were astonishingly prescient:

> **"When Cush gets to Washington he will arrive as Ron Cohen's uncle. When he leaves on Monday, everyone will be saying that Ron Cohen is Jack Figlio's nephew."**

Everyone was dazzled by Cush's wit, staying power and charming sentimentality. He went to every party for three days, was last to leave, and still got up next morning rarin' to go. He flirted with all the pretty women and had his picture taken with the Bushes—all the while giving the president an earful about how to run the country.

He cut a dashing figure in the only white tie and tails he ever wore, and made a huge impression on both presidents. The one named Bush leaned over at dinner and told the one named Cohen, "Hey, your uncle is something else, isn't he?"

Finding ourselves in agreement for perhaps the only time, I replied, "Mr. President, you have just uttered history's classic understatement."

Cush and Bush. Gridiron 2003.

At the Gridiron: President Cohen, Jill,
President Bush, Rachel and First Lady Laura Bush.

Under all this joviality and frivolity, however, Cush's thoughts rarely strayed from his middle daughter, Helen, in a hospital in Jersey. It was one of many such stays in her courageous battle with cancer, just like her mom.

Utterly in character, Cush had decided to skip Gridiron to be near her. He reluctantly agreed to go to Washington only after his whole family, including Helen, urged him to and promised to keep him apprised.

He never had a better time.

"Subsequently, he accosted everyone—friend, relative, stranger—with tales of that Gridiron weekend, how it was the most wonderful experience of his life. When I sent him a video, he watched it religiously and made all visitors sit through almost three hours.

"One pal who had been subjected to the stories so many times he felt like he had been at the dinner himself, swiped a copy of the picture of Cush and Bush, in white tie and tails, their arms over one another's shoulders, and had it made into a

business card that said, 'Jack Figlio, consultant to the President.' And he had the photo blown up, and superimposed on Bush's lapel a 'Figlio for President' campaign button."

Two years later, on the last day of Cush's life, his physician, Dr. Schwartz, visited his hospital room.

Cush, naturally, introduced him to "my Jewish nephew" and said I had been responsible for the best weekend he ever had.

"The doc said he knew all about it. He had seen the photo of Cush and Bush on the door to the waiting room of another doctor's office. With Cush, that picture was the equivalent of the ubiquitous 'Kilroy was here' signs from World War II.

"That was the night you had your picture taken with President Bush, right?" Schwartz said. Cush, for a moment, ignored how rotten he was feeling and threw out his chest to reply in mock high dudgeon:

" 'No, that was the night George Bush had his picture taken with Jack Figlio.' "

Nearly every Sunday afternoon after Vi died, Cush drove an hour each way to visit his surviving sibling, my Aunt Kay. Each time, the whole family held its collective breath—Cush loved to drive, but age had sapped his football-days reflexes.

Every weekend Kay, in lousy health herself, managed to pull together in her little kitchen a feast of Brobdingnagian proportions—salads, pastas, meats, desserts. She never knew how many might show up since there were no formal invitations, so she never chanced running out of food. If I happened to be anywhere within a 50 mile radius of the house in West

Caldwell, I knew better than to skip Sunday dinner. Like the investigative reporter her nephew never was, she would find out … and you never wanted to be on the receiving end of the dread "Kate look."

But she could never, ever, aim that withering glare at Cush.

"She would start laughing before he could cross the threshold, knowing the jokes were arriving, at last. Poor Aunt Kay—she heard those corny things so many hundreds of times … but she always laughed. Who knows whether she still really thought they were funny, or she was tickled just to be with her beloved brother, the guy who commanded center stage in every room he ever walked into."

Jack Figlio's musical passion was his ukulele, which all but disappeared in his huge hands. He knew just enough chords to accompany the singing at our family's annual Christmas Eve parties, and his enthusiasm and endurance more than compensated for a rather glaring shortage of musical talent.

Cush always insisted I sit beside him, and we croaked our way through old songs, familiar and obscure. My voice was marginal, but even then I knew all the words and sang them with gusto. He particularly liked my renditions of *"Red River Valley" and "Down by the River Side,"* which, intentionally or forgetfully, he thrust upon me repeatedly through the evening.

Every once in awhile he would declare a breather, ostensibly to replenish his plate and his wine glass but mostly to rest his throbbing fingers.

"Ah, those fingers, bent in every conceivable direction by the athletic heroics of his youth and

the arthritis of his antiquity. He joked he couldn't hitch-hike anymore because no driver could figure out which way he wanted to go. And those wayward digits ultimately prevented him from playing the ukulele—my loss, really, because now there was nothing to drown out my off-key rendition of "Red River Valley."

One day, couple of years after Cush died, a Fed-Ex box arrived a few days before Christmas. Connie and Barbara (middle sister Helen had finally succumbed to cancer) had sent their dad's precious ukulele.

Carefully and lovingly wrapped, it contained a note saying I could keep it for one year, then must pass it on to the next cousin.

Yeah. Fat chance anybody will be able to pry Unc's uke from my fingers.

Which of course his daughters knew all along.

🦉 🦉 🦉

"It's okay to feel sorrow at our loss, but please revel in the knowledge that his life was so long, so full, so magnificent, and that he touched so many. We will be entertaining each other with Cush stories so long as there is a breath of life in any of us.

"So mark well the footprints left on our world by this gentle giant, for we will never, ever be blessed with his like again.

"Arrividerci, Custandine. Io te amo."

And that's how I said "goodbye" and "I love you" to my Uncle Cush.

🦉 🦉 🦉

Chapter 45

AT LAST, "GOODBYE"

So, do you remember how I came to donate 40 gallons of blood over more than half a century? (*A Pint for My Pop*"). Because so many total strangers had given blood for the surgery to repair Dad's heart?

Here's the rest of the story.

🍦 🍦 🍦

In January 1958, when dad was in Minneapolis for the operation, I was taking finals at Illinois. Mom would keep me posted, and I was to fly up when the exams were over.

But right in the middle of the next-to-last exam, Comparative Religions, the proctor interrupted to deliver a note Mom had phoned to my rooming house.

"Come right away," was the ominous message.

So worried out of my skull that I didn't think to call and have the hospital track her down — cellphones wouldn't become ubiquitous for three decades — I took off that night on a tiny Ozark Airlines propeller plane into a classic, full-blown Midwest blizzard.

It was a cozy quartet for the harrowing ride, pilot, co-pilot, stewardess and me. We might have been the only four ninnies in the whole Midwest who would even consider venturing out on such a night.

The cabbie dropped me at the front entrance of the University of Minnesota Hospital near midnight. I handed him the last of my cash — a 20 dollar bill.

At an information desk in the deserted lobby, a sweet-faced woman flashed a warm, unmistakably center-of-America smile at the snow-flecked stranger standing before her.

Her smile disappeared when I said, "Maurie Cohen's room, please. My dad."

After what seemed like eons she finally whispered, "I'm so sorry, Mr. Cohen. Your father passed away this morning."

Just like that, my life as a "carefree kid" screeched to a halt and I suddenly became "the man of the family." In the coming days too many well-intentioned people would remind me of that, over and over, in precisely those bitterly depressing words.

I can't say my father's death was unexpected. We all, especially Maurie, had known how dangerous this surgery was. But my pop had been through hell his entire lifetime and always emerged from the darkness smiling— and alive.

Through other surgeries, through countless visits to endless medical specialists, through the many nights we could hear him croak and wheeze as his scarred heart pumped furiously to keep him alive.

Perhaps it was self-delusion, perhaps self-protection, but I had allowed myself to believe he magically would emerge into a brand new world of long walks and tennis matches and vacations that didn't involve packing his suitcases with Digitalis.

Now here was his kid in a strange hospital, struggling to imagine life without my daddy.

"Where I can find my mom?" I asked the information lady when I could trust myself not to bawl.

"She left around noon to fly back home."

Now this simply is too cruel. Mom's message had been, before my rooming-house owner mangled it:

"Come **home** right away."

So I am standing alone in the world in a strange city in the middle of a blizzard, broke and heartbroken. What the hell am I supposed to do now?

The kind woman hands me her phone.

"Dial 9 for an outside line," she says gently. "Call Mom. No charge."

As I dial she picks up another phone and calls upstairs. Presently a woman dressed in white appears like an angelic apparition and slips into my hand a plastic bag bulging with bills and coins. The nurses on my dad's floor, who of course had fallen hopelessly in love with Maurie, had turned their purses inside out for his grief-stricken son.

The kindness of this wonderful city washed over me like a torrent. First, gallons of blood donated to a stranger. Now, $75 in a plastic bag for that stranger's kid. How could one attempt to fathom such selflessness, such kindness?

While I was in the taxi back to the airport, Uncle Mac changed out of his pajamas and drove a few miles from his house in Hillside to Newark Airport and paid for my flight back home.

At the door of our garden apartment in West Orange several hours later, Mom and my sis fall into my arms, all of us sobbing uncontrollably.

Somehow we muddle numbly through the next few days, a blur of sympathy visits by friends and relatives bearing hugs and heat-and-eat casseroles. The irony is not lost — my mom had been feeding these people old-fashioned Italian meals only forever.

We buried Daddy in the Jersey meadowlands of East Rutherford, in the shadow of the Manhattan skyline. A few steps away was the grave of his mom, Rebecca, who had died 40 years earlier when Maurie was a child, as well as the side-by-side plots of Eli and Malka, his grandparents.

My middle name is Eli, and Zen named her daughters Rivka and Sara Malka, after my dad's mom and grandma.

What a pity that my father, a kind, gentle, generous, erudite man everyone adored, never got to meet his grandchildren and great-grandchildren. He would have loved them fiercely. And they would have loved him fiercely, right back. Just like everyone he ever touched.

After the well-wishers and the casseroles disappeared, I sank into deep melancholy as I sought answers for the unanswerable.

Why hadn't I delayed my exams to help deal with a family crisis, and been there with them at the hospital? Dad had always been so thoughtful of his kids; how could his kid be so thoughtless? The new "man of the house" sure was doling himself a lot of flunking grades.

And I was angry because I had been deprived of a proper goodbye, a last hug. I had blown the chance to tell him I loved him, and how much I would miss his wise counsel and our wonderful man-to-man talks.

And how lucky I had been to have a dad so universally loved.

So we are near the end of his story, and this memoir. Grab a comfortable chair, my darling grandkids, and I will tell you about the impossibly delayed goodbye.

🍦 🍦 🍦

Flash ahead to winter, 2014, fifty-six years after Dad's death. Jill and I are cleaning out the basement to make space for her art studio.

Part of the reclamation project involves a virtual archaeological dig, sifting through bygone relics, discovering possessions so hoary we don't even recall them. Vowing to discard and recycle lest we be buried in nostalgia and tsatskes, I drag several cardboard boxes out from under the basement stairs.

Blowing away a quarter-century of accumulated dust, I see two words scrawled, in black Magic Marker, "Bedroom Books."

"So that's where they ended up," I mutter. I had packed them away back in 1989 when, planning to move to Virginia so Jill and I both could be closer to work, we put our Maryland house on the market. That never happened, because until you dip an exploratory toe into the real estate cesspool you can't appreciate how much you love your home.

Thus did the temporary storage area under the basement stairs became permanent, the boxes of books soon buried beneath suitcases and duffel bags in various states of disrepair.

I open the first box and discover a number of books I hadn't even realized were missing. Plus a few I had abandoned hope of ever finding. Plus a few that don't look familiar, at all.

Tucked amid the musty volumes is an unfamiliar rectangular brown and yellow box marked, "Colo Shoes." I flip the lid and there, neatly lined up facing the same direction, are about five dozen 4-by-6 inch envelopes, each neatly slit up one side, some on the left side, some on the right. I pop one open; it is addressed to my uncle, Private Max Cohen, A Battery 310, Camp Tyson, Tenn.

Embossed on the front of the envelope is the return address: Imperial Outfitters, 846 Broad Street, Newark, N.J.

That was our family's business, a retail store (See "Dad, Imperial and Christine Jorgensen.") At the top left corner of the envelope, my dad had signed, in ink, *Maurie Cohen.*

The purple 3-cent stamp, a silver eagle with wings uplifted in the "V for Victory" symbol of World War II, has this cancellation stamp: Newark, N.J. Nov. 4, 1942, 7:30 PM.

That letter is 75 years old.

Nowadays a stamp costs 47 cents. And the state's abbreviation would be the capital letters TN, no punctuation. And don't even think of mailing a letter to Camp Tyson. It closed in 1945 near the end of World War II, when its main product, barrage balloons, no longer were needed.

Barrage balloons? My reporter's curiosity sends me to Hermione, my Google lady, who informs me they were large rubber balloons shaped like a blimp. Lacking motors, they had been sent aloft tethered to stout metal cables, in a genuine triumph of wishful thinking — perhaps enemy pilots would be dumb enough to ram them and crash.

Before he went off to fight in Italy, Mac must have helped manufacture these strange weapons of war — against a German invasion of America's Atlantic shoreline that never came.

Uncle Mac, who served in World War II
making Barrage Balloons.

So after all these years, I have connected posthumously with my dear uncle who while I was growing up never discussed his war exploits.

Back to the letters: Most were from my dad, some in his scrawl, some in my mom's sweetly precise oval hand. Even those, however, were written with my dad dictating to her. No mistaking his writing style.

Occasionally there is one from Sam, the oldest brother. There even were a few in my childish scribble, filled with spelling and syntax errors that belied the grammatical nitpicker I would grow up to become. I'm sure Mac forgave me; his only nephew was 6 at the time.

I have no idea of how I came to possess that shoebox, its contents in remarkably good condition even after seven decades. I can only presume that when Mac died in the late 1980s my Aunt Norma gave it to me as the oldest surviving family member. If so, I had never opened the box. And she, the only one would or could have shed any light, had died a few years earlier.

As I begin reading my dad's letters I get the weird sensation he is behind me on the couch peering over my shoulder, urging me to deliver his words with the requisite dramatic flair.

A self-educated high school dropout, Maurie read voraciously. He peppered conversations with almost casual references to Greek gods, Russian tsars, and obscure (to me) European novelists. His choices had sent me scurrying to his thesaurus and his encyclopedia, for he never, ever would translate for me. Look it up, he would say.

I read the first letter aloud to Jill. It is witty and fun; that some phrasing is a trifle antiquated only enhances the charm. If this is a harbinger, we are in for hours of sweet pleasure.

So sweet, in fact, I decide I must ration the letters in order to heighten anticipation. (Kind of like the times in my dreams that I put off going to Po'Boy's). But how will I resist the lure of that shoebox, tugging at my sleeve like a jar of licorice jellybeans?

I phone Diane; she, too, is surprised to learn of the treasure. Now I am certain no one else alive has ever read these letters.

Di drives down a few weekends later from New Jersey to share our gift. In the family room we alternate reading them aloud, giggling delightedly as Dad's familiar phrasings propel him back to life.

I open an envelope postmarked Feb. 22, 1943:

"Dear, dear Ishkabibble (dad's pet name for his younger brother):

"I've been telling the little phoofer (dad's pet name for me) about the mysterious and sinister code messages in the night, and he is rapturously under the impression that his uncle is a mighty hero at least as great as Barney Baxter. (May the good Lord exterminate him from the comic sheet). He believes, poor deluded soul, that you have naught but to snap your fingers, and huge balloons rise majestically into the air." (Those barrage balloons again!).

"But the thing that delights him most is the secret codes that you use. That places you in the same select circle as Captain Midnight (a Marvel Comics superhero) and his crew. Of course, I spare no lies, to nurture his hero worship."

Then it is my sister's turn. Hers was postmarked April 28, 1943.

"Dear Max,

"I've just been touched lightly—oh, very lightly, as with a fairy's wand, by the breath of war. I witnessed a blackout from our roof top. As the lights dimmed and then expired completely, a giant hush, heavy and ominous, descended as tho impelled by a psychic force to synchronize with the blackness. The world seemed to wait, supine and quivering, as though awaiting a terrible blow—gruesomely resigned, and it seemed to me, almost eager for the blow.

"Alone and apart in my solitary vigil, I was filled with a mad and intense desire to see the bombs descend, to hear the crash and to see the flame of the exploding dynamite, to see the black, sullen darkness and quiescence shattered by shrieks of mortal terror, cries of pain and anguish, confusion, noise, and bedlam. Just as when a group of shy people are gathered and an embarrassed silence falls upon them, they long for any sort of diversion to lift the heavy pall. And the eerie numbness that had encompassed the earth seized upon me. It was a scene of madness, pathos, and grandeur, and I longed for you to share it with me.

"Altho if we had been together, one of us probably would have giggled."

I take over reading that letter, in Mom's cursive handwriting:

"Your pictures were a great joy and a rare delight. Let me know in your next letter what size film your camera takes so I can send you some. I have been hearing from all sides about how tough a routine a soldier undergoes, but after looking at your pictures, replete with idleness, indolence, and Huck Finn-laziness, I am convinced that you have reformed the Army. Or is this just another manifestation of the peculiar Cohen genius of avoiding anything which remotely resembles hard work?"

When it's Di's turn again, she falls silent for several long moments, then hands me a single scrap of paper.

"Dear Mil, Mac, Sam, Dad, Ron, Di, Norma, Marcia, Stu, and Pop—and certain others. It's been so nice knowing you. M."

Mil is Millie, my mom. Mac and Sam, his brothers; Dad is his father, Joe; Ron and Di, of course, are his kids; Norma, Mac's wife; Marcia and Stu, Mac's kids. The "Pop" is a repeat—clearly Maurie is failing, his handwriting growing progressively weak.

This is written on a scrap of 8 X 11 paper, torn from the chart on which nurses record a patient's vitals: Date. Time. Temperature. Blood Pressure. IV Drips.

Maurie's request to his nurse for writing paper had been delivered with the embossed words, "University of Minnesota Hospital."

Then somehow, life draining away, he had summoned this burst of strength.

And, at last, I had my goodbye.

❦ ❦ ❦

EPILOGUE

Three chapters in this book deal with how I almost got fired from my first three jobs — each time on the first very day.

Ultimately, luck ran out. In 1986, a full 26 years after my third close encounter with unemployment, UPI got around to firing me.

My love affair with the best job I ever had ended unhappily, igniting a controversy that surprisingly was not confined to the UPI family. Although I had labored largely in behind-the-scenes anonymity through my career, my dismissal nevertheless generated a brief but intense earthquake and aftershocks throughout the news industry.

In keeping the story alive for several weeks, The New York Times and The Washington Post wrote headlines like these:

— *Popular UPI Managing Editor Fired.*

and,

— *Following Staff Uproar, UPI Tries to Re-hire Fired M.E.*

and,

— *Cohen Spurns UPI's Offer to Come Home*

For the record, when that offer was tendered my response was a series of outrageous demands for compensation, editorial independence and a big-time contract with a non-firing clause. I knew the new owner never would agree.

In the end, I got what I really wanted: An agreement that, in addition to a token financial settlement (I called it my "Plastic Parachute"), contained his written pledge not to sue to block our UPI book.

In fact, I was a lot better off "spurning" that insincere attempt. The UPI I had loved for a quarter-century was a far different creature now. The Scripps-Howard Co., whose founder had created the United Press 75 years earlier, wearied of underwriting skyrocketing losses. By the early 1980s, the red ink flowed at $12 million, then $14 million, then $18 million a year.

Desperate to unload it and unable to interest a more traditional buyer, Scripps in 1982 handed the keys to two neophyte entrepreneurs from Tennessee — and sweetened the pot with $5 million in operating cash. It was worse than a fire sale: The closest Doug Ruhe and Bill Geissler had ever come to running a media company was a Chicago-area UHF station with a notoriously weak signal.

Thus, few were shocked when amateur hour commenced immediately. The new owners hired inept cronies; shoved aside executives who were well-known and respected in the business; sold far below market value precious UPI assets; unfathomably stiffed the IRS on required quarterly tax payments; laid off veteran journalists; bounced a payroll; and, in 1984, filed for Chapter 11 bankruptcy protection.

Complicating matters was a fierce internecine battle pitting Ruhe and Geissler against Luis Nogales, a young media executive they had handpicked to be UPI's president. Nogales soon became convinced the owners were wrecking the company with their garage sale of prized assets, slashing staff, and closing bureaus, and ill-concealed attempts to break UPI's labor union. Even should there be a miraculous financial recovery, the company would be a mere shadow.

As managing editor I made a decision that ultimately would cost my job: If UPI were headed for the graveyard, we would cover its demise and write its obituary, without fear or favor.

I assigned my best investigative reporter, long-time Unipresser Greg Gordon, to a hastily created "UPI beat." Over a two-year period, we wrote and sent to our newspaper and broadcast clients almost daily stories uncovering the company's internal struggles.

Although "Joe and Jane Reader" do not know nor care exactly how information reaches them, my decision transfixed the news industry. Had anybody ever waved his company's dirty laundry so publicly?

In 1989, three years after I left UPI to begin a new career at Gannett, McGraw-Hill published the book I co-authored with Greg Gordon, who by that time also had been fired—by a subsequent owner—for refusing to let his bosses see and sanitize final pre-publication proofs.

"The book will be out in a few weeks," he told them. "Buy a copy, boys, and we'll autograph it for you."

The author's first book, published 1989.

"Down to the Wire: UPI's Fight for Survival" was a critical success and won a basketful of important awards, including Business Week magazine listing it as the year's best business book. And although it fell short of bestseller status, it is regularly cited as the most important resource for those interested in the disintegration of a storied news organization.

I had struggled with how to compress that book's 400 pages into a single memoir chapter until my old friend and fellow scribbler, Dick Ryan, suggested dealing with it in an epilogue.

So, there it is.

For more details, I still have copies that I will autograph. Thirty years later, it still is a damn good read. And the books are in better condition than UPI.

❦ ❦ ❦

CPSIA information can be obtained
at www.ICGtesting.com
Printed in the USA
BVOW03*1933220617

487619BV00003B/10/P